Extinction

EXTINCTION

Steven M. Stanley

SCIENTIFIC AMERICAN LIBRARY

A division of HPHLP
New York

Library of Congress Cataloging-in-Publication Data

Stanley, Steven M.

   Extinction.

   (Scientific American Library; 20)
   Bibliography: p.
   Includes index.
      1. Extinction (Biology)   I. Title.   II. Series.
      QE721.2.E97S73   1987   575′.7   86-22027
ISBN 0-7167-5014-7

Printed in the United States of America

Book design by Malcolm Grear Designers

Scientific American Library
A division of HPHLP
New York

Distributed by W. H. Freeman and Company,
41 Madison Avenue, New York, New York 10010 and
20 Beaumont Street, Oxford, OX1 2NQ, England

      3 4 5 6 7 8 9 0 KP 4 3 2 1 0 8 9

This book is number 20 of a series.

To Al Fischer, whose brilliance and enthusiasm
have stimulated me and many others

CONTENTS

PREFACE   ix

1   MASS EXTINCTION   1

2   GEOGRAPHY AND THE AGENTS OF CATASTROPHE   21

3   EARLY CRISES AND THE DAWNING OF HIGHER LIFE   49

4   GLACIATION AND THE ORDOVICIAN AND DEVONIAN CRISES   65

5   THE GREAT PERMIAN CRISIS   91

6   THE AGE OF DINOSAURS   109

7   HOW THE MESOZOIC ERA CAME TO AN END   133

8   THE PALEOCENE: RECOVERY, THEN CRISIS   173

9   NEOGENE EXTINCTIONS: OUR RECENT HERITAGE   191

10   AN OVERVIEW   209

REFERENCES   219

ILLUSTRATION CREDITS   229

INDEX   233

PREFACE

Mass extinctions—global crises that have repeatedly swept away most species of animal life on earth—are now basic facts of geology. Each great crisis has "reset" the global biological system, in the sense that important groups of organisms have disappeared, making way for the expansion of others. For example, about 65 million years ago mammals suddenly began to assume the role vacated by dinosaurs: Mammals became the dominant land animals on earth. At first, they remained small, but before long a wide variety of species, some small and some elephantine, populated the landscape. And then, beginning about 40 million years ago, mammals too suffered a mass extinction. Obviously this was not fatal to the group as a whole. Mammals recovered to resume their prominence and to evolve in altogether new directions, including the one that culminated in the modern human species.

Two controversial ideas have stimulated a recent surge of popular interest in mass extinctions. The first is the proposal that the impact of a giant meteor or comet triggered the crisis that ended the dinosaurs' reign. The second is the hypothesis that this and other crises have been spaced at regular intervals, owing to the operation of some periodic astronomical agent. Missing from the spate of popular accounts of these issues is any comprehensive evaluation of the record of great extinctions that is being read from rocks and fossils. *Extinction* is designed to fill this void. More generally, in the process of elucidating the crises that we term mass extinctions, this book takes the reader on a trip through the history of life on earth. Mass extinctions are interruptions of the trip—but interruptions that happen to fascinate human beings.

During the past few, years, at the hands of hundreds of expert practitioners around the world, the geological record has yielded up much of its rich store of information about global crises. Collaboration is proving to be especially fruitful. For example, students of fossil plants, which are excellent indicators of ancient climates, are sharing information with students of fossil mammals and dinosaurs, and both of these groups of scientists are exchanging information with others who specialize in the study of ancient marine life. In addition, new domains of science are shedding light on mass extinction. Forty years ago, few paleontologists would have predicted that minute fossils of single-celled, floating marine organisms would today be revealing key information about the thermal history of ancient oceans. Similarly, there was no expectation that by the 1970s the geologic community in general would have converted to the long-derided view that continents have moved over the surface of the earth, occasionally fusing together or breaking apart. In fact, plate tectonics, our new body of collective wisdom about large-scale movements of the earth's crust, is now a cornerstone of paleogeography. Because mass extinctions have operated on a global scale, paleontologists who study them are now heavily concerned with the positions of ancient continents and oceans— and with the ways in which these configurations have sometimes altered the nature of ancient atmospheres and oceans in ways inimical to life.

This book, then, is about the wide variety of paleontological and geological evidence that bears on the nature of the great extinctions. I view the book as a celebration of the renaissance that has changed the face of paleontology since 1970. The first phase of this renaissance brought paleontological data to bear on fundamental issues of evolutionary biology, and we are now gaining insight into the causes of mass extinction by evaluating what kinds of organisms died out in each crisis, where they lived, and what pattern their disappearances followed in space and time.

In part, the fervent new efforts of paleontologists to unravel the puzzle of mass extinction have resulted from our chauvinistic impulse to convince the world that astronomers do not have simple answers to complex geological problems. It might still be argued that we are reacting with bias, but there is a logical rejoinder. Paleontologists have data that raise serious doubts about the idea that impacts of extraterrestrial objects (meteors or comets) have caused most episodes of mass extinction. Moreover, we have data suggesting that many of the mass extinctions resulted from certain other, more mundane causes.

In particular, I see changes in the earth's climate as the most important cause of crises in the history of life. As I explain in this book, for several crises, such as those of Late Devonian, Late Permian, Late Cretaceous, and Eocene–Oligocene time, new evidence has surfaced during just the past two or three years to strengthen the case for climatic causation.

The highly attractive visual quality of this book is largely the result of the art direction of Lisa Douglis and the skilled and persistant photo-research of Travis Amos. I thank them for their fine work and also express appreciation to Janet Wagner and Georgia Lee Hadler for their skillful and thoughtful editing. Finally, I thank Jerry Lyons for his good-humored support and wise counsel throughout the completion of this project.

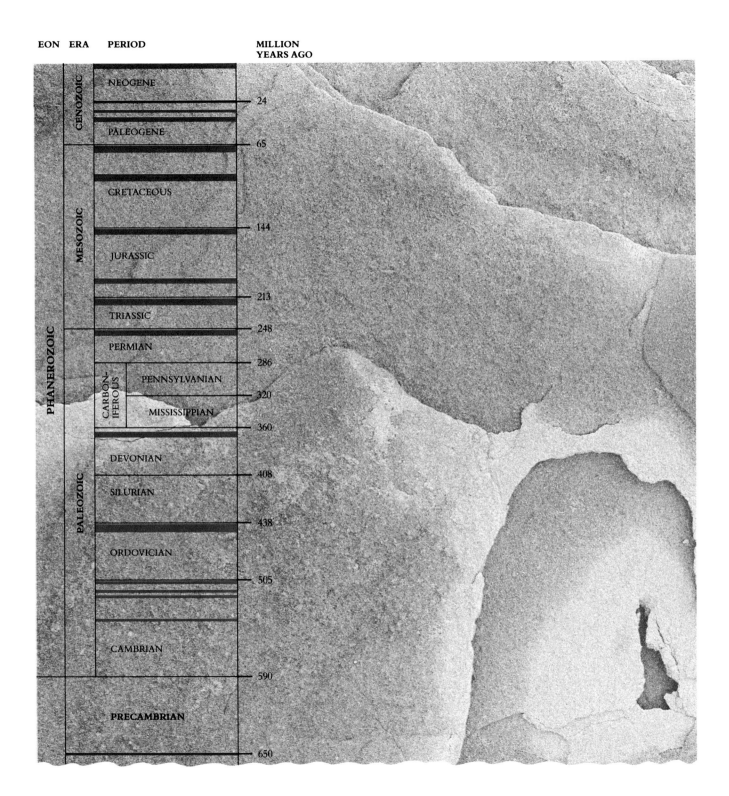

EON	ERA	PERIOD	MILLION YEARS AGO

PHANEROZOIC

CENOZOIC
- NEOGENE
- 24
- PALEOGENE
- 65

MESOZOIC
- CRETACEOUS
- 144
- JURASSIC
- 213
- TRIASSIC
- 248

PALEOZOIC
- PERMIAN
- 286
- CARBONIFEROUS
  - PENNSYLVANIAN
  - 320
  - MISSISSIPPIAN
- 360
- DEVONIAN
- 408
- SILURIAN
- 438
- ORDOVICIAN
- 505
- CAMBRIAN
- 590

PRECAMBRIAN
- 650

I MASS EXTINCTION

The great extinctions that have punctuated the history of life on earth have attracted widespread attention primarily because of humans' fascination with dinosaurs. Nearly everyone recognizes not only that the dinosaurs are extinct but also that these curious giants disappeared during a brief interval of geologic time. Nonscientists, however, frequently overlook the fact that a variety of other biological groups, ranging from flying reptiles the size of small airplanes to single-celled algae that floated in the oceans, met their end along with the dinosaurs. Paleontologists reserve the phrase "mass extinction" for biotic crises such as this one, that were relatively sudden on a geologic scale of time—confined to at most a few million years—and that swept away a wide variety of living creatures.

Since multicellular life appeared on earth, there have been fewer than a dozen biotic crises that qualify as major mass extinctions, and their victims include a minority of all extinct species. Most of the other species that have died out, numbering in the millions, have suffered piecemeal extinction; each failed to adapt to changing environmental conditions that posed problems for no more than a few species.

In fact, most of the species that have inhabited our planet died out long ago. Today, this fact jumps out at anyone who explores the fossil record in light of our knowledge of the animals and plants that inhabit the modern world. Biological surveys have left relatively little terra incognita that might actually harbor surviving populations of the species we believe to be extinct. It was not always so. Well into the eighteenth century, the living world remained quite poorly known. As a result, some scientists cogently argued that strange, and possibly extinct, creatures known from the fossil record might yet survive in unexplored regions of the globe. Theology, more than anything else, fueled opposition to the idea of extinction. The biosphere was supposed to constitute a perfect creation, and the demise of entire species

Megalonyx jeffersoni, the giant ground sloth that Thomas Jefferson studied and that was named in his honor. The animal was a harmless plant eater, representing a group of gargantuan cousins of the arboreal tree sloths. Ground sloths migrated to North America from South America shortly before the start of the modern Ice Age.

would imply imperfection. In his evaluation of the bones of *Megalonyx,* an ox-sized ground sloth unearthed in West Virginia, Thomas Jefferson adhered to the prevailing view. He suggested that the giant animal still lived in unexplored western territories of North America, "for if one link in nature's chain might be lost, another and another might be lost, till this whole system of things should evanish by piecemeal."

Not until 1786 did Georges Cuvier, the French paleontologist, establish the fact of extinction to the satisfaction of nearly all students of natural history. First he showed by skeletal comparisons that the mammoth that roamed Europe during what we now recognize as the recent Ice Age belonged neither to the living Indian elephant species nor to the living African elephant species. Second, he pointed out that the mammoth was too large to have been overlooked in the modern world. If, as was implied, the mammoth was extinct, so too must be many other fossil animals unfamiliar to students of the living world.

Georges Cuvier not only established the fact of extinction, he was first to observe that entire ancient communities of plants and animals had been swept away by what we now call mass extinctions—events that have eliminated the majority of species on earth. Actually, Cuvier hedged on the question of whether the great extinctions that he saw

Frozen baby mammoth. This unusual fossil of a species that became extinct about 10,000 years ago was preserved in the permafrost of Siberia.

recorded in sediments of the Paris Basin were truly global or only regional in scale. A creationist of the pre-Darwinian era, he tended to favor the idea that the catastrophes were regional events and that the new forms of life that replaced the old were species of the original biblical creation that migrated into the vacated area from other regions.

Even in Cuvier's day, scientists understood the elements of stratigraphic geology—the study of layered rocks, or strata. Sediments accumulate in layers, or strata, because they are laid down by discrete depositional events. For example, a single pulse of water movement, when it slows down, drops the sand or mud that it carries. Modern geologists refer to the resulting layer as a bed if it is thicker than a centimeter (about three-eighths of an inch) and a lamina if it is thinner than this. When several beds form, one on top of another, they consti-

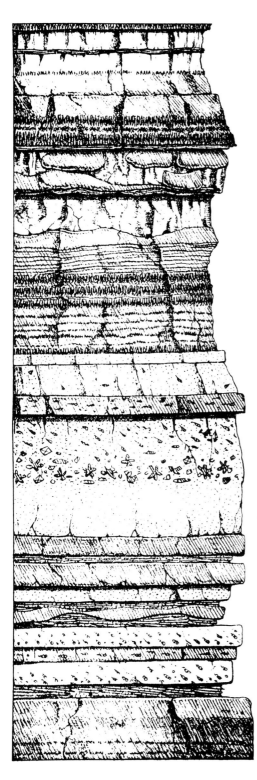

Stratigraphic sequence (left) at Monmartre, Paris, as depicted by Georges Cuvier and a coauthor in 1822. Starfish from Devonian strata (above) in New York State. The species to which they belong was originally described in the nineteenth century by James Hall, the first great North American geologist.

tute a sedimentary sequence that may turn into rock in the course of geologic time. This lithification process, which transforms mud into shale and sand into sandstone, results primarily from compaction or from cementation by minerals that crystallize from watery solution—or from a combination of these two processes. Sediments accumulate in greatest volume in the oceans, which constitute a vast depositional basin, but also settle on the land in low-lying areas such as swamps, lake floors, and river channels. In warm, shallow seas, limey sediments accumulate in great quantities, forming white beaches when they wash up along the shore. These sediments are for the most part fragments of seashells and other organically produced skeletons of calcium carbonate.

The essentials of fossilization were also understood in Cuvier's time. Fossils are remnants of ancient life. Some consist of original organic structures—usually durable features such as shells, teeth, or bones. Other fossils are nothing more than imprints of soft tissue; these include footprints and also outlines of leaves and soft-bodied animals whose final resting places were on soft sediment.

The Paris Basin, where Cuvier traced the history of life, extends along the coast of Europe from northeastern France to the Netherlands. Here, early in the Age of Mammals (in which we still live) a thick body of sediments was deposited. From the fact that some of these strata harbor fossils of marine life and others contain fossils of terrestrial life, Cuvier deduced that the Atlantic Ocean had repeatedly lapped up on the continent in this region and then receded again. It was well understood in Cuvier's day that when sediment is deposited, the younger beds are piled on top of older beds. Adopting this simple law of succession, he reconstructed the history of the basin by studying the alternation of marine and terrestrial intervals of deposition. As outlined in his *Recherches sur les Ossemens Fossiles,* Cuvier concluded that both the arrival and the recession of the Atlantic waters had wrought cataclysmic effects on organisms of the region: "Life on earth has been frequently interrupted by frightful events. Innumerable organisms have become the victims of such catastrophes. Invading waters have swallowed up the inhabitants of dry land; [at other times] the sudden rise of the sea bottom has deposited aquatic animals on land. Their species have vanished forever."

Cuvier's reconstruction of events in the Paris Basin fitted comfortably into the general concept of catastrophism, which dominated geological thinking during the eighteenth century. According to this view, the entire geological record was the product of enormous upheavals of supernatural origin, the most recent of which was the biblical flood. Catastrophism was challenged in the 1830s by the Englishman Charles Lyell, who pictured the world as a vast natural machine in a condition of steady state change: While some mountains were eroding, others were rising up, and while some sedimentary rocks were weathering away, others were forming in depositional basins nearby. In Lyell's view, life was caught up in a similar cycle without progress. Species were continually vanishing, only to be replaced by others of similar form. (Lyell avoided the question of the origin of species; long after Darwin confronted him with the evidence for evolution he opposed it, and he clung tenaciously to the idea that major living groups, such as mammals and reptiles, had coexisted through all of geologic time.) Thus, Lyell asserted that the geological record had been produced gradually, over the course of millions of years, by

The biblical deluge, as depicted in the first edition of the Luther Bible published in 1534.

the operation of everyday, earthly processes. What Charles Darwin then added was not only evidence for the large-scale transformation of life, but also an earthly explanation for the origin of species: New species arose from preexisting ones by the process of natural selection.

Our present picture of extinction draws on the ideas of both Cuvier and Lyell, although their views were poles apart. Lyell, however, is generally accorded the more prominent place in the history of geology; the everyday processes that he saw shaping the earth have indeed formed most of the rock record. Global and even regional catastrophes, important as they may be, are rare events that leave less voluminous evidence of their occurrence. For example, in the rock record representing the approximate time of extinction of the dinosaurs, there is a narrow interval of sediment that contains an unusually high concentration of iridium, an element that is extremely rare on earth but more abundant in some kinds of extraterrestrial matter. Many scientists believe that the excessive iridium represents fallout from a meteorite that crashed into the earth with effects that were fatal to the dinosaurs. Everywhere it has been found, the iridium anomaly, as it is called, is less than a meter (about 3 feet) thick. In contrast, the Age of

A hadrosaur, or duckbilled dinosaur. Hadrosaurs diversified near the end of the Age of Dinosaurs and then died out with all other dinosaurs. As large plant eaters, they were equivalent to modern antelopes and their relatives but possessed webbed feet that apparently permitted them to swim adeptly.

Dinosaurs (the Mesozoic Era, which lasted from about 250 to 66 million years ago) is represented in many parts of the world by thousands of meters of sediment that accumulated slowly or as a result of geologically minor catastrophes such as local storms or floods. Throughout this vast interval of time, millions of species appeared and disappeared from the face of the earth—far more than died out in the final mass extinction.

Today mass extinctions are not merely treated as facts of earth history, they are scrutinized by a wide variety of scientists in search of a cause—or perhaps more properly causes—for there can be little doubt that many individual mass extinctions are the product of more than one factor. For example, let us imagine that, as Cuvier believed, great biotic cataclysms have resulted from changes in the relative positions of land and sea. Then, in seeking a deeper level of understanding, we might find that these changes in relative sea level resulted from the growth of polar ice caps that locked up enormous quantities of water, or from subsidence (lowering) of the sea floor relative to the positions of continental surfaces, or from a combination of the two. At still more fundamental levels of explanation, we might investigate several conditions that led to the trapping of water in ice caps or to the depression of the sea floor. We sometimes refer to the immediate causes of mass extinction—the actual agents of death—as proximate factors. In the above example, the proximate factor is a change in sea level. We refer to the more fundamental, or remote, causes as distal factors—for example, growth of polar ice caps or subsidence of the sea floor and their underlying causes.

Cuvier identified two major biotic crises. One took place about 250 million years ago, at the end of "Primary Time," which we now term the Paleozoic Era. The other occurred about 65 million years ago, at the end of "Secondary Time," which we now call the Mesozoic Era or, less formally, the Age of Dinosaurs. This second event has long intrigued the educated public, and during the 1980s the question of what ended the dinosaurs' reign on earth has been much in the news because of the hotly debated hypothesis that calamitous changes wrought when a giant meteor struck the earth killed off the largest land animals of all time. The mystique of the dinosaurs is not all that engages our interest in their demise. What also motivates us here is anthropocentrism: It was our class of animals, the Mammalia, that were the chief beneficiaries of the catastrophe that terminated the Mesozoic Era. For more than a hundred million years while the dinosaurs ruled the earth mammals also populated the continents, but they remained small and inconspicuous by comparison. None was appreciably larger than a house cat and many were probably nocturnal. It was presumably the fierce predatory habits of some dinosaurs and the superior ability of others to compete for food and space that suppressed the evolutionary development of Mesozoic mammals.

When the dinosaurs died out, however, the mammals took center stage and underwent what is termed an adaptive radiation: the origin, from one or a small number of ancestral species, of a variety of new species adapted to different habitats and new ways of life. Having waited in the wings for more than a hundred million years, mammals underwent a rapid and spectacular diversification. Within just ten million years or so of the dinosaurs' disappearance, the ranks of Mammalia included such distinctive creatures as bats and whales and a number of terrestrial forms the size of a large dog. Not long afterwards there appeared the first species of the primates, the group to which monkeys, apes, and humans belong, and our eventual origin was simply one aspect of the adaptive radiation of this mammalian group. Had the dinosaurs survived, there is no question that we would not walk the earth today. Mammals would remain small and unobtrusive, not unlike rodents of the modern world.

Largely on the basis of major changes in the nature of life, geologists divide the vast history of the earth into formal divisions. The largest of these are known as eons. Eons are divided into eras, and eras into periods. Periods, like the other subdivisions of geologic time, vary in length, but every one spanned tens of millions of years. The final period of the Mesozoic Era—the period that ended with the dinosaurs' demise—was the Cretaceous. Periods such as the Cretaceous are divided into epochs, and epochs into ages. Most ages lasted between five and ten million years.

Our fascination with the demise of the dinosaurs should not lead us to overlook the other great extinctions of the geologic past. For example, about 250 million years ago, a more devastating event ended the era labeled Paleozoic, which means "era of ancient life". This catastrophe struck both marine life and mammal-like reptiles, which were the dominant land animals before the dinosaurs. The facts surrounding each of the great extinctions of the geologic past, through similarities and contrasts, may shed light on others. Thus, this book will consider not just the dinosaur event, but about a dozen other great extinctions as well, beginning with one that struck about 650 million years ago, at a primitive stage in the earth's biotic history, when most forms of life were aquatic bacteria and algae. The most recent crises to be discussed are ones that affected our own group, the mammals. Through hunting activities, our species may actually have been the culprit in the last of these events, which ended only about 11,000 years ago.

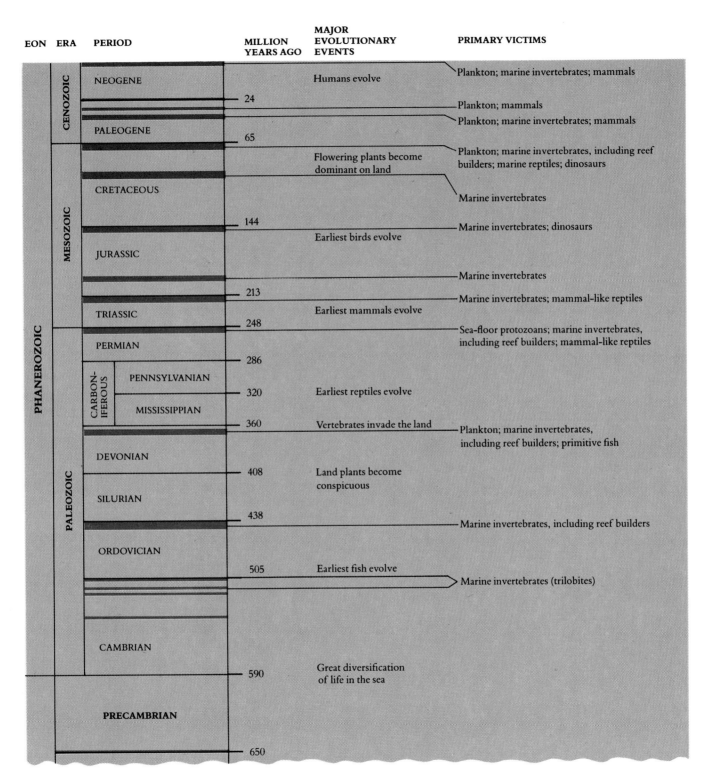

EON	ERA	PERIOD		MILLION YEARS AGO	MAJOR EVOLUTIONARY EVENTS	PRIMARY VICTIMS
PHANEROZOIC	CENOZOIC	NEOGENE			Humans evolve	Plankton; marine invertebrates; mammals
				24		Plankton; mammals
						Plankton; marine invertebrates; mammals
		PALEOGENE		65		
	MESOZOIC	CRETACEOUS			Flowering plants become dominant on land	Plankton; marine invertebrates, including reef builders; marine reptiles; dinosaurs
						Marine invertebrates
				144		Marine invertebrates; dinosaurs
		JURASSIC			Earliest birds evolve	
						Marine invertebrates
				213		Marine invertebrates; mammal-like reptiles
		TRIASSIC		248	Earliest mammals evolve	
	PALEOZOIC	PERMIAN		286		Sea-floor protozoans; marine invertebrates, including reef builders; mammal-like reptiles
		CARBON-IFEROUS	PENNSYLVANIAN	320	Earliest reptiles evolve	
			MISSISSIPPIAN	360	Vertebrates invade the land	Plankton; marine invertebrates, including reef builders; primitive fish
		DEVONIAN		408	Land plants become conspicuous	
		SILURIAN		438		Marine invertebrates, including reef builders
		ORDOVICIAN		505	Earliest fish evolve	
		CAMBRIAN		590	Great diversification of life in the sea	Marine invertebrates (trilobites)
		PRECAMBRIAN		650		

THE NATURE OF EXTINCTION

Before we become more specific in our discussion, it is necessary to grasp the nature of extinction in general. Scientists sometimes refer to the disappearance of a species from part of its geographic range as local extinction. It is preferable, however, to restrict the term extinction to the total disappearance of one or more species.

The extinction of a species amounts to the contraction of both its geographic range and its population size to zero. These two variables, geographic range and population size, which fluctuate from year to year throughout the existence of a species, are governed by what ecologists call limiting factors. Limiting factors can be grouped into a few general categories: traits of the physical environment, ecological competition, predation, and chance factors. Climate is one of the most important physical limiting factors; climatic changes have unquestionably caused many extinctions, such as the disappearance of a number of forest-dwelling antelope species from Africa about 2.5 million years ago, when the climate became drier and grasslands expanded at the expense of forests. Ecological competition between species is usually for food or space. Here and there in the world today we can see that the recent origin or immigration of a species is resulting in a decline in the distribution and abundance of another similar species. An example is the decline of the red squirrel in Great Britain during the expansion of the grey squirrel, which humans introduced in the 1920s. Similar in its effect is heavy predation upon a preexisting species by a newly arrived or newly evolved species; the impact can be severe when the victim species, because of weak defenses or ineffective modes of escape, turns out to be highly vulnerable to the predator.

Extinction is often a complicated process, however, and two or more factors must often conspire to bring it about. Probably chance factors, which are one of the limiting factors just mentioned, often play an important role in the final disappearance of species—after their populations have been diminished to small size by physical conditions, competition, or predation (or more than one of these agents). Mishaps are far more likely to have catastrophic consequences in small populations than in large ones. When only a few individuals are present, for example, there might be one year when, by chance, males fail to encounter females at mating time.

With all of this said, it must also be admitted that, although millions of species have died out in the geologic past, for only a handful do we know with a high degree of certainty the actual cause of extinction. For the vast majority of lost species, we simply cannot reconstruct either demographic history or relevant environmental changes with sufficient detail to understand what happened. The conventional wisdom holds that the constantly changing physical and biological milieu continually eliminates species, while at the same time evolution is forming others, some of which closely resemble previously existing species and some of which display novel new features. (There is not necessarily a numerical balance between disappearances and originations.) These piecemeal disappearances constitute background extinction.

The fossil record occasionally reveals that at some time many species in a particular region have died out during a very brief interval. As long as other species belonging to the same genera and families have persisted in other areas where they did not experience severe losses, however, such an event is known as a regional extinction rather than a mass extinction. As we shall see in Chapter 9, pulses of regional extinction of this kind took place both on the land and in the sea during the recent Ice Age of the Pliocene and Pleistocene epochs. The most severe marine event was in the western Atlantic Ocean and the Caribbean Sea, where the pattern of extinction—disappearance of virtually all strictly tropical species from southern Florida—implicates climatic cooling as the culprit. Our ability to identify the primary cause in this example illustrates an important point: We have a much better chance of discovering the cause of a pulse of extinction that removed many species than we do of discovering the cause of the isolated disappearance of a single species. The larger event can display a pattern of selective extinction that a single species' demise cannot.

THE NATURE OF MASS EXTINCTION

During brief intervals, mass extinctions have eliminated large numbers of species—sometimes most of the species on earth—on a global geographic scale. In the process, they have terminated many larger taxonomic groups into which species are classified. At the top of our hierarchical classification of life is the kingdom. Animals form one kingdom and plants another, and of course neither of these huge groups has been terminated by any mass extinction. In fact, extinction has befallen few phyla (singular: phylum), which represent the next category in the hierarchy below the level of the kingdom. An example of a phylum is the Chordata, which includes all animals with backbones and a few more primitive groups. The mammals (Mammalia) and reptiles (Reptilia) constitute two of the classes of chordates. These classes, in standard fashion, are divided hierarchically into orders, families, and genera (singular: genus). In contrast to phyla, many

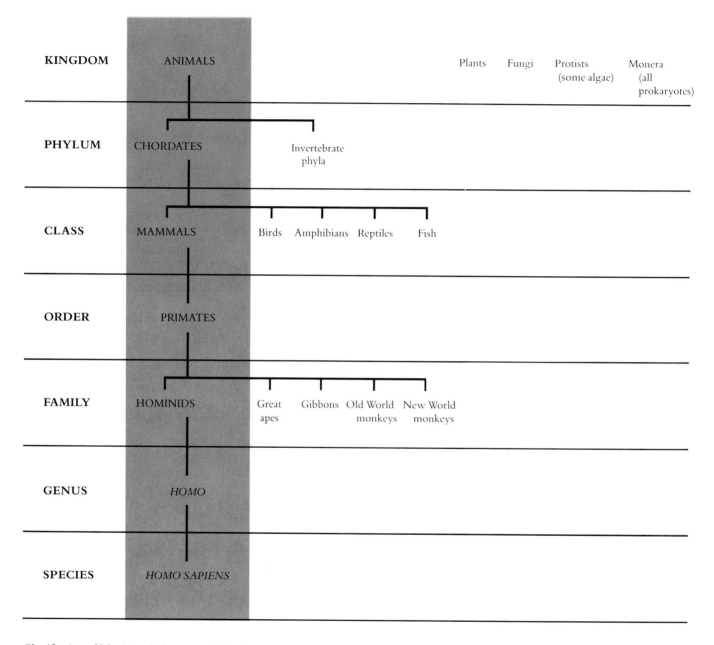

Classification of life. Animals form one of five king-
doms. A complete classification is shown for our species, *Homo sapiens*.

lower taxonomic groups have been swept away in mass extinctions. The dinosaurs, for example, constituted two orders. Traditionally, these have been assigned to the class Reptilia, but some experts assign them to a separate class along with certain of their relatives including birds and crocodiles.

The disappearance of a family or other large taxon amounts to the disappearance of all of its species. The number of species can dwindle, sometimes to zero, even by way of background extinction. Such decline is to be expected, for example, when a group of animals is confronted with a newly evolved group of predators that are especially adept at attacking it or with a newly evolved group of superior competitors. One of the best examples of the competitive displacement of one group by another is the Late Cretaceous expansion of the newly evolved flowering plants, including hardwood trees, at the expense of the conifers (cone-bearing plants) and their relatives. One competitive advantage of the flowering plants is that they reproduce rapidly and are therefore effective at colonizing bare ground. By contrast, the seeds of conifers take a long time to germinate. Before the rise of the flowering plants conifers and their relatives were the dominant plants on earth, yet today they tend to prevail only in cold or dry areas where flowering plants are unable to flourish. In addition, living species of conifers number only about 550, while more than 200,000 species of flowering plants dominate modern landscapes. Operating through competition, organic evolution on a global scale has been an important factor in the decline of particular groups of organisms such as the conifers, operating to accelerate the rate of background extinction.

An important question is whether mass extinction is truly distinct from background extinction of higher taxa such as families. To address this question, in 1982, J. John Sepkoski and David M. Raup of the University of Chicago plotted the number of extinctions per million years for families of vertebrate and invertebrate marine organisms during the last 560 million years or so. Their graph of this rate against time reveals five geologic ages for which very heavy extinction is recorded. One of these is the final age of the Cretaceous Period, during which the dinosaurs declined to extinction, or near extinction. In another paper also published in 1982, Sepkoski suggested that, in addition to these five most severe crises, there were about ten mass extinctions of second order importance during the past 600 million years. We can then ask whether the rates of family disappearance during mass extinctions really do stand out as a cluster of high rates against the low rates of background extinction that have prevailed throughout most of geologic time. The question is, were there many

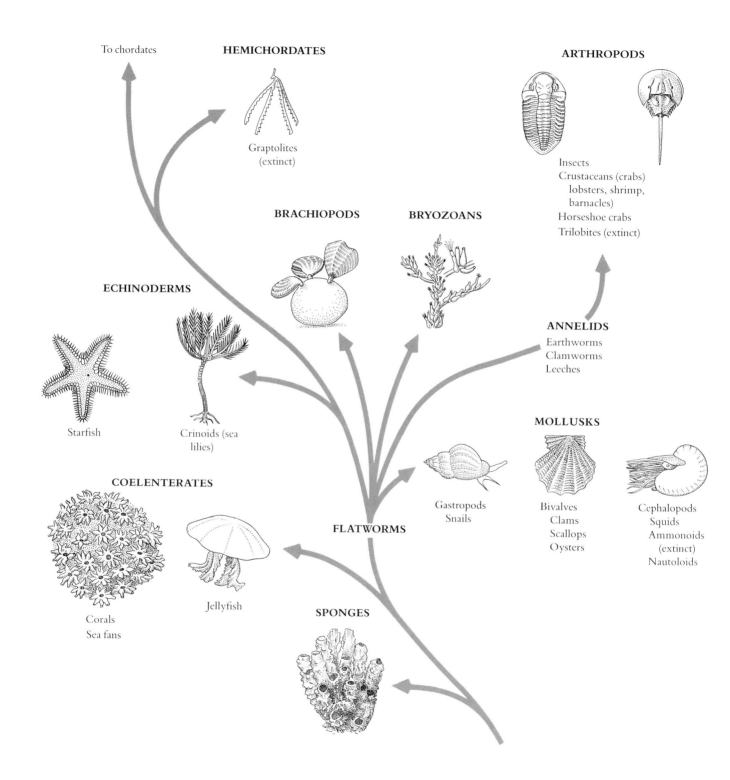

To chordates

HEMICHORDATES

Graptolites
(extinct)

ARTHROPODS

Insects
Crustaceans (crabs)
lobsters, shrimp,
barnacles)
Horseshoe crabs
Trilobites (extinct)

BRACHIOPODS

BRYOZOANS

ECHINODERMS

ANNELIDS
Earthworms
Clamworms
Leeches

Starfish

Crinoids (sea
lilies)

MOLLUSKS

COELENTERATES

Gastropods
Snails

Bivalves
Clams
Scallops
Oysters

Cephalopods
Squids
Ammonoids
(extinct)
Nautoloids

FLATWORMS

Jellyfish

Corals
Sea fans

SPONGES

Left: Major groups of invertebrate animals. All forms of life shown here have fossil records.

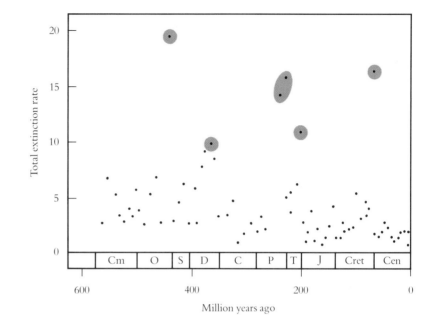

Raup and Sepkoski's plot of extinction rate (number of extinctions per million years) for families of marine animals during the past 600 million years. Colored circles indicate the five most severe crises.

ages for which rates were intermediate between low background rates and the high rates that characterize mass extinctions? If there were only a few intervals characterized by intermediate levels of extinction, we would conclude that something quite unusual happened at times of mass extinction.

The issue has not been resolved by numbers alone, in part because the number of mass extinctions is so small that statistical tests are inconclusive. James F. Quinn of the University of California at Davis scrutinized the total pattern of extinction in the graph prepared by Raup and Sepkoski and concluded that there is no compelling statistical evidence that the five peaks labeled mass extinctions are quantitatively distinct from background rates. Raup and Sepkoski have countered this challenge with the observation that high rates of extinction of families are not the only hallmark of mass extinctions. In addition,

Fragments of a branching colony of Ordovician bryo-zoans from the vicinity of Cincinnati, Ohio. Intercon-nected individuals occupied tiny pores in the stony skeleton.

these events are commonly characterized by the geologically sudden disappearance of even larger groups—orders and classes of animals—which only rarely suffer extinction at other times.

There is no question that mass extinctions can be distinguished from intervals of background extinction on qualitative grounds. For example, Robert Anstey of Michigan State University compared the pattern of extinction for animals known as bryozoans during intervals of mass extinction and intervals when low levels of background extinction prevailed. Commonly called moss animals, bryozoans are aquatic invertebrates that form colonies which attach to hard surfaces. All individuals within each colony descend, by budding, from a single progenitor. The individuals are tiny creatures, and many of them are adapted for straining food from the surrounding water. Other individuals within the same colony specialize in reproduction or in defense of the colony. Anstey found that bryozoan species characterized by complicated colonies (ones consisting of a large variety of individuals) experienced exceptionally high rates of extinction during two major biotic crises (Late Ordovician and Late Devonian). These species experienced unusually low rates at other times. We do not understand the biological reason for this contrast, but it does indicate that something abnormal was happening to bryozoans during the interval of heavy extinction. The implication is that the mass extinction was causally unrelated to background extinction.

I have conducted a similar test for a regional mass extinction in eastern North America that during the recent Ice Age decimated the group of shellfish called bivalve mollusks. The bivalves include the familiar clams, mussels, and oysters; all are housed in a hinged, two-part shell, which contrasts with the single spiral shell of a snail. The East Coast crisis eliminated many species of bivalves that were characterized by small body size, while species of large body size were much less severely affected. This fact might initially seem strange because during the same interval of time quite a different pattern characterized the coasts of California and Japan, where there was no mass extinction and, instead, low background rates of extinction prevailed. In these stable Pacific areas, species of small body size enjoyed very low rates of extinction, apparently because such species are characterized by very large populations—just as there are vast numbers of mice in the world compared to the number of elephants. What caused the mass extinction in eastern North America was regional climatic cooling associated with the onset of glacial conditions as large ice caps grew in three areas adjacent to the North Atlantic—Scandinavia, Greenland, and eastern Canada. Species of small body size are characterized by narrow temperature tolerances, and a large percentage are restricted to

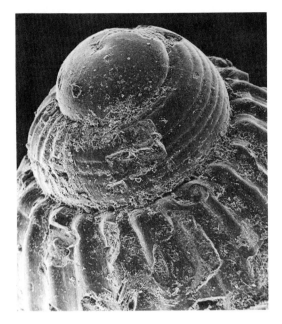

Scanning electron micrograph of the larval shell forming the apex of a Cretaceous snail shell. Small size distinguishes shells of larvae that floated in the plankton from shells that lived on the sea floor. Most species have a single type of larva.

tropical climatic zones. For this reason, small species suffered preferentially in the regional mass extinction of eastern North America; their huge populations were of little value for survival when the entire region that they inhabited cooled down.

David Jablonski of the University of Chicago has similarly shown that an abnormal pattern of mass extinction characterized mollusks in North America during the Late Cretaceous mass extinction, which eliminated the dinosaurs. Here the comparison is between the fates of molluscan species that had different types of larval development: In one type of development the animal could float in the ocean for weeks or even months, feeding all the while. In the other type, the larva could not feed and floated for only a few days or hours or not at all. Jablonski has found that species with feeding larvae, apparently because of their wide geographic dispersal, were resistant to extinction during normal times within the Cretaceous Period. Species with non-feeding larvae and narrower geographic ranges experienced higher extinction rates, apparently because of their vulnerability to local environmental change. On the other hand, during the great terminal Cretaceous extinction both groups of species suffered more-or-less equally.

These examples reveal that within four biotic crises patterns of extinction deviated from the norm. They did not simply represent an intensification of everyday background extinction but were qualitatively different. Why each was abnormal I will consider more fully in later chapters.

THEMES IN MASS EXTINCTION

Any search for the causes of biotic crises must focus not only on patterns of individual mass extinctions but also on patterns shared by several of these events. Common patterns tend to point to common agents of destruction.

One salient point here is simply that many individual crises have struck life both on the land and in the sea. The implication of this universality is that, barring some extraordinary coincidence, the explanation for the mass extinction cannot be found entirely in either the marine setting or the terrestrial setting.

A second feature, brought to light by Andrew H. Knoll of Harvard University, is that on the land, while animals have suffered repeatedly, plants have been highly resistant to mass extinction. Floral transitions, though profound, have occurred through the replacement of one major group by another over many millions of years.

A third theme, mentioned earlier, is the preferential disappearance of tropical forms of life during mass extinctions. This pattern is especially apparent for marine life in the event that marked the end of the Cretaceous Period, but is evident in many other crises as well.

A fourth characteristic of mass extinctions is the tendency of certain groups of animals to experience them repeatedly. Such groups obviously did not disappear altogether in the first crisis that affected them. Their surviving species multiplied after this event, only to be depleted by another. Three groups of marine invertebrates illustrate this kind of vulnerability, and, not coincidentally, each of them disappeared altogether in a final crisis. These groups, which will be encountered in subsequent chapters, were the trilobites, arthropods that crawled over and burrowed into the sea floor; the graptolites, animals that formed colonies on stalks, which in most cases floated in the ocean; and the ammonoids, swimming predators that possessed shells and were closely related to the living pearly nautilus. The tendency of all three of these groups to suffer mass extinction may have been related to the high rates of background extinction of these groups. Each normally experienced very high rates of turnover, meaning that their species tended to die out at high rates and to be replaced through high rates of speciation. (Speciation is the origin of a new species from a population of some preexisting species.) These high rates created instability. Even a moderate fractional increase in rate of extinction or decrease in rate of speciation caused their number of species to decline precipitously.

And, finally, the most controversial trait of mass extinctions is their alleged equal spacing, or periodicity, in geological time. It has been proposed that mass extinctions have occurred every 26 million years. The validity of this assertion is not as easily assessed as one might expect. First, the dates of the mass extinctions are not precisely known. Second, there is some question whether some intervals characterized by relatively high extinction rates constituted true mass extinctions or only times of slightly elevated background rates. Because it is difficult to envision an earthly explanation for periodicity, the notion that biotic crises are periodic has led astronomers to join the search for a cause, seeking potential agents of catastrophe in the extraterrestrial domain. The astronomers have tended to employ as a model for all crises the final extinction of the dinosaurs, which has been claimed to have been associated with iridium fallout of extraterrestrial origin. The intriguing question of periodicity will be addressed in the final chapter of this book, after discussion of the events themselves.

These events were spread over about 650 million years. The first crisis, so far as we know, victimized only algae, at a time when pri-

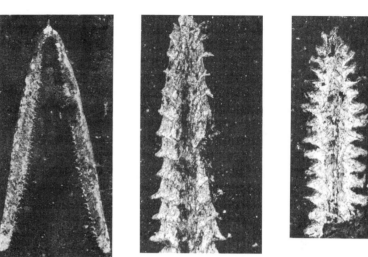

Two groups that experienced repeated heavy extinction during the Paleozoic Era. Trilobites (above) were cousins of the living horseshoe crab. Graptolites (above right, three pictures) were colonial animals that occupied fragile stalks of organic matter that are commonly preserved in fine-grained sediments. Most species floated as plankton in ancient oceans.

mordial animal life was only beginning to colonize the oceans. Multiple crises then devastated animal life during the Cambrian Period, which began about 590 million years ago. All of the known victims of the Cambrian crises were animals without backbones, and most were trilobites, arthropods that were distant relatives of modern horseshoe crabs; despite these setbacks, the Cambrian was the heyday of the trilobites. Three subsequent Paleozoic crises struck diverse groups of marine organisms. The second of these, which began more than 370 million years ago, was, as far as we know, the first mass extinction to include vertebrates among its victims, devastating large armored fish. Slightly more than 250 million years ago, the most severe crisis of all time brought the Paleozoic Era to a close, decimating life in the oceans, where casualties constituted somewhere between 75 and 90 percent of all marine species. This event was also the first to strike vertebrate animals on the land, the previous crisis having occurred at just about the time when the earliest amphibians, which had evolved from fish, were crawling up onto the land. The Mesozoic Era was punctuated by several mass extinctions, the last and most severe of which was terminal for the dinosaurs. Finally, a few episodes of heavy extinction have struck during the Cenozoic Era, affecting both marine and terrestrial life. As we shall see, these events have been linked to a long-term deterioration of the earth's climate that culminated in the cycles of glaciation and glacial retreat that have characterized the Northern Hemisphere during the past 3 million years.

EON	ERA	PERIOD		MILLION YEARS AGO	EVENTS

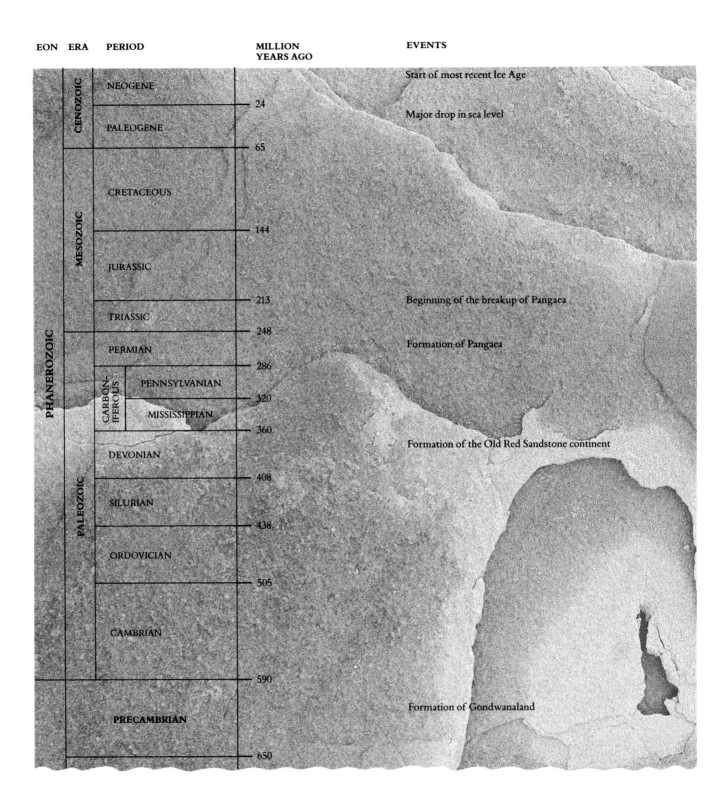

EON ERA PERIOD   MILLION YEARS AGO   EVENTS

PHANEROZOIC

CENOZOIC
- NEOGENE — Start of most recent Ice Age
- 24
- PALEOGENE — Major drop in sea level
- 65

MESOZOIC
- CRETACEOUS
- 144
- JURASSIC
- 213 — Beginning of the breakup of Pangaea
- TRIASSIC
- 248

PALEOZOIC
- PERMIAN — Formation of Pangaea
- 286
- CARBONIFEROUS
  - PENNSYLVANIAN
  - 320
  - MISSISSIPPIAN
- 360 — Formation of the Old Red Sandstone continent
- DEVONIAN
- 408
- SILURIAN
- 438
- ORDOVICIAN
- 505
- CAMBRIAN
- 590

PRECAMBRIAN — Formation of Gondwanaland
- 650

2 GEOGRAPHY AND THE AGENTS OF CATASTROPHE

Because mass extinction operates on a broad geographic scale rather than a local one, it can only be understood in the context of world geography. This chapter will review how, in the course of geologic time, major geographic features change in ways that may contribute to mass extinction. Remarkably, until the 1960s geologists were at a loss to explain the evidence of such changes, largely because it was not generally understood that continents continuously move over the surface of the earth, occasionally breaking apart or attaching to one another. Since learning about this behavior, geologists have been piecing together the details of continents' movements, with the result that we are beginning to understand the history of changes in such things as ocean circulation, the level of the seas relative to continental surfaces, and climatic patterns—all of which traditionally have been considered to have had some role in mass extinction. This chapter will evaluate these possible agents of destruction and others.

The potential proximate agents of mass extinction—the immediate causes of death—can be divided into two groups, those that represent everyday sources of mortality but somehow at times become accentuated and those that are exotic, in the sense that they do not kill off individuals and species under normal circumstances but only during mass extinctions.

Among the exotic agents that have been proposed for one or more of the great crises are sudden volcanic emissions either of poisonous gases or of darkening clouds of dust; radiation from a supernova (stellar) explosion close to the earth; and intense cosmic radiation triggered by a sudden weakening of the earth's magnetic field, which normally serves as a protective shield.

Among the mundane sources of mass extinction are global climatic change, widespread shifts in the positions of land and sea, changes in the concentration of oxygen in the atmosphere and ocean, disruption in supplies of food or nutrients, change of the salinity (salt concentration) in the ocean, and spread of turbidity (suspended sediment) throughout the oceans. It is important to note that these are everyday limiting factors—agents that also cause death and extinction on a local scale. These limiting factors may also work their destruction during mass extinctions as a result of more distal causes that are extraterrestrial in origin. Among the lethal effects that have been imputed to the impact of a large meteor, for example, are climatic cooling (from the darkening of skies by dust ejected into the atmosphere) and production of turbid water in the oceans—both kinds of change that on a smaller scale also contribute to background extinction. Similarly, any drastic change in the sun's output of radiant energy would have a devastating effect on life, but via temperature change, which on a more local scale also contributes to background extinction.

HOW CONTINENTS MOVE ACROSS THE GLOBE

Firm evidence that continents are in motion triggered a modern-day revolution in the earth sciences, giving rise to the subject known as plate tectonics. Plates are huge blocks of the earth's crust, sometimes containing continents, that move laterally over the earth's surface at the rate of a few centimeters per year—about as fast as our fingernails grow.

The idea of lateral continental movement, or continental drift as it came to be called, was hypothesized in the last century. It did not receive widespread consideration, however, until 1915, when the German geologist Alfred Wegener published the first edition of his book *On the Origin of Continents and Oceans.* What compelled all geologists' attention was the variety of arguments that Wegener and his followers advanced in favor of continental drift. The most fundamental piece of evidence was the jigsaw-puzzle fit of the modern continents into a single hypothetical supercontinent that Wegener named Pangaea. (We now know that Pangaea did exist and that it began to break apart about the time when the dinosaurs evolved.) Indications that the southern continents of Pangaea—South America, Africa, peninsular India, Australia, and Antarctica—were once interlocked were uncovered decades ago in the form of fossil evidence that particular groups of plants and animals occupied most or all of these landmasses. The most revealing fossils represented forms of life that seemed incapable of traversing broad oceans. One of these was the small reptile *Mesosaurus,* whose fossil remains are found in late Palezoic lake deposits of both Brazil and South Africa. The *Glossopteris* flora, also of late

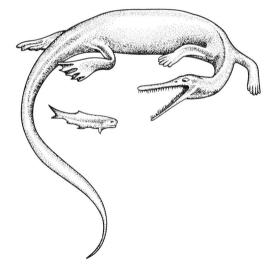

Mesosaurus, a late Paleozoic swimming reptile of small body size (length about 0.6 meters, or 2 feet) that could not have crossed large oceans, but is nonetheless found in lake deposits of both South America and Africa. Its distribution suggests that the two continents were united at the time of its existence.

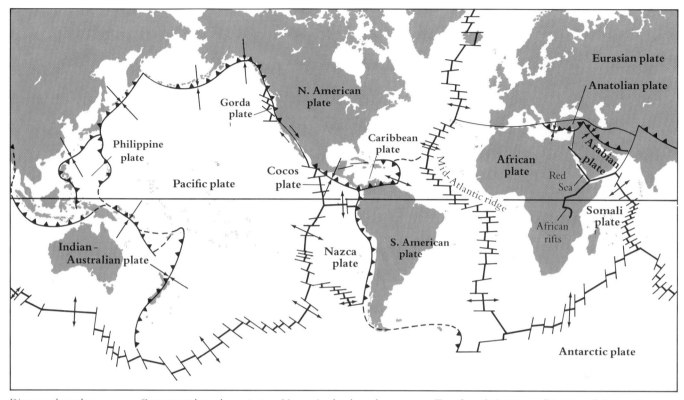

Divergent boundary ——— Convergent boundary ▲▲ Uncertain plate boundary ---- Transform fault ——— Direction of plate motion →

Plates that form the outer shell of the earth today. Some plates, such as the Indian–Australian plate, contain continents. Others, such as the Pacific plate, are entirely overlain by oceans. Any two adjacent plates are in motion relative to one another. Some move away from each other along midocean ridges, some converge along subduction zones, and others slide past each other. Midocean ridges, such as the mid-Atlantic ridge, are offset by faults.

Paleozoic age, is even more widespread, occurring on all of the southern continents. This terrestrial flora is named for a treelike plant having unusual tongue-shaped leaves and pea-sized seeds that could not possibly have blown across oceans to disperse the genus throughout the southern continents had the continents been positioned as they are today. A slightly younger fossil fauna characterized by particular kinds of terrestrial mammal-like reptiles also exists in most of the southern continents, with similar geographic implications.

Supporting evidence comes from the rock record. Early proponents of continental drift pointed out the remarkable similarities in the sequences of late Paleozoic and early Mesozoic rocks found on the southern continents. On each of these continents, sediments deposited by glaciers are overlain by coal beds harboring the *Glossopteris* fossil flora; these, in turn, give way upward to desert deposits that include sand dunes hardened into rock; and finally, at the top, there are dark

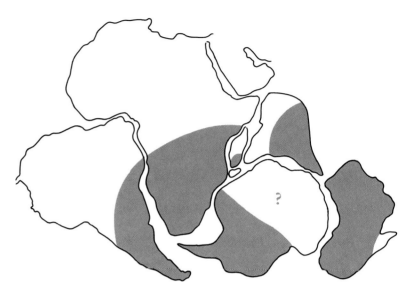

Distribution of the late Paleozoic *Glossopteris* fossil flora on the modern continents makes sense if these continents were united as Gondwanaland. Several groups of plants constitute this flora. The name *Glossopteris* means "tongue fern," with reference to the shape of this plant's leaf (photo).

rocks formed by the cooling of lava. It would have been a remarkable coincidence for precisely the same sequence of rock-forming events to have occurred independently on widely separated continents. Scratches that the glaciers gouged into bedrock offer an additional kind of evidence. They reveal that the direction of glacial movement in areas like southeastern South America, southern Australia, and India would require that the glaciers had spread inland from the ocean if the continents had been in their present positions. Because glaciers are continental features that do not move from sea to land, this is impossible. A more reasonable pattern emerges when the landmasses are assembled into a supercontinent; then southern Africa becomes a center from which glaciers radiated to the other regions.

We now recognize that more than 600 million years ago, the southern continents that share so many paleontological and geological features were united to form a supercontinent that has been named Gondwanaland. Shortly before the Age of Dinosaurs began, Gondwanaland, by virtue of northward movement, became attached to North America and Asia to form Pangaea. For almost half a century, the diverse lines of evidence favoring the idea of continental drift failed to gain widespread favor. Only for the Southern Hemisphere, where geologists were directly confronted with the strongest evidence, was the concept of drift widely accepted. The primary source of opposi-

Glaciated areas of Gondwanaland continents in their present positions. Arrows show directions of glacial movement. With continents in their present positions, these directions are problematical, implying that glaciers moved from oceans onto land.

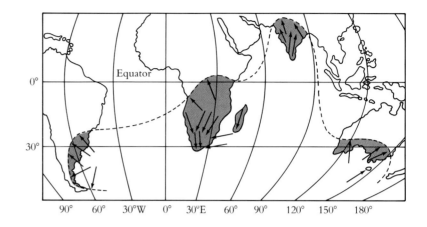

tion in North America and Europe was the argument of geophysicists that the lateral movement of continents was physically impossible. Shortly after the publication of Wegener's book, studies of the refraction of earthquake waves within the earth revealed that the continents did not rest in isolation on the denser rock of the earth's mantle (the interior zone below the earth's crust). Rather, the continents form only part of the earth's crust; a thinner and somewhat denser layer of crust lies between them, beneath the waters of the ocean. After calculating the great resistance of the oceanic crust, geophysicists concluded that no imaginable force could cause the continents to plough through it so as to drift over the mantle.

Suddenly, in 1962, a new model of continental movement obviated the geophysicists objection to the drift hypothesis. In fact, the new proposal was more than a model of continental movement. What Harry Hess of Princeton University suggested was that the entire crust of the earth is in lateral motion—not only the continents, but with them the crust beneath the seas. The idea was that new crust is being formed along the great submarine mountain chains known as midocean ridges and spreading in either direction. Along the axis of a midocean ridge is a deep valley. The mid-Atlantic ridge and valley rise above the sea surface on Iceland, providing a spectacular view of these structures and confirming the idea that they are the site of crustal formation. Here, crust is formed as dark lavas derived from the mantle rise toward the surface. There is tension where the newly produced crust spreads laterally in two directions. As a result, long fissures form, and slices of crust drop downward along these breaks to form a

Thingvellir graben in Iceland. This rift in the earth's crust is a segment of the mid-Atlantic ridge that has been elevated above sea level. Vertical faults bound the central valley, and lava periodically rises along them and spreads over the valley floor.

valley. Intermittently, more lava rises up to fill the fissures, adding more crust.

We now recognize that the upper part of the earth's mantle, the rigid zone immediately below the crust, forms and spreads laterally with the crust. The crust and this attached portion of the mantle constitute the lithosphere. Below them is the asthenosphere, the lower zone of the mantle, which is of doughy consistency.

Given the fact that the surface area of the earth is unchanging, if new lithosphere is forming and spreading along midocean ridges, then old lithosphere must be disappearing in other regions. These turn out to be deep-sea trenches, elongate depressions where the greatest depths of the oceans are found. The oceanic lithosphere on one side of a trench descends into the earth's mantle, angling downward beneath the lithosphere on the other side. When the descending lithosphere

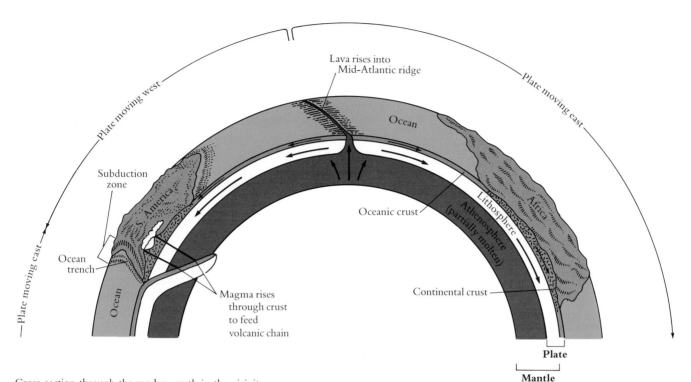

Cross-section through the modern earth in the vicinity of the southern Atlantic Ocean. South America and Africa are moving apart due to sea-floor spreading along the mid-Atlantic ridge. Oceanic crust is being subducted beneath South America, melting and releasing magma of relatively low density that rises to form deep-seated igneous rocks and also volcanoes in the Andes.

reaches great depth, it melts. Thus, the lithosphere is consumed by the asthenosphere, but the least dense components of the melted lithosphere rise upward through the doughlike mantle as magma. Some of this magma emerges at the surface, where it forms volcanoes. As a result, long chains of volcanoes, such as those that constitute the Aleutian Islands, stand alongside deep-sea trenches. The process of lithospheric descent and consumption is known as subduction, and the band of ocean floor along which it occurs is termed a subduction zone.

Harry Hess originally supported his model of crustal movement with a variety of circumstantial evidence. A high rate of heat flow from the mantle along the midocean ridges, for example, accorded with the idea that hot material was moving up from the mantle here to form new crust. Similarly, the origin of earthquakes in the mantle adjacent to subduction zones squared with the idea that a plate margin was descending here by fits and starts. (Hess was not aware that the upper mantle moves with the crust.) The definitive test, however, was based on the magnetism of the deep-sea floor. As many rocks form,

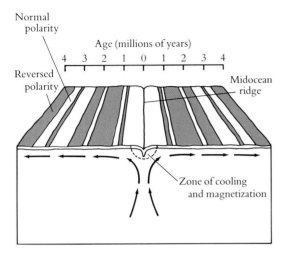

Normal
polarity

Age (millions of years)

Reversed
polarity

Midocean
ridge

Zone of cooling
and magnetization

Formation of new oceanic crust along a midocean
ridge. As iron-rich crust cools upon formation, it is
magnetized by the earth's magnetic field. Occasional
reversal of the polarity of the magnetic field results in
striping of the magnetic polarity of the newly formed
crust parallel to the ridge.

the magnetism of their iron-rich mineral grains becomes aligned with the lines of force of the earth's magnetic field. For unknown reasons, the earth's magnetic field reverses its polarity at intervals that are irregular but frequently in the order of a hundred thousand or a million years. Intervals of polarity like that of the present, when a compass needle points north, are described as normal. The times when a compass needle would have pointed south are called reversed. It was reasoned that if new crust is indeed forming at a midocean ridge and spreading in both directions away from it, then the crust nearest the ridge should display normal polarity; farther from the ridge, a band of reversed polarity should be encountered; and still farther out, another band of normal polarity. As it turned out, measurements of seafloor magnetism revealed the predicted pattern of magnetic striping parallel to midocean ridges. It is difficult to explain the origin of this configuration by any mechanism other than the origin and lateral spreading of crust at midocean ridges.

Midocean ridges and subduction zones divide the lithosphere into plates. Some plates carry continents with them, while others include only oceanic crust. Some plates are relatively small, but one is so large as to underlie most of the Pacific Ocean. Plates move away from one another along midocean ridges and converge along subduction zones, where the margin of one is subducted beneath the margin of another. In other places, plates neither move apart nor converge, but slide past one another along enormous faults. Their movement is driven by convection in the underlying mantle. Heat generated by the decay of radioactive materials in the mantle drives this convective motion, which takes the form of huge rotating gyres; hotter, less dense mantle material flows upward, and cooler mantle material flows downward to replace it. Where two adjacent gyres flow toward the surface and diverge, they produce a ridge system and new crust is formed. For reasons that are not entirely understood, convection patterns within the mantle shift occasionally, terminating the activity of some subduction zones and ridge systems and causing others to form.

Within some plates are continents, which consist of low-density crust that is locked into the oceanic crust and moves with it. Thus, continents are passengers in the conveyor belt system of plate tectonics. Some ridge systems pass from ocean basins onto continents, which they rend apart. This is achieved only with difficulty because continental crust is much thicker than oceanic crust. For this reason, incipient rifting is sometimes abortive, with convective patterns in the mantle shifting before a continent is divided. The Red Sea has recently formed where continental crust has been successfully rifted apart. A neighboring spreading system passes into Africa, where it is forming

Diagrammatic cross-section of the earth's mantle, showing huge convective cells that bring magma toward the surface along midocean ridges and cause subduction of the crust where two plates converge.

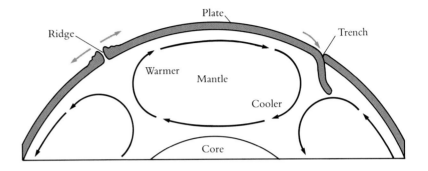

the great rift valleys, some of which harbor huge lakes such as Tanganyika. The continent of Africa is being put to the test, and it will be several million years before it will be apparent whether it will fragment along the rift valleys or hold together until the rifting ceases.

Some faults along which plates move past one another also pass onto continents. The most famous of these is the San Andreas Fault, movement along which is bringing Los Angeles and San Francisco closer together. Los Angeles sits near the margin of the Pacific plate, which is moving northward relative to the North American plate, on which San Francisco rests.

When a continent comes to lie along a subduction zone, a mountain chain forms. Because of the buoyancy afforded by its low density, the continent cannot be subducted. Instead, oceanic crust is subducted beneath the continental margin. The result is that a chain of volcanoes forms along the continental margin a short distance inland. A conspicuous example is the Cascade Range of the Pacific northwest, where subduction is occurring. The volcanic activity and a buildup of granites and other igneous rocks of low density below the volcanoes are responsible for the growth of mountains. Volcanoes build up the surface of the earth directly, whereas the rocks of low density that form within the crust as rising magma hardens build mountains indirectly; they cause the earth's surface to rise as they are buoyed up by more dense rocks below. Mountains also form when two continents collide along a subduction zone; neither continent can be subducted, but the margin of one may be wedged beneath the other to form a mountain chain. This is the way in which the lofty Himalayas have been forming after peninsular India, a fragment of Gondwanaland that moved northward, collided with Asia and began to pass beneath it. We speak of the juncture between two continents as a suture.

The Himalayas are the tallest mountain range on earth. Northward movement of the Indian–Australian plate has wedged the peninsula of India beneath the crust of southern Asia, elevating it and bending it into huge folds such as the ones shown here.

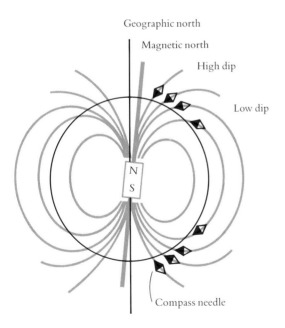

The earth as a bar magnet. Magnetic lines of force intersect the earth's surface at progressively lower angles toward the equator.

Paleomagnetism—rock magnetism— provides the most important evidence for reconstructing continental movements of the distant past. The angle of inclination of the lines of force of the earth's magnetic field varies with latitude. The magnetism imparted to rocks when they form has the angle of inclination of the magnetizing lines of force. This means that the magnetism frozen into a rock reveals the rocks' latitude at the time of formation. As noted above, rock magnetism also has a polarity, and this reveals the orientation of the rock with regard to the magnetic pole. Thus, if the rock has been immobile within continental crust, we can establish both the latitude and the orientation of that segment of crust for the time when the rock formed. What, unfortunately, we cannot determine from paleomagnetism is longitude—position along an east–west line.

HISTORY OF CONTINENTAL MOVEMENT

We have only fragmentary knowledge of continental movements prior to 700 million years ago. The history of continental movements since that time, while complex in detail, has been dominated by just a few important events. Gondwanaland, the great southern continent, was in existence at the start of this interval, but about 600 million

In Middle Ordovician time (right), the continents were widely dispersed. Gondwanaland, the large southern continent, began to encroach on the South Pole; Scandinavia and North America were far apart. By late Early Devonian time (below), Gondwanaland had crossed the South Pole, and North America and Greenland were attached to Scandinavia, with a mountain chain marking the suture zone.

MIDDLE ORDOVICIAN

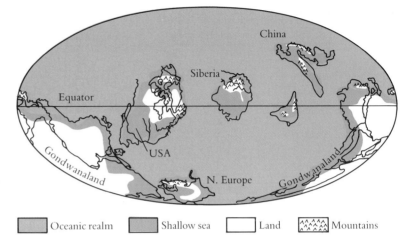

☐ Oceanic realm   ☐ Shallow sea   ☐ Land   ☐ Mountains

years ago it was equatorial in position, as were most other sizeable landmasses. It subsequently moved southward and late in the Ordovician Period, about 450 million years ago, it encroached on the South Pole. Other continents remained at lower latitudes. Among these, North America and Greenland had been attached to each other for

LATE EARLY DEVONIAN

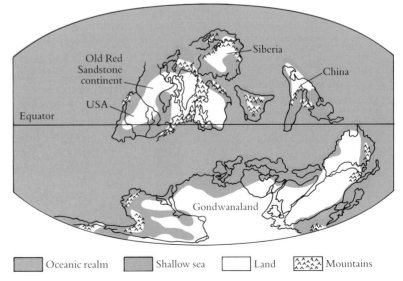

☐ Oceanic realm   ☐ Shallow sea   ☐ Land   ☐ Mountains

In Late Permian time, nearly all of the earth's continental crust was united to form the supercontinent Pangaea, which extended from pole to pole.

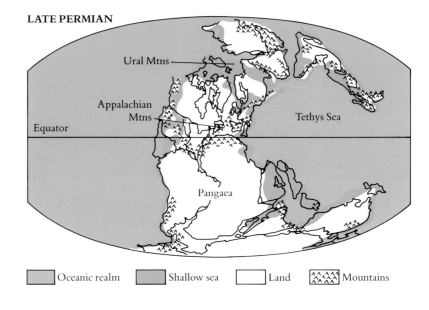

LATE PERMIAN

Ural Mtns

Appalachian
Mtns

Equator

Tethys Sea

Pangaea

☐ Oceanic realm   ☐ Shallow sea   ☐ Land   ∧∧∧ Mountains

hundreds of millions of years. During mid-Paleozoic time, they became sutured to Europe to form the large Old Red Sandstone continent, named for the Old Red Sandstone, a deposit that accumulated in freshwater environments in northern Great Britain shortly after the suturing event. The Old Red Sandstone accumulated to the east of mountains that were formed during the suturing process; similar deposits were laid down to the west of newly formed mountains (the ancestral Appalachians) in New York State and eastern Canada.

During late Paleozoic time, a more momentous suturing event took place: Gondwanaland moved northward and united with the Old Red Sandstone continent to form the bulk of Pangaea. The attachment of Asia to Europe along the Ural Mountains completed this supercontinent shortly thereafter.

Once fully formed, Pangaea was short-lived. It began to break apart early in the Mesozoic Era and by mid-Mesozoic time had been severed along an axis in the vicinity of the Mediterranean and Gulf Coast. Thus, Gondwanaland was separate from the northern landmass once again. Its subsequent history has been one of fragmentation. A look at where its fragments are today reveals the pattern of its breakup: The Atlantic Ocean was born with the rifting apart of South America and Africa (along with the separation of North America,

In Early Cretaceous time, Pangaea was beginning to fragment along new rift zones. The incipient Atlantic and Indian oceans were present, but continents were still clustered much more closely together than today.

EARLY CRETACEOUS

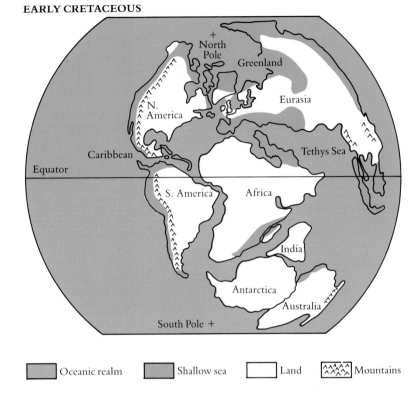

Oceanic realm	Shallow sea	Land	Mountains

Greenland, and Eurasia in the north); Antarctica and Australia parted company with the rest of Gondwanaland, drifted south, and eventually separated from one another; and peninsular India broke away from Africa and slid northward, colliding with Asia some 15 million years ago to form the Himalayas.

CAUSES OF SHIFTS IN SEA LEVEL AND CLIMATE

During all these vicissitudes, seas were alternately spreading over continents and receding and climates were alternately deteriorating and ameliorating. Plate movements were in part responsible. Changes in the rate of midocean spreading have probably caused the seas to rise

Mackay glacier, which caps a large region of Antarctica, the continent now positioned over the South Pole.

and fall relative to the level of continental surfaces. The reason is that midocean ridges owe their elevation to the high rate of heat flow from the mantle. When these structures become especially numerous or the average global spreading rate happens to increase, then their expanded volume will displace water in the ocean basins, causing it to rise higher over continental surfaces. Calculations indicate that this must be a slow process, however, and it turns out that many major changes in sea level have been much more rapid. Sedimentary rocks reveal that throughout the world, shorelines have sometimes dropped tens of meters (tens of yards) in a few tens of thousands of years. It may be that the only mechanism capable of producing such dramatic changes is the melting and thawing of ice on the land. The growth of glaciers, removing water from the global hydrological cycle, lowers the level of the oceans. The volume of glaciers that formed during the recent Ice Age locked up enough water on the land to depress sea level by about 100 meters (about 325 feet). Some geologists believe that nearly all drops of sea level that have been both rapid and pronounced have resulted from melting and thawing of glaciers—sometimes large, continental glaciers like those of the recent Ice Age and sometimes small mountain glaciers. In addition, many geologists have favored the idea that the lowering of sea level has killed off large numbers of animals restricted to shallow sea floors, which have shrunk in area.

Subsequent chapters of this book will review a variety of evidence suggesting that the growth of glaciers has often been associated with global climatic change, another potential agent of mass extinction. Furthermore, glacial growth has been related to the positions of continents. The reason is quite simple. Continental glaciers grow only on continental surfaces and their growth is initiated only at high latitudes. Thus, glaciers have developed only when continents have been situated at or near polar regions. When glaciers grow, their white surfaces increase the earth's albedo, which is the proportion of incoming sunlight that is reflected from the earth's surface. This has the effect of further cooling the earth in the glaciated region and possibly in regions far away, through the influence of winds and ocean currents.

At certain times when continents have been stationed at very high latitudes, their climates may nonetheless have been too warm to accumulate glaciers. Ice expansion may then have been initiated only by global cooling caused by some external influence. One possibility, which is all but impossible to substantiate from the rock record, is that the sun's output of radiation has fluctuated enough to influence earthly climates and the extent of glaciation.

Also, there have inevitably been changes in the degree to which the greenhouse effect has operated to warm the earth. Carbon dioxide and other compounds in the earth's upper atmosphere act in the same manner as the glass of a greenhouse. They permit solar radiation to pass to the earth's surface. Once the radiation turns into heat, however, these same compounds inhibit it from escaping from the lower atmosphere. The greenhouse effect has received much publicity following the discovery that the burning of fossil fuels and other forms of combustion carried out by the civilized world have raised levels of atmospheric carbon dioxide to the degree that the world has been warming significantly during the present century. In earlier times, several factors in the natural environment may have caused levels of carbon dioxide to fluctuate strongly enough to alter world temperatures. One of these is the abundance of plants, which consume carbon dioxide as they carry out photosynthesis. Another is the area of sediments exposed above sea level, where their weathering consumes carbon dioxide. Unfortunately, these variable are difficult to evaluate for the geological past.

AGENTS OF BIOLOGICAL CATASTROPHE

Having a general picture of the factors that alter climatic conditions and sea level, we can now consider the degree to which these kinds of large-scale changes and others contribute to biotic crises. First, we will consider two agents of extinction that have received a great deal of attention over the years. One of these, the geologically sudden lowering of global sea level, is a mechanism that I believe has been granted far too much importance as an agent of mass extinction for marine life. A second, global climatic change, I judge to have been the single most important proximate agent of mass extinction. Two others apply primarily to the marine realm: level of dissolved oxygen and the salt content of the oceans. I will also briefly discuss the previously mentioned idea that the dinosaurs died out in a crisis of extraterrestrial origin.

When the Seas Have Retreated

Traditionally, one of the most popular explanations for mass extinctions in the ocean has been that species occupying the sea floor have been eliminated when global sea level has dropped, draining shallow seas from the surfaces of continents. For perspective here, one must recognize that our present world is one in which the oceans stand lower in relation to the continents than their historical average. This means that continental shelves—the expanses of shallow sea floor

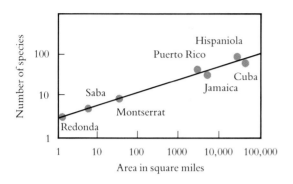

Species-area curve for amphibians and reptiles of West Indian islands. The number of native species increases markedly with island area.

where oceans lap up on the continents like soup on the broad lip of a bowl—are narrower now than at most times in the past. Today only a few broad lake-like oceans occupy continental surfaces (an example is Hudson Bay which exists only because during the recent Ice Age a continental glacier depressed the earth's crust in eastern Canada; the rebound process is not yet complete). At many times in the past, large areas of continents have been inundated by shallow seas; and it is the occasional recession of these seas on a large scale that some geologists believe to have caused widespread destruction of the life of shallow sea floors. We shall refer to this idea as the species–area hypothesis because it is based on the observation that the number of species that can occupy a region correlates with the area of suitable habitat in the region.

The obvious limitation of the species–area hypothesis is that it can provide only a partial explanation for the crises that we observe in the marine ecosystem. Many of these events affected not only bottom-dwelling life but also pelagic life—organisms that floated or swam above in the water over areas that extended far beyond the margins of continents.

There is much evidence that even for sea-floor life, lowering of sea level cannot have caused losses nearly as severe as those that occurred in the great mass extinctions. One basic question here is how many species can share a given space. For vertebrate life of islands, the answer is commonly expressed graphically as a plot of the numbers of species that occur naturally on islands of various areas. For mass extinctions of the past that coincided with lowering of sea level, we often can estimate reduction of sea floor area and reduction in number of bottom-dwelling species. Unfortunately, what we do not know for life of the sea floor is the configuration of the species–area curve, which would allow us to determine whether a given reduction of sea floor area could account for a given reduction in number of species. The problem is that in the modern world there are very few geographic regions where we have a thorough knowledge of life on shallow sea floors. Also, as I noted previously and will discuss more fully in a later chapter, regions like the western Atlantic Ocean have experienced heavy extinction during the recent Ice Age. As a result, they support impoverished faunas today that fail to manifest their true ecological capacity.

We can, however, follow a more restricted approach—one that leads to the conclusion that changes in the area of shallow sea floor have not played a major role in global marine mass extinctions. Here we simply take note of the enormous diversity of life existing today on certain small areas of shallow sea floor that have been intensively

Examples of the many species of gastropod mollusks (snails) that are endemic to the tiny Hawaiian archipelago.

studied. One of these is the tiny Hawaiian archipelago, where hundreds of species of shelled mollusks inhabit shallow seas. About 20 percent of these are endemic to the small Hawaiian biogeographic province, which means that they have no additional area in which to live. Another key region is the slender continental shelf that fringes the western coast of the Americas from the tip of Chile to Alaska. This is not like the broad shelf along eastern North America that is building seaward as sediments eroded from the land are expanding to produce a broad, depositional prism. Rather, the shelf along the western coast is a narrow shoulder of the continent that is commonly jolted by earthquakes and uplifted; for much of its length, it stands along a deep submarine trench, where the oceanic crust beneath the Pacific is underriding the adjacent continent. Fossil seashells preserved along this slender shelf reveal that the marine mollusks of the region suffered little excessive extinction during the recent Ice Age, and in this small but biotically stable region, we find a luxuriant fauna today. The shallow water species of marine mollusks, nearly all of which are restricted to the eastern Pacific, number about three thousand. This large total seems all the more remarkable when we note that the area of shallow sea floor here shrank even beyond its present narrow size during the recent Ice Age, when sea level fell as massive glaciers grew on the land. That so narrow a fringe of shallow sea floor can support

Distribution of Oligocene seas across Eurasia before the global lowering of sea level in mid-Oligocene time—an event that caused little extinction of marine life.

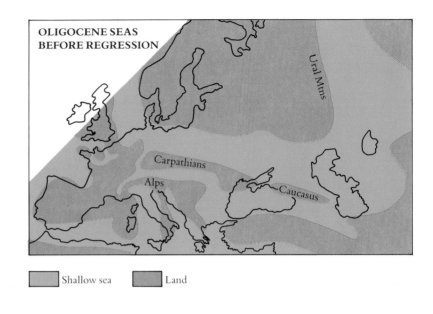

OLIGOCENE SEAS BEFORE REGRESSION

Ural Mtns

Carpathians

Alps

Caucasus

Shallow sea   Land

so many species argues against the idea that regression of seas from the land (as geologists term seaward shift of a shoreline) has devastated bottom-dwelling marine life in the distant past.

The species–area hypothesis did not arise through sheer speculation. On the basis of observations in the field, paleontologists have long linked two of the great extinctions, the ones that brought the Paleozoic and Mesozoic eras to a close, to depression of sea level throughout the world. During the final geologic period of each of these eras (the Permian Period and the Cretaceous Period) global sea level had stood higher than it stands today, lapping up over broad areas of the surfaces of continents. Early in Permian time, shallow seas stretched from Texas to Wyoming, for example, and early in Cretaceous time, a vast interior seaway spanned the length of North America, from the Arctic Ocean to the Gulf of Mexico. For many years, it was believed that sea level dropped at the end of each of the Permian and Cretaceous periods, evacuating shallow seas from many areas. In recent years, however, it has become apparent that at the very end of Cretaceous time the seas were not receding, and there is debate as to whether they were falling or rising at the close of the Permian. As I will describe shortly, other major biotic crises definitely occurred at times when sea level was not falling.

Even more damaging to the species–area hypothesis is the fact that at certain times when sea level did fall dramatically throughout the world there were no great extinctions. One of these times was mid-way through the Oligocene Epoch (Late Paleogene), slightly more than 30 million years ago, which on a geological scale of time was only yesterday. According to Peter Vail and other geologists of the Exxon Production Research Company who have been charting sea level changes in great detail by studying the sediments lying beneath continental shelves, sea level at this time dropped to a much lower position than at any other time in the past 200 million years. Before this time, seas had spread over much of the continent of Europe, and when they fell, the sea surface stood more than 100 meters (more than 300 feet) below its present level. In subsequent chapters I will review this and other relatively innocuous drops in the level of the world's oceans.

The Role of Climatic Change

There is one simple fact that makes climatic change a likely general agent for mass extinction. This is the relative ease with which a change in global temperatures can eliminate myriads of species. Two aspects of mass extinction are important in this light. One is that on two levels its impact is comprehensive. The first level is that of the species. Here we can simply remind ourselves that, by definition, for a species to become extinct, its population size must decline to zero. If a species is both populous and widespread, this is a tall order—quite a different matter even from a severe dwindling of abundance, from which re-covery is possible. The second level of comprehensive loss is at the level of the higher taxonomic group. As we have already seen, mass extinctions characteristically eliminate large numbers of families—and sometimes even whole classes—by terminating every last one of their species. These conditions place a heavy burden on causal hypotheses, many of which seem to come up short unless the causal agents operate in conjunction with other destructive agents.

The advantage of temperature change as an agent of extinction is that it permeates the environment on a global scale. Its effects are virtually inescapable. This is evident in the modern world in the man-ner in which climate controls the geographic distributions of species. Mass extinction is geographic, not local, in scale, and temperature is the primary limiting factor controlling the geographic disposition of life. Thus, we can readily envision what would happen if the tropics cooled below the thermal tolerance of most or all of the species be-longing to certain large taxonomic groups. Reef-building marine or-

Tropical coral reef at Ant Atoll in the Pacific, teeming with life near the ocean surface.

ganisms offer an example because they have been almost entirely restricted to tropical zones throughout their long and frequently disrupted history. As one travels northward beyond the Florida Keys, the modern Caribbean reef community, dominated by corals, dies out suddenly in the vicinity of Miami. Even areas to the immediate south, including the entire Caribbean, are marginal with respect to the temperatures necessary to support reef growth. There is no doubt that if this region were to experience a drop in mean annual temperature of 7 or 8°C, the reef community would be destroyed.

This argument that temperature is a likely agent of biotic crisis (an argument that we can formulate even before we examine the records of particular disasters) follows the traditional hypothetico-deductive method of science. We may never actually prove the validity of a hypothesis. If, however, we erect many hypotheses (ideally, every conceivable one) and all but one (in this case, the idea that temperature change has been the dominant immediate agent of mass extinction) are deficient when we test their predictions against patterns of extinction, then that one surviving hypothesis must be favored. The nonclimatic potential agents of mass extinction that are not relegated to secondary or insignificant roles by this approach are, for the most part, of extra-terrestrial origin (such as a jolt of cosmic radiation) or of unlikely terrestrial origin (such as the emission of noxious volcanic gases on a global scale). These are agents with the necessary destructive potential; the likelihood of any one having played a prominent role must be assessed on the basis of (1) the probability that it could have come into play, and (2) the degree to which its predicted impact on life and environments matches patterns that we observe in the geologic record.

There is one typical pattern of mass extinction that is compatible with the idea that climatic change is the dominant agent of mass extinction, but is difficult to reconcile with most alternative hypotheses: Major crises tend to wreak especially heavy devastation in the tropical zone, at least within the marine realm. This pattern is evidenced in the marine realm by the reef-building community, which has been transfigured repeatedly as a consequence of mass extinction. During the Cambrian period, the major reef builders were primitive calcareous algae and strange cone-shaped creatures of unknown biological relationships. Neither of these forms survived into middle Paleozoic time, when a community of sponges and corals assumed the dominant role, only to be decimated by mass extinction. In late Paleozoic time, other types of sponges and algae prevailed. After they were set back by the extinction that marked the end of the Paleozoic Era, the group of corals that builds reefs in the modern world came to the fore. Even the success of these corals was not uninterrupted, however. In mid-Cretaceous time, a strange group of bivalve mollusks related to burrowing cockles and clams evolved cone-shaped shells in the manner of corals, and through superior competitive abilities, these animals displaced corals as the dominant reef builders. It was only when the aberrant bivalves died out with the dinosaurs that corals resumed their preeminence, which they have maintained to the present day.

Some paleontologists have suggested that the vulnerability of reef builders and other tropical marine groups to major crises reflects a general narrowness of adaptation of tropical species. While some tropical species may be specialized with regard to food preferences, this generalization does not hold for many. For example, it appears that species of burrowing bivalve mollusks that live at high latitudes occupy the same general variety of environments and eat the same variety of foods as species that live at low latitudes. Nonetheless, in the crisis that ended the Mesozoic Era, the burrowing bivalves, like the reef-building rudist bivalves, experienced heavy losses only in the southern sector of North America. They were devastated in the Gulf of Mexico, but were virtually unscathed 1500 kilometers (about 950 miles) to the north, in North Dakota, where shallow seas flooded the continent both before and after the crisis.

There is a simple model of mass extinction via climatic change that predicts the observed tendency of tropical species to suffer especially

During mid-Cretaceous time, when polar regions were warmer than today, breadfruit plants grew in Greenland. Their leaves closely resemble those of the modern Pacific breadfruit plant (see page 44), with its edible fruit.

heavy losses. This model is based on the fact that global climatic cooling can totally eliminate the tropics, but is not likely to destroy other climatic zones. If the earth cools substantially, nontropical zones can simply migrate toward lower latitudes and, where there are no barriers, life of these zones can migrate as well. The equatorial zone, however, must simply cool down; it has no place to go. Thus, a major episode of global cooling should be expected to devastate tropical life. By the same token, global warming should eliminate species adapted to polar climates, which must warm up in the absence of a place to migrate. This model is strengthened by its ability to account for a temporal pattern that is often discerned for ancient biotic crises—a

A modern Pacific breadfruit plant.

pattern in which a single mass extinction occurs as a series of pulses. It may simply have been that each pulse occurred when temperatures reached the thermal threshold of a particular set of organisms.

At certain times in the past, the equatorial zone was probably substantially warmer than it is today. Fossil plants show, for example, that during mid-Cretaceous time, 30 or 40 million years before the dinosaurs' demise, the state of Wyoming experienced subtropical conditions, except at high altitudes, and breadfruit plants grew in Greenland. Similarly, before a moderately severe global biotic crisis occurred slightly less than 40 million years ago, southeastern England was cloaked in tropical jungles resembling those of modern Malaysia. It seems only reasonable to conclude that at times such as these the equatorial zone was also warmer than at present, and I suggest that we refer to its condition as supertropical. The implication is that at such times the equatorial region was inhabited by species that could not survive there (or anywhere else on earth) today.

The evidence that not long ago England was much warmer than today represents one fragment of a large body of information about ancient climates provided by fossil plants. Especially for the last 100 million years or so, when modern flowering plants (including hardwood trees) have flourished, plants have been regarded as the thermometers of the past. Where they have left a good fossil record, they are our best source of information about ancient climates. As will be described in subsequent chapters, plant fossils and also sedimentary deposits left by ancient glaciers show that climatic cooling did, in fact, occur at several times of global biotic crisis. Twenty years ago, we had no such evidence for even a single crisis.

Oxygen and Salt in the Oceans

The concentration of dissolved oxygen is one of the limiting factors in the ocean that has been thought to have varied on a large enough scale at times to have contributed to mass extinction. In deep marine basins, waters that are positioned below the level of stirring by surface waves can become anoxic, meaning depleted of oxygen, when the oxygen consumed in the decay of organic matter is not replenished by an influx from the atmosphere. Anoxic waters, which today are found at the bottoms of deep, stagnant lakes, seem also to have characterized the deep sea at certain times in the past. In contrast, the deep sea today is well supplied with oxygen by cold, dense waters that are descending from the surface near the earth's poles and flowing toward the equator. As a result, a large variety of animals occupy the deep-sea floor. At some past times, when the earth's poles have been much warmer, water has not descended to the deep sea at a rapid rate, and the deep sea has become anoxic and largely devoid of life. During some of these intervals oxygen-depleted waters have expanded upward so far that even shallow arms of the ocean that have spread over continental surfaces have had anoxic conditions in their deeper zones. This can be seen from the widespread abundance of fossils of bottom dwelling animals and from the accumulation of black muds, the high organic carbon content of which reflects an absence of aerobic (oxygen-utilizing) bacteria. In oxygenated habitats, these microbes decompose organic matter.

The question is whether the anoxic zone can expand even to shallow waters and thus eliminate life throughout large areas of the ocean. Here, it can be argued, is the problem with the idea that anoxic conditions have served as an important agent of mass extinction. Mass extinction has virtually always struck life of shallow marine habitats, and yet wave activity stirs the upper 10 meters (30 feet) or so of the oceans, charging it with atmospheric oxygen. Barring a major drop in the concentration of oxygen in the atmosphere, waters shallower than this should virtually always have served as a refuge for vast numbers of species.

The salt concentration, or salinity, of water at all times excludes some species from those nearshore habitats where seawater is diluted by freshwater from streams and rivers. Water masses that are permanently brackish or have fluctuating salinities are inhospitable to most species of marine life. Bays and lagoons, for example, tend to support few species. Can such a limiting factor become global in its effects, destroying huge numbers of species, genera, and families? The mechanism most often considered is the evaporation of shallow seas—a process that leaves sodium chloride and other salts high and dry on the land, while the evaporated waters return to the oceans via rainfall. Obviously, these returning waters dilute seawater, but by how much? Most calculations suggest that the volume of salt precipitated during a brief interval of geologic time has hardly ever been sufficient to lower the salinity of the oceans enough to cause heavy extinction. Even so, we cannot rule out the possibility that some species that are particularly sensitive to salinity have died out during minor perturbations of the salt balance of natural waters.

Iridium and Bombardment from Outer Space

Since 1980, much excitement has been generated by the suggestion of a group of scientists at the University of California at Berkeley that a large meteor crashed into the earth about 65 million years ago, causing the extinction of the dinosaurs and many other kinds of animals in the crisis that ended the Mesozoic Era. The primary source of evidence for this possibility, mentioned earlier, is the presence in many areas of the world of an unusually high concentration of the element iridium in a sedimentary interval that is just a few centimeters or a few tens of centimeters (up to about a foot) thick and is positioned at the boundary between rocks representing the Mesozoic and Cenozoic eras.

Advocates of the impact hypothesis invoke a number of lethal consequences for the arrival of a large meteor. Among these are acid rain and global temperature changes resulting from alteration of the earth's atmosphere. Whether some of the alleged changes could actually contribute significantly to extinction is doubtful because they are unlikely to kill more than a small fraction of the individuals of any species. An example is the generation of turbidity in the oceans (the condition in which water is murky with suspended sediment). A meteor landing in the ocean would send large volumes of sediment up into the water column. On the other hand, were a meteor to land in shallow water, where heavy extinction is commonly concentrated, the settling time would be brief—probably a matter of days—and the layer coating the life of the sea floor would be relatively thin. Nearly all species can forego food for such a brief interval, and many have efficient mechanisms for expelling unwanted sediment from their respiratory currents. There are other forms, such as some species of corals, that are relatively sensitive to an accumulation of sediment; but even these inevitably include many colonies of individuals that live upside-down above the sea floor or in the shelter of other organisms. The total annihilation of such a species means that every single polyp (tentacled, budlike individual) of every one of its billions of colonies must die out—an unlikely prospect.

In Chapter 7 I will review the evidence for the lethal impact of an extraterrestrial object at the end of the Mesozoic Era. For now, it will be sufficient to note that there are no firm geological data suggesting that earlier mass extinctions resulted from this kind of event. In fact, for some of these events there is evidence opposing this idea— evidence of more mundane causation. This is documentation in the earth's sedimentary record of climatic changes resulting from movements of continents over the surface of the globe.

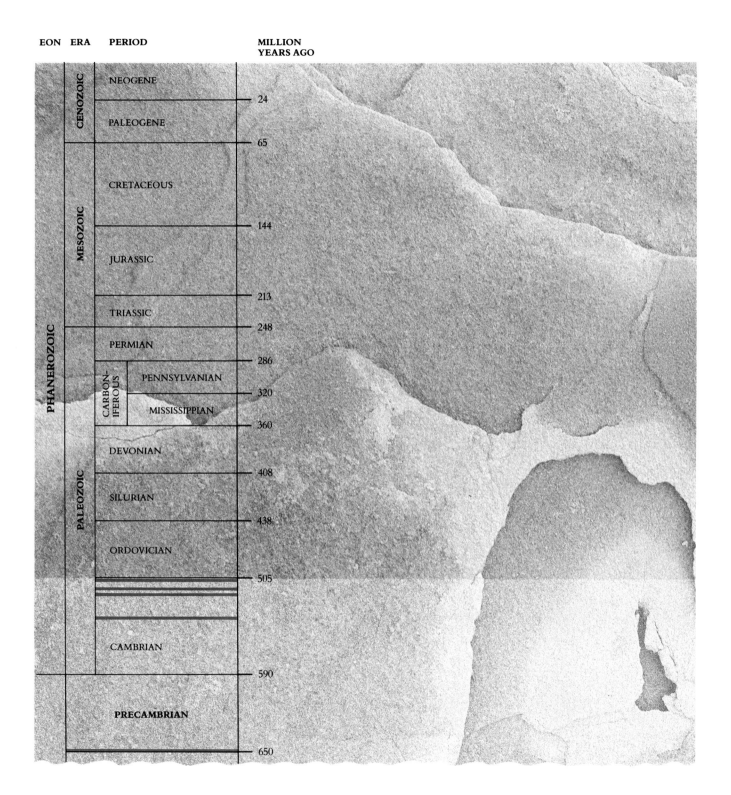

EON	ERA	PERIOD		MILLION YEARS AGO
PHANEROZOIC	CENOZOIC	NEOGENE		
				24
		PALEOGENE		
				65
	MESOZOIC	CRETACEOUS		
				144
		JURASSIC		
				213
		TRIASSIC		
				248
	PALEOZOIC	PERMIAN		
				286
		CARBON-IFEROUS	PENNSYLVANIAN	
				320
			MISSISSIPPIAN	
				360
		DEVONIAN		
				408
		SILURIAN		
				438
		ORDOVICIAN		
				505
		CAMBRIAN		
				590
		PRECAMBRIAN		
				650

3 EARLY CRISES AND THE DAWNING OF HIGHER LIFE

To glimpse the earliest known mass extinction, we must travel back more than half a billion years in geologic time to just before the transition between the two fundamental divisions of earth history. The first of these intervals was dominated until almost its very end by single-celled organisms. This early interval is informally termed the Precambrian in recognition of the fact that it was followed immediately by the Cambrian Period. It was during Cambrian time that multicellular life first left a rich fossil record because many groups of animals evolved durable—and thus readily preservable—skeletons. The Cambrian, then, is the first period of the second great division of earth history—the eon known as the Phanerozoic, which means the interval of well-displayed life.

PRECAMBRIAN LIFE

The first mass extinction thus far recorded, which took place shortly before the dawning of Phanerozoic time, differed from later crises in one important way: The victims were of limited biological variety. There is no contradiction here with our earlier definition of mass extinction; it is simply that life, even in the oceans, had not yet diversified greatly. There were only a few kinds of organisms to be subjected to catastrophic environmental change. As for most later crises, however, the evidence surrounding this early mass extinction is compatible with the idea that climatic change was the primary agent of extinction.

Precambrian time began with the origin of the earth, about 4.6 billion years ago, and the oldest fossils yet discovered are about a billion years younger than this. Not surprisingly, these earliest forms are prokaryotes, the group to which the most primitive living cells

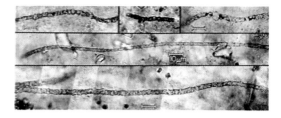

Filamentous algae (top) of the type that form stromatolites. These particular chains of cells are of late Precambrian age. Cross-sections of fossil stromatolites (bottom) of late Precambrian age. Layers are clearly visible within the columnar growths.

belong. Prokaryotes are single-celled organisms that lack a nucleus and that do not have their genetic material organized into chromosomes. They constitute the kingdom Monera, which is split into two divisions: the Schizophyta (traditionally called bacteria) and the Cyanophyta (formerly known as blue-green algae). Like algae and higher plants, cyanophytes conduct photosynthesis that results in the release of molecular oxygen. Early prokaryotic fossils are of two types: microscopic remnants of cells and large, layered structures called stromatolites. The cell remnants include nearly spherical forms and filaments constituting chains of cells. Some of these structures apparently represent schizophytes and others represent cyanophytes, but it is difficult to determine to which of these groups some fossil material should be assigned. Stromatolites were (and are still today) built primarily by filamentous cyanophytes.

Nowhere in the fossil record has a true mass extinction of prokaryotic organisms been uncovered, and these groups continue to thrive today. The cyanophytes did, however, decline markedly in abundance early in the Phanerozoic Eon. Previously, the stromatolites that they produced, sometimes cabbagelike and sometimes reeflike, had carpeted vast areas of shallow sea floor. Their fossil record in this early interval is voluminous and sometimes spectacular. While a graduate student at Johns Hopkins University, Peter Garrett developed a strong case that it was the diversification of animal life early in Phanerozoic time that caused the stromatolites' decline. The kinds of filamentous cyanophytes that formed the early stromatolites exist today, but seldom do they flourish sufficiently to produce stromatolites. To construct one of these structures, they must grow into a thin mat of sticky, tangled filaments on the sea floor and then trap particles of sediment. Through the layer of sediment thus formed they then send a few filaments to produce another mat. It is the alternation of organic-rich and organic-poor layers that gives the mound-shaped stromatolite, the product of upward growth, its layered internal structure. In the modern world, the growth of stromatolites is usually thwarted by the presence of grazing and burrowing animals, such as snails and worms, that destroy algal mats. Under controlled conditions, in which these kinds of animals have been fenced out of areas where filamentous cyanophytes occur, the latter have been successful at forming mats. Nature herself has actually conducted similar experiments, with the same results. Stromatolites flourish today only in two kinds of marginal marine environments, which are hostile to most forms of animal life. One is the supratidal zone—the narrow fringe of territory that is neither land nor sea but that is exposed to the baking sun or to rain, except when occasional storms inundate it with marine

Living stromatolites exposed during low tide at Shark Bay, Western Australia, where the water is too saline for destructive animals to flourish. The larger stromatolites here are the size of a large upholstered hassock.

waters. Here, where neither terrestrial nor marine animals thrive, cyanophytes have the opportunity to construct stromatolites, at least in tropical areas like the Great Bahama Bank, which provide the warm temperatures necessary for the growth process. The organisms that build stromatolites are incredibly hardy: Dry them out and they become dormant; add water and they come back to life. The second kind of habitat that fosters stromatolite growth is a marginal marine lagoon whose waters are so much saltier than those of the open ocean that few animals can survive. Bodies of water of this type develop in hot, arid environments where the high rate of evaporation and weak communication with the open sea cause the salt concentration to rise to a toxic level. The best example is Shark Bay in Western Australia where, in the near absence of damaging animal life, stromatolites flourish in the intertidal zone and below.

While stromatolites grew rampantly on late Precambrian sea floors before the evolution of destructive animals, other kinds of cyanophytes lived a planktonic life, which means that they floated in waters shallow enough to be well illuminated by sunlight. At this early stage of earth history, all floating organisms were plantlike forms—what we term phytoplankton. Floating animals, or zooplankton, which today include such forms as protozoans and minute crustaceans, had not yet evolved. Fossil evidence reveals that about 1.4 bil-

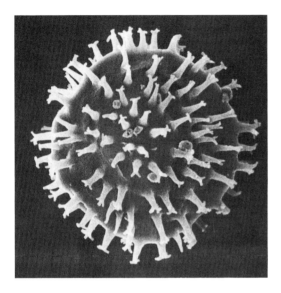 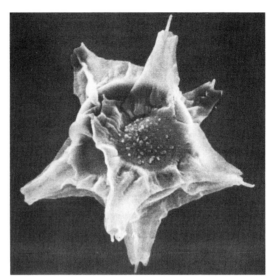

Examples of acritarchs, the group that suffered the first known mass extinction in earth history. Acritarchs are the durable dormant stages of single-celled algae.

lion years ago, at least 2 billion years after prokaryotic life evolved, the modern kind of cell came into being: Eukaryotic algae joined the cyanophytes as aquatic plankton. Unlike prokaryotes, eukaryotes possess a nucleus and their genetic material is segregated into chromosomes. Thus, they comprise not only many single-celled organisms and algae, but all multicellular plants and animals.

The evidence for the existence of the eukaryotic cell about 1.4 billion years ago is based primarily on the size and wall structure of fossil cells. Many eukaryotic algae have spiny or complexly textured cell walls. Studying both flattened cells preserved in dense shale, a highly compacted rock, and three-dimensional cell remains preserved in chert, an uncompacted sedimentary rock consisting of finely crystalline quartz, the Soviet paleontologist B. F. Timofeev and J. William Schopf of the University of California at Los Angeles have documented a change in the spectrum of sizes of algal cells about 1.4 billion years ago. Before this time, there were few cells with diameters larger than 10 micrometers (1 micrometer = 1×10^{-6} meter) and almost no cells reaching 60 micrometers across. Sizes below 20 micrometers typify prokaryotic cells today, and the first appearance in the fossil record of many larger cells is taken to signal the advent of the eukaryotic condition. Nearly all of the large, eukaryotic cells are assigned to the group of algae know as acritarchs. This is thought not to be a homogeneous taxonomic group, but a collection of eukaryotic forms whose biological properties cannot be easily ascertained from their preserved remains.

THE FIRST GREAT EXTINCTION?

The fossil record of the acritarchs reveals what was perhaps the first great extinction. From a humble beginning about 1.4 billion years ago, the acritarchs diversified to the point where, after about 700 million years, they included many species. This expansion has been documented by Gonzalo Vidal of the University of Lund, Sweden, and Andrew Knoll of Harvard University. They have also observed that the diversification of the acritarchs came to an abrupt halt, about 650 million years ago. On a geological scale of time, this crisis occurred slightly before the Phanerozoic Eon began, about 590 million years ago. While these authors have documented the crisis in detail only in Scandinavia, where about 70 percent of the flora disappeared, they have advanced two kinds of evidence that the event was truly a mass extinction. First, the kinds of plant and animal life that disappeared did not reappear after the crisis; in other words, the disappearances were true extinctions, not temporary emigrations. Second, the same kind of decline is documented in the fossil records of Africa and Australia.

Vidal and Knoll note a temporal correspondence that is potentially of great importance. The acritarch extinctions coincided with what may have been the greatest episode of continental glaciation in the entire history of the earth. This event left deposits of gravelly sediments ploughed up by glaciers in a remarkable number of areas, including Greenland, Scotland, Scandinavia, the Soviet Union, China, and Australia. Surprisingly, some of these regions were apparently positioned at low latitudes at the time of glaciation. For example, Australia, according to interpretations based on rock magnetism, was located near the equator. From our modern perspective, it seems remarkable that about 650 million years ago glaciers spread across large areas of Australia not far from the equator. In contrast, during the recent Ice Age, which began about 3 million years ago, large continental glaciers (as opposed to smaller glaciers of mountain valleys) have been confined to high latitudes, being centered in Canada, Greenland, Scandinavia, and Antarctica. (As we shall see in Chapter 9, glaciers have waxed and waned during the recent Ice Age, and they will return again.)

As Vidal and Knoll have suggested, the temporal coincidence of the acritarch extinctions with exceptionally widespread glacial activity

Evidence of late Precambrian glaciation in Australia.
The scratches on ancient bedrock resulted from the
movement of glaciers with rocks frozen into their
lower surfaces. The man is examining a boulder within
coarse sediment that was ploughed up and then deposited by the glacier.

raises the possibility of causal connection. Such a connection is not
firmly established, and yet the pattern is consistent with a theme introduced in Chapter 2: the correspondence between mass extinction
and climatic change.

TRILOBITES APPEAR AND DISAPPEAR

The first mass extinctions that afflicted the animal world followed
rapidly upon the initial evolutionary diversification of higher animals.
Higher animals, as opposed to higher plants, are inherently vulnerable
to mass extinction. The first primitive multicellular animals appeared
on earth sometime very late in Precambrian time. The dating of their
origin is hindered both by the imperfection of radiometric dating
techniques and by controversies as to what geological features constitute actual fossil remains. For years, paleontologists have scoured the
Precambrian record in search of a very ancient record of animal life.
Candidates for early animal fossils in sedimentary rocks include tube-
shaped structures that might constitute burrows of wormlike animals.
Claims of biological origins for such structures older than a billion
years are automatically suspect. Structures that are universally accepted

Reconstruction of some of the invertebrate animals represented by fossils of latest Precambrian age. These animals differ from creatures of the modern world, and their biological relationships and modes of life are controversial.

to be animal fossils are relatively abundant in rocks dated at between 700 and 800 million years. These forms include the tracks, trails, and burrows of soft-bodied animals that moved over and through sand and mud. They also include imprints of soft-bodied animals that have been variously interpreted as jellyfish, segmented worms, and forms of life not closely related to any known taxonomic group of younger age. Lacking armor or bodily support from hard, mineralized structures, these animals appear to represent an early stage of animal evolution, when predatory animals were small and primitive.

The Cambrian Period, the first period of the Phanerozoic Eon, was marked by the presence of numerous animals with skeletons; the base of the Cambrian approximately corresponds to the time when such animals first evolved. The earliest skeletonized animals were tiny creatures whose dimensions are generally measured in millimeters (1 millimeter = 0.04 inch); many would have been quite unfamiliar to a modern-day zoologist, but some belonged to classes of sponges and mollusks that still exist. After these small forms of life had ruled the

Early Cambrian trilobite of the olenellid group, the most primitive trilobites. The segmentation of these animals resembles that of many other arthropods, including pill bugs and centipedes.

sea floor for perhaps 15 million years, the trilobites made their appearance. These arthropods—three-lobed, as their name suggests—had sturdy, calcified skeletons that left an excellent fossil record. Many species of trilobites crawled on and burrowed through sea floor sediment with their numerous legs, each pair positioned beneath a segment of the external skeleton, and the rare preservation of trilobite mouth parts, which were also located on the underside of the body, reveals that they consumed small food objects. Perhaps some were micropredators, feeding on minute animals, and others fed on organic detritus; we will never know the range of their diet. Other trilobites, especially those known as agnostids, spent their life in the water above the sea floor. These were mostly small forms that presumably floated in the water but engaged in modest swimming movements. Their fossil occurrence over broad geographic areas reflects the fact that they were carried great distances by ocean currents. In fact, many types of agnostids that occur in North America are also found in Asia and Australia.

Early in the Cambrian Period the trilobites rose to a dominant ecological position on shallow sea floors. Before the end of the period, however, they suffered at least four mass extinctions, three of which are especially well documented. The first crisis for the trilobites appears to have taken place at the end of the interval of time known as the Early Cambrian Epoch. At this juncture, the oldest group of trilobites, the olenellids, died out, and they were not alone. Also disappearing was a strange group of organisms, thought to have been animals rather than plants, that were the primary builders of the world's first organic reefs. These creatures, known as archaeocyathids, secreted vaselike skeletons with the configuration of a cone within a cone, the two cones being perforated by holes and connected to one another by partitions. Although this early mass extinction has not been well studied, it represents the first of the already mentioned series of crises that decimated reef-building communities of tropical seas.

The three other mass extinctions of trilobites, which took place during the Late Cambrian Epoch, have been much more carefully investigated by the study of sedimentary rocks and their fossils on the continent of North America, and at least one of the crises has also been shown to have struck in Australia. The North American rocks reveal that as the Cambrian Period progressed, marginal seas lapped farther and farther up onto the continent, which at the time was generally low-lying and devoid of uplands. In the United States, rocks representing the earliest Cambrian are restricted to eastern and western zones where mountains now rise up. As the later Cambrian seas

X ray of a trilobite hidden within a piece of shale. The antennae are visible, as are some of the limbs, extending beyond the carapace.

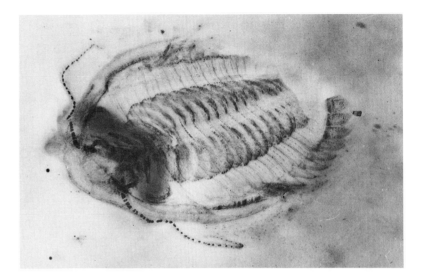

Reconstruction of archaeocyathids, strange, cone-shaped reef-builders that failed to survive beyond Early Cambrian time.

spread farther inland, calcium carbonate sediments, which are typically restricted to tropical climatic zones, accumulated on their shallow floors. Eventually these turned into limestone. Most limestone consists primarily of particles of calcium carbonate derived from the fragmentation of skeletons of several types of marine organisms. Today mollusks, calcareous algae, and sea urchins are among its most important contributors. Calcium carbonate sediment becomes consolidated into limestone by cement that also consists of calcium carbonate and often has been dissolved from the sediment itself and reprecipitated between the grains. Organic reefs are limestone structures that have solid frameworks even as they stand on the sea floor—frameworks formed primarily by corals and calcareous algae that cement themselves to one another. It is not surprising that carbonate sediments accumulated over large areas of North America during the Late Cambrian because, as revealed by rock magnetism, North America at that time sat astride the equator. Trilobites that lived in the shallow waters that flooded the continent were adapted to tropical conditions, and during most of Late Cambrian time their aqueous habitat occupied all but a small island in the continental interior.

Each of the three Late Cambrian mass extinctions terminated a major adaptive radiation of trilobites: Each event caught the animals when they were flourishing. The effects of these crises were focused not only on the trilobites, however. At least one of the crises also

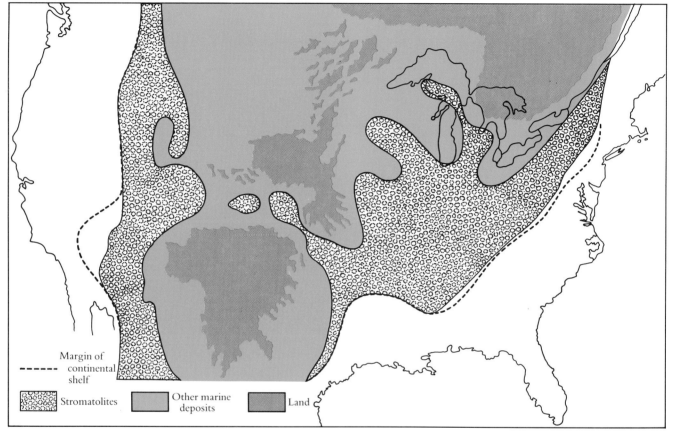

LATEST CAMBRIAN

Margin of
- - - continental
shelf

Stromatolites   Other marine   Land
                 deposits

Broad distribution of shallow seas and stromatolites across the North American continent during Late Cambrian time.

decimated the brachiopods, which are double-shelled animals known informally as lamp shells, and at least one also took a heavy toll on the conodonts. Conodonts were animals that left an abundance of tooth-like structures in the fossil record and, through a single fossil occurrence of bodily impressions, are now known to have been eel-shaped swimmers.

THE SEARCH FOR A CAUSE

Allison Palmer of the Geological Society of America has analyzed the pattern of the Late Cambrian mass extinctions in great detail through his field work in the western United States. At intervals of just a few centimeters he has carefully sampled strata spanning the rock records

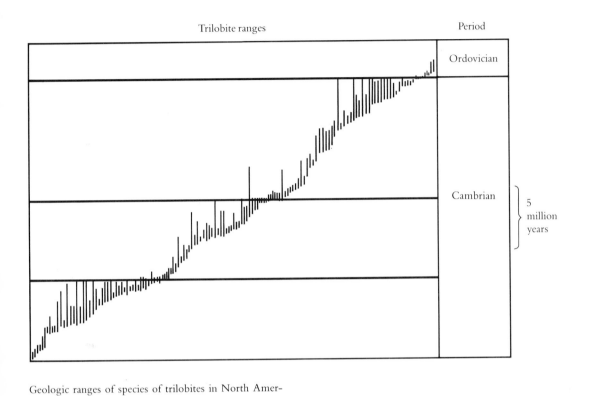

Geologic ranges of species of trilobites in North America during the latter part of Cambrian time. Each bar represents one species. Three mass extinctions are indicated by horizontal lines.

of mass extinctions. The trilobite fossils gathered in this way reveal the same kind of pattern for all three mass extinctions. Examining samples collected upward through stratigraphic sections, Palmer has found that suddenly, within an interval of a centimeter or less (less than 0.5 inch), most of the genera that existed before each crisis disappear from the record, never to reappear. Two or three of the genera survived the crisis and, along with a few genera that invaded from some other region, these forms went on to flourish, as evidenced by their great abundance in the fossil record. Very quickly, one of the new genera came to dominate the fauna at a time that must be regarded as the climax of the extinction event, a time when only one type of animal—known in the field of ecology as an opportunist—seems to have been well adapted to the changed environmental conditions. Only very slowly did the fauna rediversify, by the evolution of new species.

Sedimentary rocks of Cambrian age do not contain radioactive minerals suitable for accurate radiometric dating, but such minerals in igneous rocks reveal that the Late Cambrian Epoch lasted about 20 million years, and from this we know that the trilobite extinctions were separated by intervals of a few million years. In contrast, it can-

Conodonts, the minute tooth structures of extinct eel-like animals. Imprints of the entire conodont animal are very rare in the fossil record, but teeth are common.

not have taken more than a few thousand years, or perhaps much less, for deposition of the centimeter of limestone that records the sudden disappearance of the fauna struck down by each of the three mass extinctions. Each of these narrow intervals has attracted detailed examination. A search across each of the first two crisis intervals has failed to locate any anomalously high concentration of iridium that might implicate an extraterrestrial meteor or comet. For each of the three crises, the nature of the narrow interval differs from location to location, but for the first two there is no evidence of a break in deposition of marine sediment that would signal the evacuation of shallow seas from the broad surface of the North American continent.

Limestones in Utah representing the interval of a Late Cambrian mass extinction. The arrow points to the level in the rock at which numerous trilobites suddenly disappeared. There was no interruption of sediment accumulation at the time of extinction.

James F. Miller of Southwest Missouri State University has, however, documented the existence of a surface of erosion at the position of the third episode of extinction in North America. He concludes that seas at this time drained from large areas of the continent. A similar marine withdrawal has been noted in Scandinavia, which seems to confirm the idea that at this time there occurred a global lowering of sea level. This episode marked the end of the Cambrian Period and the start of the Ordovician. Miller has noted that rocks dating from slightly after the end of the Cambrian in South America contain sediments of glacial origin, the definitive characters of which are scratched and faceted cobbles and boulders that were sculpted as they slid along at the bases of moving glaciers. Presumably the growth of glaciers early in the Ordovician Period trapped a considerable volume of water on the land in the form of ice, causing sea level to decline throughout the world. Presumably also, the expansion of glaciers coincided with widespread cooling, at least on a regional scale.

Withdrawal of shallow seas, though it may have occurred at the time of the final crisis of the Late Cambrian, fails as a causal explanation for this event. If it were an effective agent of extinction, then it should have caused severe losses midway between the first and second of the Late Cambrian mass extinctions; geologists have long recognized that at this time shallow seas disappeared from most areas of North America.

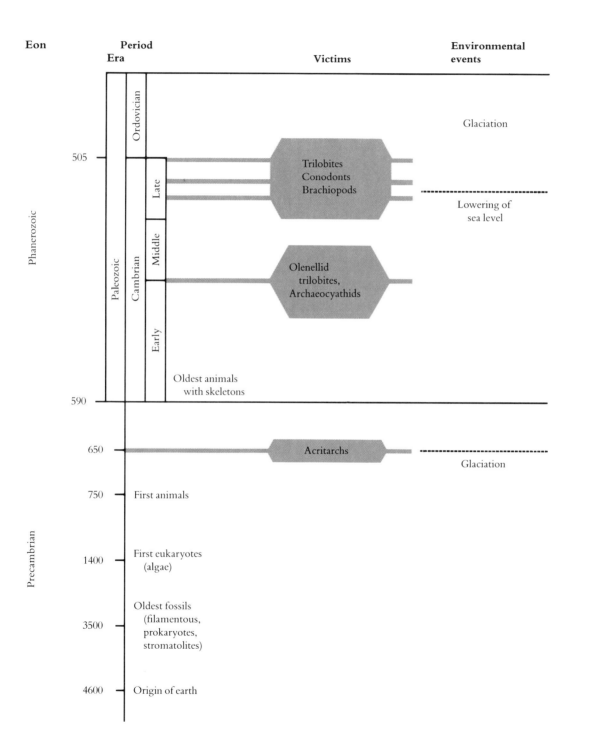

Eon	Period Era	Victims	Environmental events

Ordovician — Glaciation

505

Trilobites
Conodonts
Brachiopods

Lowering of sea level

Olenellid trilobites, Archaeocyathids

Oldest animals with skeletons

590

650   Acritarchs

Glaciation

750   First animals

1400   First eukaryotes (algae)

3500   Oldest fossils (filamentous, prokaryotes, stromatolites)

4600   Origin of earth

Phanerozoic — Paleozoic — Cambrian (Late, Middle, Early)

Precambrian

Major events of Precambrian and Cambrian time. Colored horizontal bars depict mass extinctions.

Allison Palmer has joined Michael Taylor of the United States Geological Survey and James Stitt of the University of Missouri in entertaining the hypothesis that the catastrophes of Late Cambrian time occurred when cool waters from deep zones of the oceans spread up onto the continent and eliminated all but the hardiest species of marine life. Deep waters are not only cold, they are often also depleted in dissolved oxygen; Palmer and Taylor have proposed both chilling and oxygen starvation as possible agents of extinction. There is, however, a fundamental problem with the oxygen hypothesis: the apparent impossibility of maintaining low oxygen levels in the upper 15 to 20 meters (about 50 to 65 feet) of the water column of a broad, unrestricted sea. In this zone, waves stir the waters sufficiently to keep them well supplied with atmospheric oxygen. Not only were large areas of sea floor on the North American continent shallower than this, but many planktonic agnostid trilobites—a group also affected by the crisis—must have floated close to the surface.

The idea that cooling of the shallow Cambrian seas caused the crises enjoys some empirical support. First, it appears that most of the trilobites that recolonized these environments evolved from a group known as the olenids. A key observation, then, is that the olenids were ordinarily the denizens of cool, offshore sea floors and also of shallow habitats in Scandinavia, which is believed at that time to have been positioned at a higher latitude than North America. These patterns of occurrence suggest that the olenids went largely unscathed because of their tolerance of cool conditions, and that their descendants were able to colonize the impoverished shallow seas in the aftermaths of the mass extinctions because they were tolerant of the cool conditions that then prevailed. Limestone deposition continued without interruption at many locations during the crises, so conditions may have remained marginally tropical. A second piece of evidence, advanced by Michael Taylor, is that near the end of Cambrian time, the trilobite faunas of western North America became more uniform between the shoreline and the submarine continental margin. During the second-to-last age of the Cambrian, a distinctive group of species had inhabited nearshore environments. During the final age, these environments came to be occupied by genera that were more widespread—ones able to live not only near the shore but also farther offshore, presumably in cooler waters. This change may have signalled the beginning of a large-scale thermal transition. Unfortunately, we have no idea what may have caused climates to cool repeatedly during Late Cambrian time.

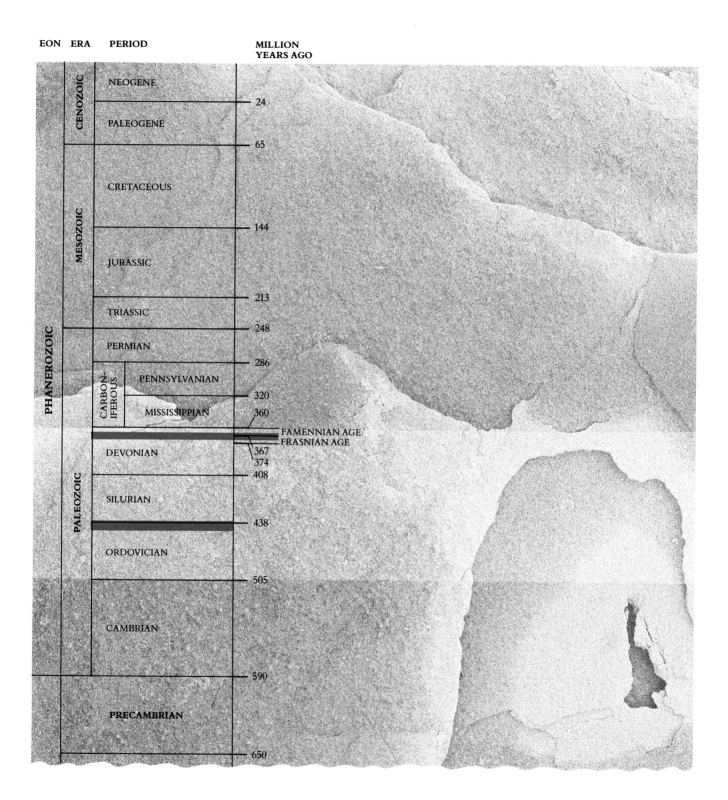

EON	ERA	PERIOD		MILLION YEARS AGO
PHANEROZOIC	CENOZOIC	NEOGENE		
		PALEOGENE		24
	MESOZOIC	CRETACEOUS		65
		JURASSIC		144
		TRIASSIC		213
				248
	PALEOZOIC	PERMIAN		
		CARBON–IFEROUS	PENNSYLVANIAN	286
			MISSISSIPPIAN	320
				360
		DEVONIAN		FAMENNIAN AGE / FRASNIAN AGE / 367 / 374
		SILURIAN		408
		ORDOVICIAN		438
				505
		CAMBRIAN		
		PRECAMBRIAN		590
				650

4 GLACIATION AND THE ORDOVICIAN AND DEVONIAN CRISES

The final mass extinction of the Cambrian Period marked a major change in the history of life. Whereas the trilobite is the natural biological symbol of the Cambrian, the ensuing Ordovician Period is not so easily characterized. Following the crisis that marked the end of the Cambrian, life rebounded just as it had after the earlier mass extinctions of trilobites. This time, however, the expansion was broader. Groups of animals that had played minor roles in Cambrian seas now assumed prominence, and altogether new groups appeared. Trilobites recovered to a degree, but during the Ordovician Period—and forever after—they remained less diverse and played a lesser role in the ecosystem.

The rich fauna that emerged after Cambrian time suffered three mass extinctions during the Paleozoic Era—the first at the end of the Ordovician Period (about 440 to 450 million years ago), the second near the end of the Devonian Period (about 360 to 370 million years ago), and the third at the end of the Permian Period (about 250 to 255 million years ago). This final event brought the Paleozoic Era to a close. These three extinctions rank among the five greatest of all time in level of devastation within the world's oceans. Each of these crises eliminated a higher percentage of preexisting marine families than did the later Cretaceous event, famous for having swept away the dinosaurs.

This chapter describes the Ordovician and Devonian crises, and the following chapter, the Permian event. What is striking about these Paleozoic crises is that all three share a large number of patterns, each of which emerges as a theme of these chapters. Patterns of extinction suggest that climatic cooling was for each event the dominant agent of mass extinction, and geological evidence indicates that each event occurred during the onset of a glacial episode, triggered when a large continent approached or passed over one of the earth's poles.

The expansion of new forms of marine life after the
Cambrian Period. Families that originated in Cambrian
time are labeled the Cambrian fauna. A dramatic adaptive radiation during the Ordovician Period produced a
great increase in the diversity of life.

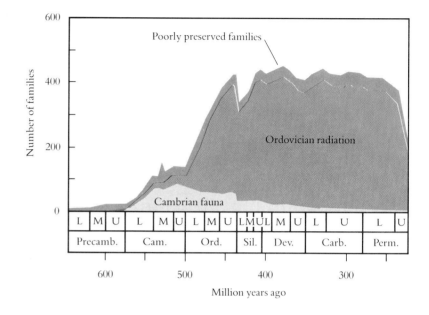

Before examining the nature of each mass extinction, it is necessary
to review the dramatis personae—the groups of organisms that populated the world when the event began.

THE ORDOVICIAN RECOVERY

Trilobites never regained the prominence they enjoyed during the
Cambrian Period. There is little question that their reduced success
resulted from the great expansion of other forms of life. Possibly
the primary reason was the appearance of a new kind of predator:
the nautiloid, ancestor of all squids and octopuses. Living pearly
nautiluses, which are actually a group of closely related species, are the
sole surviving nautiloids. In contrast to modern coiled forms, early
nautiloids were small and had straight or gently curved conical shells.
Like virtually all of their descendants within the molluscan class
Cephalopoda, the ancestral nautiloids were almost certainly mobile
predators, swimming by jet propulsion and snaring their prey in a
battery of tentacles before tearing it apart with an underbiting but
otherwise parrotlike beak.

Nautiloids, relatives of the modern squid and octopus, were swimming predators that assumed a major ecological role in Ordovician seas. Nautiloid shells are divided into gas-filled chambers by partitions, some of which are visible in the fossil (top) from which the outer shell has been partly worn away. Many Ordovician nautiloids, including the fossil shown, had straight shells, in contrast to the sole surviving nautiloid genus, the pearly nautilus (middle), which is shown in a rare underwater photograph in nature. The squid (bottom), also shown in life, is a type of cephalopod that lacks a shell and swims much more rapidly than the pearly nautilus.

Only recently has it been discovered that nautiloids underwent a dramatic but localized adaptive radiation near the end of Cambrian time. This event is recorded in the sedimentary record of China and apparently was confined to the region in which this country was positioned late in Cambrian time, a region whose ancient location remains ill-defined. Given this Cambrian origin, it is quite possible that in earliest Ordovician time the nautiloids got the jump on the trilobites, in an evolutionary sense, diversifying rapidly and then, by virtue of their predatory habits, suppressing the trilobites' recovery. Before the end of the Ordovician Period, some straight-shelled nautiloids attained lengths of almost 3 meters (about 10 feet). Nearly all groups of trilobites that lived after the Cambrian could roll up in the manner of a pill bug, but this behavior, while providing temporary protection for the soft underbelly, was no permanent solution for escape from a persistent and powerful attacker such as a nautiloid. Modern crabs, in contrast, are fully housed in a boxlike exoskeleton that is formed by the folding of the carapace under the body while the legs remain free for locomotion; crabs are much less vulnerable to predators than are trilobites.

The rapid post-Cambrian expansion of other kinds of marine life than nautiloids perhaps also braked the reexpansion of the trilobites by populating the seas not only with new kinds of predators but also with competitors for food and space. Many of the groups of animals that became diverse and populous in Ordovician seas remained so until the end of the Paleozoic Era, some 200 million years after the Ordovician came to a close. They formed the cast of characters that were featured in the three great Paleozoic episodes of mass extinction.

Among the animals that came to flourish during the Ordovician Period were other molluscan groups, chiefly gastropod and bivalve mollusks. These are the animals that produce seashells. Gastropods comprise snails of all types, including those that live in freshwater and terrestrial settings; bivalves include clams, mussels, scallops, oysters, and their relatives. The gastropods had achieved a substantial evolutionary beginning during the Cambrian, but the bivalves were rare before mid-Ordovician time. By Late Ordovician time, however, a wide variety of bivalves were present, some burrowing in the sediment and some resting on the surface.

Brachiopods, known informally as lamp shells, were especially diverse and abundant on Ordovician sea floors. Although not mollusks, brachiopods are double-shelled marine animals that bear a superficial resemblance to bivalves, and like most bivalves they strain their food from the water. Despite temporary setbacks by heavy extinction, brachiopods sustained their success throughout the Paleozoic

A fossil trilobite that died and was preserved in an enrolled, protective posture.

Era to the degree that they are the most abundant macroscopic fossils in rocks of this age. Today brachiopods are well represented in only a few areas—most notably the shallow waters fringing New Zealand—and many live beneath rocks or in crevices within coral reefs.

During the second half of the Ordovician Period, distant cousins of the brachiopods, the bryozoans, formed stony colonies, some of which were massive and some of which had fingerlike branches. Bryozoans of the modern world form less substantial colonies; many encrust hard surfaces, including the hulls of boats.

Starfish also made their appearance during Ordovician time, and their record, although meager because of their weakly developed internal skeleton, is adequate to reveal that all of the major groups alive today evolved at this early time. There can be little doubt that the Ordovician starfish, like their close living relatives, were carnivores that everted their stomachs to digest the prey that they held with hydraulically operated suckers arrayed along their arms.

Crinoids, informally known as sea lilies but actually closely related to starfish, established a foothold on Ordovician sea floors that they did not relinquish until the Paleozoic Era came to an end. From that

Typical Ordovician brachiopods. Known as lamp shells because some species resemble Aladin's lamp, these double-shelled animals are unrelated to bivalves. They are the most abundant macroscopic fossils of Paleozoic rocks but are relatively uncommon today.

time to the present, they have been uncommon in most marine settings. This foothold was a literal one: Most crinoids attached themselves to the sea bottom with a rootlike holdfast, spreading their arms to strain food wafted their way by water currents.

Also colonizing the surface of Paleozoic sea floors following a notable adaptive radiation in Ordovician time was a group of corals called the Rugosa. These corals are so named for the exterior roughness of the stony calcareous cup that housed their tentacled bodies. Unlike most modern reef-building corals, the rugose corals were, for the most part, solitary rather than colonial—the horn-shaped cup of each individual was not connected to another cup. In fact, few of these early corals were reef builders. A fourfold symmetry of the bladelike internal partitions of the rugose cup distinguishes it from the cup of a modern coral, which has sixfold radial symmetry, and it is not certain whether modern corals evolved from rugose corals or separately, from naked sea anemones. The rugose corals may have died out near the end of the Paleozoic Era without leaving descendants.

The reef builders of shallow Ordovician seas comprised other kinds of corals known as tabulates because of the horizontal platforms

Crinoids, or sea lilies, originated during the Ordovician Period. Shallow-water groups diversified greatly as the Paleozoic Era progressed, but later declined in abundance. Stalked forms that attach to the sea floor are restricted to deep water today, apparently because they are vulnerable to heavy predation by shallow-water predators, including fish. As shown in the underwater photograph, crinoids spread their arms to sieve small food particles from the water.

within the tube-shaped cups that constituted their skeletons. The tabulates included a variety of colonial forms, some resembling organ pipes and others having moundlike or encrusting shapes. These were not the builders of the first well-developed reefs of the Ordovician Period, however. This was the role of massive colonies of bryozoans. Only later did tabulates join in reef construction, along with robust branching and encrusting colonial animals known as stromatoporoids. The evolutionary relationships of the stromatoporoids remained problematical until the 1960s, when the discovery of their descendants living on Caribbean coral reefs showed them to have been sponges. These descendants, which constitute a previously unrecognized class of sponges, have skeletons that in many diagnostic ways resemble those of the stromatoporoids. The dense nature of these skeletons allows for only very slow growth in comparison to the growth rates of reef-building corals, which secrete porous skeletons. It is apparently their slow growth that makes these curious sponges weak competitors for space on modern reefs, so that most find room to grow only beneath corals or in caves and crevices.

We know comparatively little about the forms of life that floated and swam above Ordovician sea floors. Plankton, the life that floats in seas and lakes, must have been abundant in Ordovician waters. We have little direct evidence of their existence, however, because most planktonic groups lack durable skeletons of the type that are likely to leave fossil records. We do know, however, that among the algae that served as food for many marine animals were many varieties of acritarchs, the single-celled algae that were set back by extinction near the end of Precambrian time. Also persisting from earlier times were the conodonts which, as we have seen, were eel-like swimmers whose

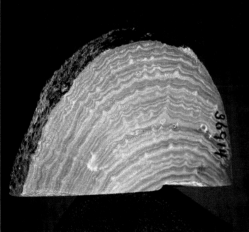

Most rugose corals (top right) were solitary "cup corals" rather than colonial animals, and were not major contributors to reefs. In contrast, tabulate corals were colonial reef-builders. The example shown (top left) might be compared to a massive colonial reef-building coral of today, though the Ordovician and modern coral groups are only distantly related. Stromatoporoids (above) of the sort that encrusted skeletons of dead animals, as part of the reef community, are now known to have been sponges. The bumps on the surfaces of their colonies were sites of expulsion of the water, from which they strained their food.

teeth are commonly found fossils. Ordovician strata also offer an excellent fossil record of the colonial graptolites, most types of which were passive floaters that strained food from the water.

The general adaptive radiation of invertebrate animals (animals without backbones) that took place during the Ordovician Period produced what might be described as the Paleozoic marine fauna: Most of the classes that evolved or diversified at this time survived until the end of the era, joined by only a few others.

THE LATE ORDOVICIAN CRISIS

Very close to the end of the Ordovician Period, extinction struck marine life on a global scale with what, in geological time, must be regarded as great suddenness. Nearly a third of all existing brachiopod families disappeared—and this was the group that had left the most conspicuous fossil record in Ordovician rocks. In addition, many other prominent groups disappeared, including groups of conodonts, trilobites, bryozoans, and much of the reef-building fauna. In fact, organically constructed reefs are quite rare and poorly developed in the oldest rocks of the next period, the Silurian. So severe were the losses that it appears that in all of Phanerozoic time—nearly 600 million years—the crisis of the Late Ordovician may have been exceeded

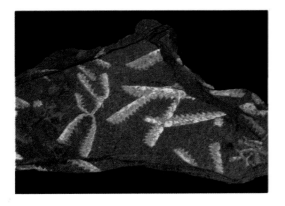

Ordovician graptolites. Most commonly found flattened within compacted black shales, fragile colonies of most graptolite species floated in the ocean.

in impact on marine life only by the event that brought the Paleozoic Era to a close.

Heavy extinctions took place not only on Ordovician sea floors, but also in the waters above. Here the graptolites were reduced to low diversity. The pattern of their extinction merits our special attention in that it suggests the spreading of cool temperatures equatorward from the poles. David Skevington of Cambridge University has shown that during Early Ordovician time graptolites had been distributed geographically in a normal fashion, with some species confined to low latitudes and others to high latitudes. As the Ordovician progressed, however, the zones of occurrence of particular species became compressed toward the equator and reduced in number. At the end of the period, what species remained were confined to low latitudes. Peter Sheehan of the Milwaukee Public Museum has offered evidence that, on the sea floor, brachiopods experienced similar geographic changes: Faunas adapted to the cold conditions of deep-water environments and high latitudes spread into shallow seas closer to the equator toward the end of Ordovician time.

SOUTH POLAR GLACIATION

Thus, geographic evidence suggests the spread of cool temperatures from high latitudes. Only recently, however, have we understood why this pattern developed. Late in the 1960s, a team of French geologists led by Serge Beuf reported a remarkable discovery in northern Africa: glacial deposits of Late Ordovician age. These deposits are coarse conglomerates with cobbles and boulders, many of which bear scratches that are the hallmark of glaciation. The scratched stones had been transported at the base of glaciers, where they scraped against surfaces that the glaciers were overriding. Also present are underlying rock surfaces that had been scoured and scratched by glacial movement. It might seem surprising that the Late Ordovician glaciation was recognized only recently. The explanation is simple: Found primarily in the Saharan Desert, the glacial evidence was overlooked for many years.

The cause of this major episode of continental glaciation is revealed by the evidence of rock magnetism: Late in Ordovician time the super continent Gondwanaland moved over the South Pole. In a polar position, the land mass cooled to the degree that it accumulated glaciers. In fact, it is not unlikely that every time a continent has moved over a pole during the most recent billion years of earth history it has become glaciated.

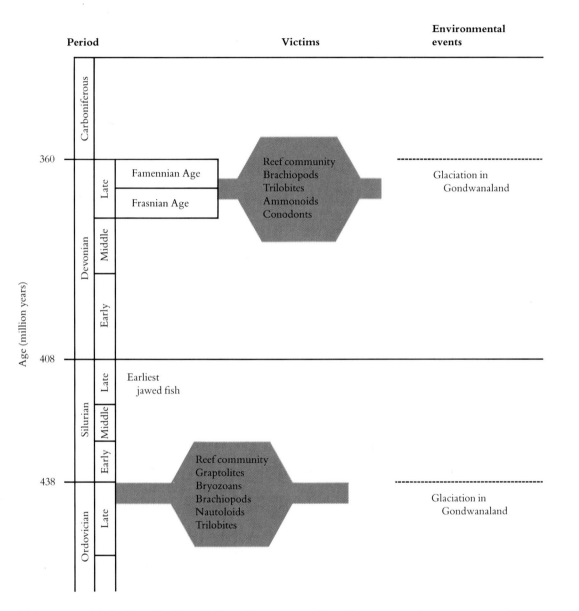

Major events of Ordovician, Silurian, and Devonian time. Colored horizontal bars depict mass extinctions. In Late Ordovician time, the north African region of Gondwanaland was positioned at the South Pole and accumulated large glaciers.

As we have seen, there are two major concomitants of continental glaciation. One of these is widespread cooling. The other is a lowering of sea level throughout the world. As glaciers grow, they remove a large volume of water from the global hydrological cycle—which is to say, from the oceans—and lock it up on the land. Thus, we would predict that the Late Ordovician glacial episode should have lowered

A map of Gondwanaland in Late Ordovician time,
showing the South Pole and the area of glaciation.

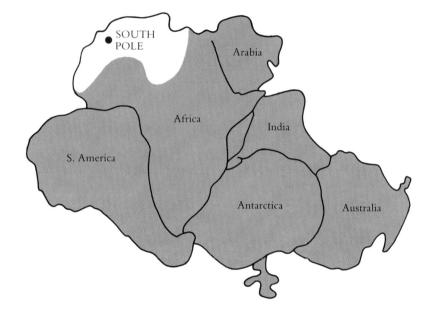

sea level while altering climates. The rock record bears out this prediction, revealing that at the time of the Late Ordovician glacial activity,
regions that previously had been inundated by shallow seas were evac-
uated.

Hypothetically, we might invoke either or both climatic change
and sea-level lowering to explain the mass extinction that brought the
Ordovician Period to an end. During the most recent glacial interval,
however, repeated global lowering of sea level has not caused heavy
worldwide extinction. As I will discuss in Chapter 8, life of shallow
seas suffered during the recent Ice Age only in areas where temperatures dropped. The Ordovician record itself offers corroborating testimony. It permits us to conduct the critical test, which is to examine
what happens when sea level falls without apparent climatic change.
Late in Early Ordovician time, shallow seas, which had for some time
flooded most of North America, withdrew to the margins of the continent. Large areas that were previously marine were left high and dry.
The critical question is, how did this change impinge on marine life?
In fact, it had no significant effect: Life went on. This controlled ex-
periment—albeit one conducted millions of years ago without human
planning—indicates that, without climatic change, a drop in sea level

Calcareous algae of the type that flourished in warm Paleozoic seas.

will have little effect on sea floor life as long as some shallow seas continue to fringe continents.

Peter Sheehan, who seems to have been the first scientist to link the Late Ordovician extinction with the glacial event, cites as support for this idea an observation of Arthur J. Boucot of Oregon State University: The marine faunas of the early segment of the following period, the Silurian, are markedly cosmopolitan in distribution. This geographic pattern suggests that the crisis interval was associated with climatic cooling. There are two possibilities. First, the mass extinction may have preferentially eliminated animal groups that were narrowly adapted with regard to temperature conditions, leaving a residue of cosmopolitan forms. Second, in the aftermath of the crisis, seasonally cool temperatures may still have extended to low latitudes. Both of these conditions imply that climatic cooling accompanied the transition to the Silurian Period.

Another feature of the marine realm immediately after the Late Ordovician crisis was that limestones accumulated at a reduced rate. Like reefs, which were virtually absent after the crisis, limestones form primarily in warm seas where calcium carbonate, the principal component of both reefs and limestones, is readily produced. Another event that seems to have reflected a temperature drop was the disappearance of an important group of calcareous green algae, which today are restricted to warm seas.

LIFE EXPANDS AGAIN

As the Silurian Period progressed and then gave way to the Devonian without large-scale biotic disturbance, invertebrate marine life once again recovered by way of adaptive radiation. This rebound took place at a relatively low taxonomic level. The terminal Ordovician crisis had for the most part removed families, genera, and species, and it was primarily multiplication of surviving groups at these taxonomic levels that constituted the recovery. By contrast, most phyla, classes, and orders survived the crisis.

Expanding to attain greater ecological prominence, nonetheless, was the community of reef builders, in which the dominant members were now tabulate corals and stromatoporoids; rugose corals and bryozoans were restricted to minor roles. Reefs of Silurian and Devonian age are found in many parts of the world, including the Great Lakes region of the United States, where many occur in rocks now buried below the surface although they lie exposed in some areas, such as in the Chicago region and the lower peninsula of Michigan. In western

Reconstruction of a mid-Devonian reef in New York
State. The primary reef builders are tabulate corals, but
cone-shaped, solitary rugose corals stand above them
on the left and stalked crinoids spread their arms upward on the right. A giant nautiloid and the largest
species of trilobite of all time rest on the sea floor in
the foreground.

Canada, subsurface reefs of this age, being porous like many other
ancient reefs, harbor economically important reservoirs of petroleum.

Among the new forms of life that evolved during middle Paleozoic
time were the ammonoids and the jawed fish—both predatory
groups. The ammonoids appeared in mid-Devonian time as coiled
cephalopod mollusks that resembled the modern pearly nautilus. Descendants of the straight-shelled nautiloids, ammonoids had among
their new traits septa—partitions within the shell—that were convoluted rather than planar where they met the outer wall of the shell. It
is probable that ammonoids, which died out with the dinosaurs, were
swimming predators, as are nautiloids and living cephalopods. The
shells of modern-day cephalopods are chambered structures filled
with gas that offsets the weight of the shell material, producing neu-
tral buoyancy for swimming. Similarity of form and ancestry points
to a similar condition in the ammonoids.

Jawed fish had an earlier origin, the oldest known representatives
being of Late Silurian age. They were preceded by jawless fish, whose
fossil record extends back into the Cambrian. With jawless fish able to
consume only small items of food, the evolution of jaws greatly expanded the ecological role of fish, though the earliest jawed fish were

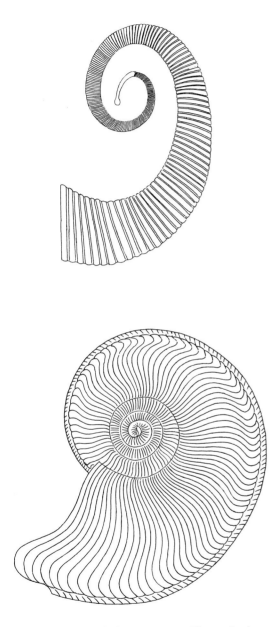

Primitive ammonoids from Germany. These animals descended from the nautiloids and, like them, were swimming predators. Ammonoids reached their evolutionary zenith during the Age of Dinosaurs.

only a few centimeters long. Some of the early jawed fish occupied freshwater habitats; and in Early Devonian rocks of freshwater origin, the first placoderm jawed fish make their appearance in the geologic record. The placoderms are of special ecological importance because in the course of the Devonian they not only invaded the marine realm, but also diversified to include representatives as long as 10 meters (about 30 feet). The head region was armored with massive bone, sectors of which formed powerful bevel-edged jaws, whereas the posterior portion of these animals was naked of rigid armament and flexible for swimming. These monsters of the deep, which are especially well preserved in marine shales of northeastern Ohio, transformed the marine ecosystem by virtue of their ability to attack large prey. In fact, it is probable that the largest placoderms fed on smaller ones as well as on sharks. Sharks by this time were also highly diversified, and impressions of their bodies are preserved today in rocks with the bony fish. (Sharks then, as now, had skeletons of cartilage.)

It was also during middle Paleozoic time that higher organisms first invaded the land on a large scale. Because animal life is nourished by plant life, animals made their evolutionary beachhead only after plants had colonized lowland areas. The first plants were nothing more than leafless, rootless stalks that drew moisture and nutrients from the soil through simple underground stems. The very earliest of these were presumably semi-aquatic, forming marshes in standing water. Exactly when plants made their way onto dry land remains uncertain (it may even have been during Ordovician time), but before the end of the Devonian Period the descendants of these pioneers stood as tall trees that formed the world's first forests.

Very near the end of the Devonian Period, vertebrate animals joined higher plants on the land. Representing this event is *Ichthyostega,* an animal whose remarkable anatomy places it in an evolutionary position between Devonian fish and amphibians, the class of animals that includes toads and salamanders—creatures that spend their early lives in water and then metamorphose into terrestrial adults. *Ichthyostega,* whose remains have been collected from sedimentary rocks of freshwater origin in Greenland, is a true "missing link." It had legs for walking on land but retained a swimming tail and the distinctive tooth structure of its piscine ancestors. *Ichthyostega* probably lived so late in the Devonian Period that it escaped a great mass extinction that had occurred a bit earlier. This crisis, which forms our next topic, spanned the boundary between the Frasnian and Famennian ages—a boundary positioned about 7 million years before the end of the Devonian Period.

Evolutionary history of early fish. Lobe-finned fish possessed lungs, which they passed on to amphibians. Sharks and placoderms gave rise to no other major groups. The sharks, fast swimmers whose bodies are supported by cartilage rather than bone, have survived, whereas the placoderms, with their bony armor, died out during the Paleozoic Era.

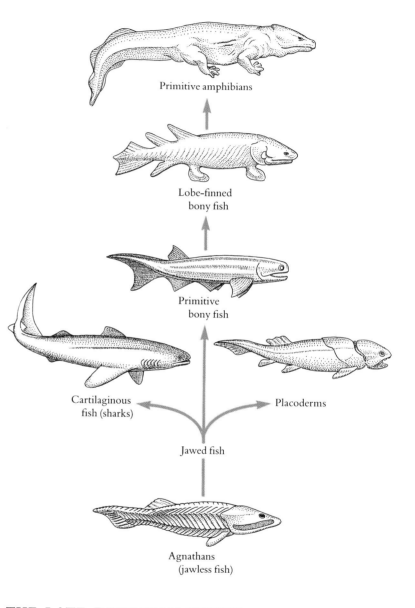

Primitive amphibians

Lobe-finned bony fish

Primitive bony fish

Cartilaginous fish (sharks)

Placoderms

Jawed fish

Agnathans (jawless fish)

THE LATE DEVONIAN EVENT

The crisis that occurred near the end of the Devonian Period, like the one at the end of the Ordovician, struck primarily within the marine realm. The higher plants which had become well established on the land during Devonian time, seem not to have been adversely affected. Among the marine groups that suffered heavily were certain types of

Armored head of *Dunkleosteus* (left), the largest placoderm of all time, which reached a length of some 10 meters (about 30 feet) in the Late Devonian seas in the region of Cleveland, Ohio. Reconstruction of *Ichthyostega* (right), the earliest known amphibian. This Late Devonian animal had the feet of an amphibian but a finned tail resembling that of its fish ancestors.

brachiopods, trilobites, conodonts, and acritarchs. There is much evidence that this crisis, like that of the Late Ordovician, resulted primarily from widespread refrigeration with the onset of an interval of continental glaciation. This appears to explain what is perhaps the most striking aspect of the Late Devonian crisis: the decimation of the reef community that had flourished for a hundred million years or so, since mid-Ordovician time. Although this community had recovered from the terminal Ordovician event, the second crisis brought about its demise. After the Devonian, neither tabulate corals nor stromatoporoids ever again functioned as major reef builders. In fact, throughout the remainder of the Paleozoic Era—more than a hundred million years—reef growth was relatively feeble; no other group took over the role with great success until corals of the modern type evolved early in the Mesozoic Era.

The temporal pattern of the Devonian crisis has been a source of controversy. Digby McLaren, former director of the Geological Survey of Canada, has maintained that the mass extinction is recorded along a single bedding plane—at a single parting of strata that marks a geologically instantaneous catastrophe throughout the world. Several other paleontologists have advanced evidence that the mass extinction was instead spread over several million years.

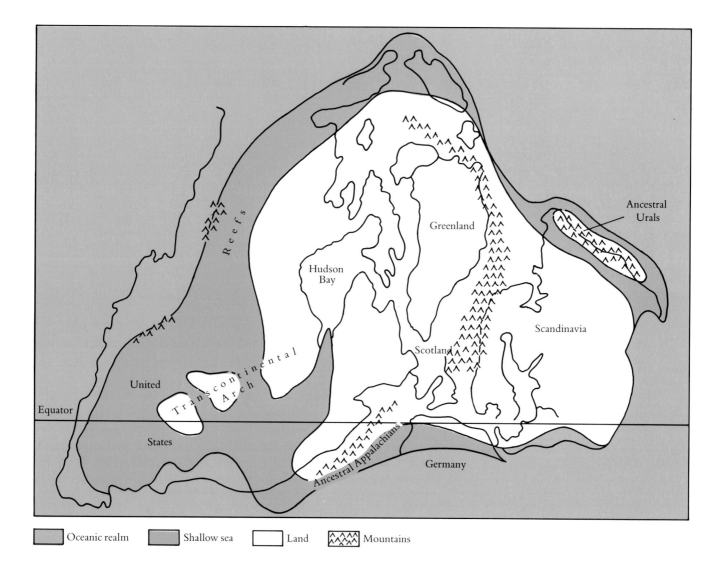

Oceanic realm   Shallow sea   Land   Mountains

The Old Red Sandstone continent of Late Devonian time. New York State, where a rich fauna of marine life was fossilized, lay near the equator.

One area that has offered evidence of a protracted crisis is upper New York State, where rocks of Late Devonian age are especially well exposed. This is where the science of geology was first practiced on a grand scale in the United States; here, during the middle part of the last century, James Hall studied the thick sequence of Late Devonian sandstones and shales. We now know that the reason that these deposits accumulated to such great thickness was that they were being shed at a rapid rate by erosion of the ancestors of the modern Appalachian

Mountains. These were rugged uplifts that were being forced upward as North America and Europe collided. (Not until the Mesozoic Era, when the combined landmass was rifted apart, was the modern Atlantic Ocean formed.) The ancient supercontinent that came into being when North America and Europe were sutured together is known as the Old Red Sandstone continent, in honor of the Old Red Sandstone, a deposit that accumulated in Great Britain throughout the Devonian Period. The Old Red deposits formed in lowlands to the east of the ancestral Appalachians. To the west, sediments eroded from the mountains settled in river valleys and in an adjacent sea in what is now New York State. This juxtaposition may seem strange, but then, as at many other past times, seas flooded much of the North American continent. During Late Devonian time, marine waters spread eastward from the west coast all the way to a zone of lowlands in front of the mountain belt along which North America and Europe joined. These seas were interrupted only by a large island or two in the central United States—positive topographic elements along what is known as the Transcontinental Arch, a ridge that persisted throughout most of the Paleozoic Era. The area that is now northeastern Ohio was positioned far from shore, and here, in moderately deep water, sharks and huge, fearsome placoderm fish swam above sea floors on which dark mud slowly accumulated.

George McGhee of Rutgers University has undertaken a thorough study of the Late Devonian invertebrate fauna that occupied the marine waters west of the ancestral Appalachian mountain belt, as recorded in the thick sequence of strata now visible in the gorges and roadcuts of New York State. It is his estimate that the mass extinction that occurred near the end of the Devonian swept away at least 70 percent of the invertebrate species of this region. Plots of species occurrences within the strata indicate that heavy extinction began during the Frasnian Age and continued into the succeeding Famennian interval, the final age of the Devonian, spanning perhaps 7 million years. In collaboration with other workers, McGhee has conducted a systematic search for high concentrations of iridium in the shales of New York State that represent the critical interval of time, but the results have been negative. Thus, there is no evidence of an extraterrestrial agent having caused the crisis.

There have been additional studies indicating that the Late Devonian crisis was spread over several million years. In one of these, J. Thomas Dutro of the United States Geological Survey has demonstrated a gradual decline of brachiopods, beginning in mid-Devonian time, in a nearly continuous stratigraphic sequence in New Mexico. Similarly, Paul Copper of Laurentian University in Canada has uncovered a protracted interval of global decline for the atrypoids, a major group of brachiopods that disappeared in the Frasnian–Famennian crisis. Of the 12 atrypoid genera and subgenera alive at the start of Frasnian time, three disappeared near the end of the early Frasnian interval and five more near the end of the middle Frasnian interval. Only the remaining four, plus one that apparently evolved in mid-Frasnian time, died out near the end of the Frasnian. Furthermore, Copper has concluded that there are no stratigraphic horizons thought to coincide with the Frasnian–Famennian boundary that reveal the sudden mass death of atrypoids, even on a local scale. For quite a different group, the ammonoids, Michael House of the University of Hull in England has documented heavy extinction, apparently in a series of pulses, throughout Frasnian and Famennian time.

It was not only invertebrate life that was victimized by the Late Devonian event. Fish experienced such heavy losses that the nature of the ecosystem in waters above the sea floor was profoundly altered. In fact, most species of marine fish failed to survive the Devonian Period. In the seas that spread westward from the ancestral Appalachian Mountains, for example, the especially large and fearsome species of placoderms disappeared. The few placoderm groups that survived into the Carboniferous Period, which followed the Devonian, died out quickly, leaving the role of large swimming predator to the sharks which, perhaps in response, seem then to have diversified substantially. The fine-grained, black deposit of northeastern Ohio known as the Cleveland Shale harbors an especially diverse placoderm fauna, as well as a large flora of acritarch algae, providing further evidence that the Late Devonian crisis did not occur during a brief geological moment at the Frasnian–Famennian transition: The Cleveland Shale is of Famennian age. In a doctoral dissertation at the University of California at Los Angeles, E. Reed Wicander showed that it was only after the time of deposition of the Cleveland Shale that the acritarchs declined to low levels of diversity, from which they never rebounded. The same was true for the placoderms.

EVIDENCE OF COOLING

George McGhee's data from New York State reveal another remarkable fact. While other groups of marine life were declining during the crisis, one group, the glass sponges, were diversifying. These are a group of sponges, still populating the oceans today, that secrete skeletons of silica. An important attribute of these animals, noted by

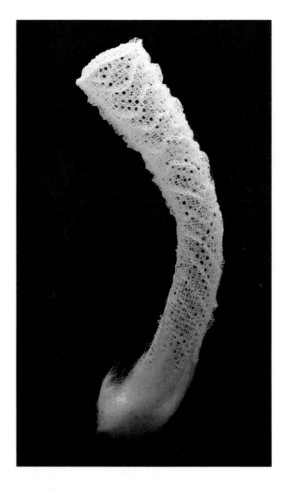

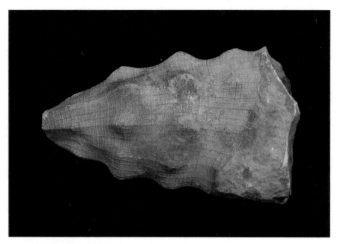

One of the many kinds of Late Devonian glass sponges that flourished in New York State when other groups of animals were dying out. An impression of the mesh-like sponge skeleton is visible in the brown sandstone (right). The skeleton of a modern glass sponge is shown for comparison (left).

McGhee, is that they tend to thrive in cool waters, often living at considerable depths in modern seas, where their thermal requirements are satisfied. During the biotic crisis in New York State, the expansion of the glass sponges was, however, within shallow seas. As McGhee has observed, this pattern suggests that the seas were becoming cooler, to the benefit of the sponges but at the expense of the previously flourishing representatives of other biological groups. There is no question that before this time the waters had been warm: Rock magnetism reveals that during Late Devonian time New York State lay very close to the equator.

Could it be that near the end of Devonian time an episode of global cooling affected even tropical seas? This has been suggested not only by George McGhee, but even earlier by Paul Copper, who called attention to the fact that, while tropical forms of life were devastated by the crisis, faunas of higher latitudes were not. At this time, Gondwanaland lay far to the south, and the South Pole was, in fact, positioned within the segment of this supercontinent that consisted of what is now South America. Although there is only a poor record of marine life spanning the crisis interval, we do know that groups of animals that flourished at these high latitudes before the crisis remained alive afterwords. Nothing like the destruction of the tropical coral reef community took place.

The collapse of the reef community is especially well displayed in the rocks of western Canada and western Australia, where enormous reefs grew in mid-Devonian time and none remained at the period's

Topographic expression of the huge Late Devonian reef of Western Australia. A marine basin lay to the left of the sinuous reef front. It is remarkable that this structure, which formed more than 350 million years ago, still stands in relief above the surrounding terrain.

close. In Canada, some Devonian reefs today are exposed at the earth's surface and others lie far below, often serving as petroleum reservoirs. More spectacular reef outcrops are seen in the Canning Basin of Australia, around which enormous reefs stand in topographic relief, much as they once grew above the ancient sea floor. Before them, now barren in the hot sun, sits the basin that was once deep in water. Most of the reefs of the Canning Basin, which today are positioned near the coastline of Western Australia, were part of a huge Devonian barrier reef that today stretches for at least 350 kilometers (about 220 miles) along the Canning Basin and that in life may have been much longer. It is a curious irony that this "great barrier reef" of the Devonian occupied the continent that in modern times is fringed by the Great Barrier Reef, the longest reef tract in the world today.

The Devonian reef system of Western Australia once lay buried beneath younger sediments, but has been exposed by erosion. In a few places, small pinnacle reefs rise up from the basin floor. In life, they grew to the sea surface. Muddy sediments accumulated over large areas of the basin. The vertical dimensions of the reefs reveal that during reef growth the basin floor in front of the living reefs lay as much as 300 to 400 meters (about 1000 to 1300 feet) below sea level. Coarse limestone debris occasionally broke from the reefs and spilled down their flanks into nearby areas of the basin. Fossils preserved in the basin sediments reveal that the basin waters were occupied by a variety of swimming and floating animals, including fish, nautiloids, ammonoids, and conodonts. The reefs themselves were produced primarily by the dominant reef builders of the day—tabulate corals and stromatoporoids—with algae playing a secondary role.

When the global extinction struck, near the time of transition from the Frasnian Age to the Famennian Age, the coral–stromatoporoid reef community was destroyed in Western Australia, as elsewhere. Then, around the margins of the Canning Basin, a remarkable transformation took place. A new phase of reeflike growth began, with stromatolite-building cyanophytes playing the dominant constructional role. Stromatolites had been sparsely developed in the original reef, but following the mass extinction they flourished. From the history of the stromatolites during early Paleozoic time—once abundant, the stromatolites' decline coincided with the diversification of animal life—their resurgence in the late Devonian is easily understood. Not only was competition for space in shallow-water habitats suddenly relieved, but it is likely that the kinds of animals that had been stifling the growth of stromatolites for more than a hundred million years by eating and boring through them were drastically diminished in variety and number. The stromatolites had a reprieve, until animal life experienced an evolutionary recovery shortly thereafter.

The death of the huge Devonian reef was rather sudden, at least on a geological scale of time. As was discussed in the first chapter of this book, however, this does not necessarily imply that the agent of extinction was imposed suddenly. A general trend of climatic deterioration could, for example, have caused sudden extinction when it brought temperatures down to the minimum requirements for tabulate corals and stromatoporoids, which probably approximated those for modern reef corals. The reefs of western Canada also seem to have died out rather abruptly. Here the occurrence of black shales on top of the reef deposits has suggested to some paleontologists that the reef builders might have been killed off by the spread of anoxic conditions—in which free oxygen is absent and organic matter, left unoxidized by bacteria, imparts the black color of carbon to the muds in which it is buried. As described in the previous chapter, however, wave agitation sustains high levels of dissolved oxygen in shallow water by exposing it to the atmosphere. It is far more plausible that the black shales were superimposed on the reefs: The latter had been growing upward to maintain a position close to sea level while the edge of the basin along which they were growing was subsiding under their weight. What may have happened is that continued sinking of the region after the reefs were dead lowered them into the basin, where in deep water black muds settled over them.

Search for a high concentration of iridium in the Australian reef sequence has yielded only one possibly significant spike, but this isolated occurrence of an unusually high concentration is positioned in a stromatolitic layer that is stratigraphically higher—and therefore younger—than the Frasnian–Famennian boundary. Furthermore, the algae in this layer are of a type that characteristically trap heavy metals. This iridium anomaly seems, therefore, to be unrelated to the extinction event.

Returning to the paleontological evidence, we observe that rugose corals also contributed to Devonian reefs, and A. E. H. Pedder of the Geological Survey of Canada has shown that both the reef-building and non-reef-building members of this group were devastated in the Late Devonian crisis. By his tabulation, 148 shallow-water rugose species have been described from late Frasnian strata in one or more parts of the world, and of these, no more than six survived into the Famennian. (There may have been even fewer if one or two Famennian species have been misidentified.) Species characteristic of deep-water deposits, though fewer, fared better: Of ten known Frasnian species, three or four persisted into Famennian time. As has happened after many other mass extinctions, the decimated group then rebounded with a dramatic adaptive radiation. Before the end of Famennian time, perhaps 10 or 12 million years after the climax of the crisis, at least 14 new families and dozens of new species of rugose corals populated shallow seas. The fact that these dramatic events were concentrated in warm, shallow seas, while corals adapted to deep, cool waters were not severely affected, is consistent with the observation that the Late Devonian crisis was for the most part a disruption of tropical ecosystems.

Still another aspect of the tropical bias of the Late Devonian mass extinction is reminiscent of something that happened during the Late Ordovician crisis: Calcareous green algae, which today are restricted to warm seas, experienced heavy extinction.

Finally, George McGhee has noted that whereas marine fish were among the primary victims of the Late Devonian event, freshwater fish were not. Freshwater fish being adapted to seasonal temperature changes, would be expected to have been more resistent to cooling than were marine fish, whose normal habitat would have been more stable.

RENEWED GLACIATION

The preceding paragraphs have summarized a variety of evidence suggesting that an interval of climatic cooling may have been the primary cause of the Late Devonian mass extinction. Having been in possession of this incriminating evidence for several years, we now also have direct evidence of climatic deterioration: glaciation in Gondwanaland. For many years the facts here were in question. There were reports only of possible glacial deposits, perhaps of Late Devonian age, in South America. Recently Mario V. Caputo and his professor John C. Crowell, of the University of California at Santa Barbara, have confirmed the reality of glacial deposits, which are located for the most part in northern Brazil, and have shown the age of these deposits to be Late Devonian. More precisely, associated fossil algae indicate a Famennian age for most of the deposits, and their glacial origin is confirmed by the presence within them of pebbles and cobbles that were smoothed and scratched as they slid along while frozen into the undersurfaces of glaciers. In addition, shales associated with the gravelly glacial deposits contain dropstones, which are isolated pebbles and cobbles that could only have reached their sites of deposition, in quiet water far from shore, by floating across the water while frozen into buoyant ice. When the ice melts it releases the stones, allowing them to sink to the bottom.

Thus, a strong case emerges that climatic cooling was the dominant agent of Late Devonian mass extinction. Inasmuch as the glacial deposits of this interval that have thus far been dated are Famennian in age, it remains possible that the Frasnian segment of the mass extinction took place during the early stages of climatic deterioration, before continental glaciers had developed. An alternative possibility is that glaciation began in Frasnian time but has not yet been detected in the rock record.

Since the middle part of the last century, late Paleozoic glacial deposits have been recognized in southern continents that constituted Gondwanaland, although the reality of the supercontinent was not universally accepted until the 1960s. Even after this acceptance, however, glacial deposits were unequivocally recognized only in post-Devonian Paleozoic systems (the Carboniferous and Permian). It was tempting to assume that glaciation began before the end of Devonian time because rock magnetism revealed that at this time Gondwanaland moved over the South Pole again. Yet the sector of the supercontinent that first assumed a polar position during Devonian time was the re-

Movement of the position of the South Pole with respect to Gondwanaland during the Paleozoic Era. It was actually Gondwanaland that moved, and it encroached on the South Pole twice, in Late Ordovician time and in Late Devonian time.

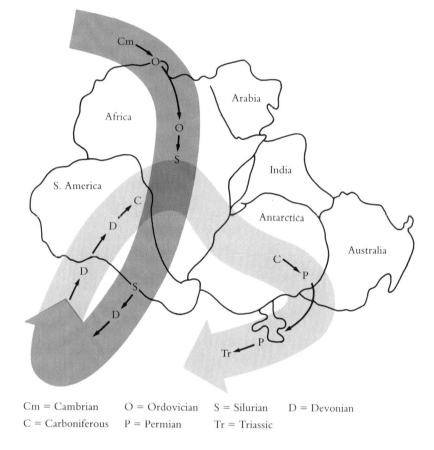

Cm = Cambrian	O = Ordovician	S = Silurian	D = Devonian
C = Carboniferous	P = Permian	Tr = Triassic	

gion now constituting northern South America, and South America had until recently yielded only uncertain evidence of glaciation. The findings of Caputo and Crowell offer dramatic confirmation of our suspicions.

Within Gondwanaland, the locus of glaciation shifted approximately with what we know from rock magnetism to have been the position of the South Pole. During Late Devonian time, glaciers formed on Gondwanaland first in South America and then migrated across southern Africa and Antarctica to Australia, via which Gondwanaland exited from the pole.

What is remarkable about the Late Devonian events just described is that they constitute a repetition of the earlier Paleozoic pattern: During Late Ordovician time, Gondwanaland had moved over the

South Pole and accumulated continental glaciers. At about the same time, a mass extinction struck marine life, with heaviest impact in the tropics. Glaciation continued until mid-Silurian time when, according to the reconstructions of Caputo and Crowell, Gondwanaland moved off the pole. Then, late in the Devonian Period, Gondwanaland moved over the pole once again, initiating a new interval of continental glaciation, and a second mass extinction struck. Again the greatest effect was in the tropical zone.

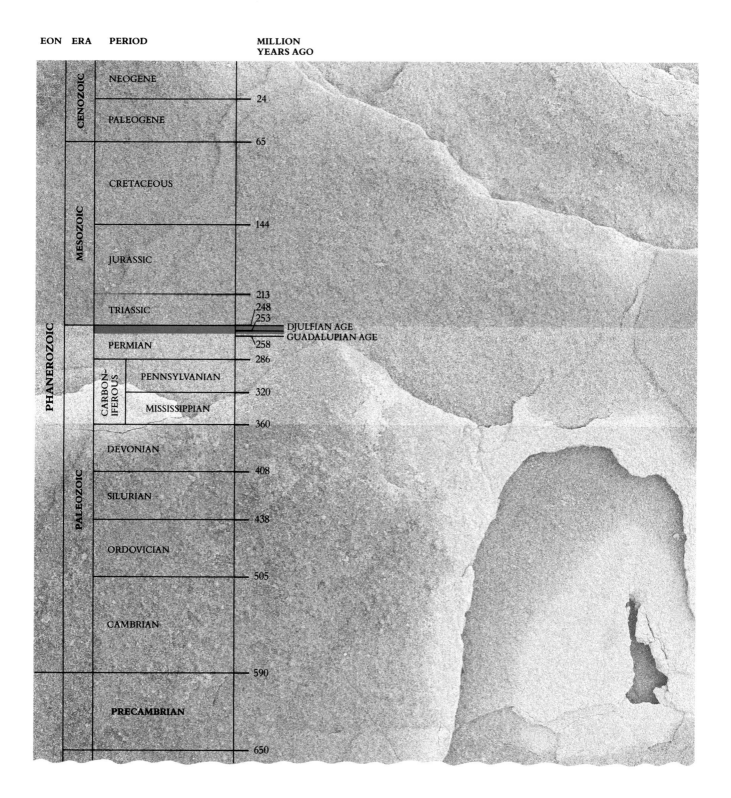

EON	ERA	PERIOD		MILLION YEARS AGO
PHANEROZOIC	CENOZOIC	NEOGENE		
				24
		PALEOGENE		
				65
	MESOZOIC	CRETACEOUS		
				144
		JURASSIC		
				213
		TRIASSIC		248
				253
	PALEOZOIC	PERMIAN		258
				286
		CARBON-IFEROUS	PENNSYLVANIAN	320
			MISSISSIPPIAN	360
		DEVONIAN		
				408
		SILURIAN		
				438
		ORDOVICIAN		
				505
		CAMBRIAN		
				590
		PRECAMBRIAN		
				650

DJULFIAN AGE
GUADALUPIAN AGE

5 THE GREAT PERMIAN CRISIS

The Late Devonian crisis left an impoverished fauna in the oceans, but an evolutionary rebound during Carboniferous and Permian time once again brought life in the world's oceans to a high level of diversity. At the same time, a complex ecosystem featuring large, mammal-like vertebrates colonized the land, marking a major advance over Late Devonian time, when vertebrates were first crawling up onto the land. Then, between about 250 and 255 million years ago, in Late Permian time, the long, peaceful interlude after the Late Devonian crisis was disrupted by what appears to have been the most devastating mass extinction of all time. About half of all families in the marine realm disappeared, and vertebrate faunas on the land were decimated. This collapse of the ecosystem remains unexplained. It did, however, display a number of patterns that resemble those of the late Ordovician and Devonian crisis. These patterns include a tendency for tropical life to suffer most severely and a reduction in the rate of accumulation of tropical limestones. As we shall see at the end of this chapter, these similar features suggest a climatic cause.

RECOVERY IN THE SEAS

Many of the prominent taxonomic groups of the late Paleozoic interval that preceded the Permian crisis were ones that had flourished before the Late Devonian crisis—brachiopods, for example, and ammonoid, bivalve, and gastropod mollusks. Also successful again were the bryozoans, but whereas most of those present in early Paleozoic time had been so-called "stony" forms with heavily calcified skeletons, those of the late Paleozoic were for the most part lacy forms that stood upright on the ocean floor and waved about, resembling the

A lacy bryozoan (left) of late Paleozoic age. This was a fan-shaped colony that stood upright on the sea floor, waving in water currents from which the minute, interconnected individuals of the colony extracted particles of food. Fusulinid foraminiferans (right) of late Paleozoic age. These single-celled creatures resembled amoebas with skeletons. The skeletons, which are often so abundant as to constitute the dominant components of limestones like the one figured here, superficially resemble grains of rice but are actually elongate spirals.

sea fans (the "soft corals") of today. The crinoids, or sea lilies, reached their pinnacle of success during the first half of the Carboniferous Period when they formed vast submarine meadows in the shallow seas that flooded much of the North American continent.

Corals were also present on late Paleozoic sea floors, but they were not successful reef-building varieties. In fact this was not a time of luxuriant reef growth. As has happened time and again in earth history, a way of life vacated by extinction remained poorly exploited for millions of years. Evolution may abhor a vacuum, but it often takes a long time to fill it. In Late Carboniferous time, calcareous algae shaped somewhat like potato chips formed small mound-shaped reefs in warm, shallow seas, but otherwise there were virtually no reefs built of solid organic skeletons until the Permian Period, when a motley association of algae, sponges, and bryozoans assumed this role in a rather modest way.

With the disappearance of the armored placoderm fish came an ascendancy of bony fish, which more closely resembled fish of the present, and also of sharks. Possibly because of predatory pressures from these groups and the ammonoids, which were armed with tentacles and beaks, trilobites continued to decline to the point where they were quite uncommon by Early Permian time.

An important group that emerged after the Late Devonian crisis was the fusulinid foraminiferans. Foraminiferans are amoeba-like, single-celled organisms with skeletons. They thrive in modern oceans, their skeletons being found in almost any handful of sand or mud from the sea floor. The fusulinids were unusually large members of this group. Their typical shape was like a grain of rice, and some were several times as large. It is generally assumed that in the manner of similarly large foraminiferans today, the fusulinids harbored algae in their protoplasm—symbionts that served as food.

One important group for which we have little fossil evidence for the late Paleozoic interval is the phytoplankton—floating single-celled algae. The acritarchs left a fossil record of high quality because they produced cysts; these resting spores had heavy, readily preserved cell walls. In the aftermath of their sharp decline during the Late Devonian crisis, whatever groups of algae floated abundantly in the oceans left virtually no fossil record.

LIFE ON LAND

The difference between the marine ecosystem that existed before the Late Devonian crisis and the one that developed thereafter was minor compared to the transformation that took place on the land. As was mentioned earlier, forests of tall trees had come into being before the crisis. At present we have no evidence that these were affected by the event, although this may in part reflect the relatively poor fossil record of plants. What we do know is that as the Carboniferous Period progressed, swamps spread over broad lowland areas on a scale never seen before, and the plants that grew within them—trees that lived in standing water, like modern cypresses—left woody remains that turned to peat and then to coal. It is the voluminous coal deposits formed in this way in the state of Pennsylvania that gave the Late Carboniferous the name "Pennsylvanian" in the United States. The plants that formed the so-called coal swamps were for the most part trees that reproduced by means of spores, in contrast to modern trees, such as hardwoods and conifers, which reproduce by seeds. The living descendants of Carboniferous spore-bearing trees are all much smaller and less conspicuous. The closest relative of the predominant coal formers, the lycopods, is *Lycopodium*. Commonly called club moss, this plant will fit comfortably in a flower pot.

The decline of the lycopod trees came early in the Permian Period and can be attributed at least in part to a global trend toward drier climates, as revealed by dune and salt deposits of Permian age. This resulted in part from a progressive lowering of sea level during Per-

Lycopod tree of Carboniferous age (left), compared to its closest living relative, the club moss, *Lycopodium*. In contrast to the Carboniferous lycopods, whose bulky remains accumulated in swamps to become the dominant constituents of the vast coal deposits of Carboniferous age, living lycopods (right) are the size of small ferns. The one shown here is growing at the base of a modern tree. Both the fossil and living forms display a spiral of leaves and leaf scars on the stalk or trunk.

mian time, which not only drained broad continental surfaces but left many inland areas far from the ocean and starved for water, much as the Gobi Desert is today. Interestingly, one of the groups of plants that expanded as the swamp flora declined was one that today commonly prevails on dry terrain: the conifers, or cone-bearing plants, which include the pines, firs, and spruces. These and other gymnosperm ("naked seed") plants formed what is sometimes termed the

Mesophytic Flora—the flora that went on to flourish during most of the Mesozoic Era.

Animal life in the terrestrial realm experienced even more sweeping changes. Insects had evolved in mid-Paleozoic time, but it was not until late in the Carboniferous that they resembled those of the modern world in range of adaptations. Higher on the evolutionary scale, vertebrate animals first made their way onto the land at the time of the Late Devonian mass extinction, or just a bit later. As amphibians, these animals and their immediate descendants were tied to water for their reproduction, laying eggs there like toads, salamanders, and other terrestrial amphibians of the present world. Despite this limitation, late Paleozoic amphibians attained great diversity; some were hulking herbivores the size of a pig.

Very late in Carboniferous time, vertebrates took another major evolutionary step forward with the origin of the reptiles. Modern reptiles differ from amphibians in a number of skeletal structures, but some late Paleozoic species are intermediate in form, leaving experts uncertain as to how to classify them. Unfortunately, the fossil record will never reveal which of these species possessed one critical reptilian adaptation: the amniote egg which, by providing nutrition within a protective shell, liberated reptiles from dependence on water for reproduction and allowed them to colonize highlands and regions lacking large bodies of water.

Reptiles themselves then underwent great changes. In the course of the Permian Period they came more and more to resemble mammals. The changes were partly dental in nature, with highly differentiated teeth replacing the rather uniform sets of teeth of early reptiles. Important, too, were advances in locomotory mechanics—especially the placement of the limbs more directly beneath the body, so that the ancestral reptilian crouching posture gave way to a more upright stance. Many Early Permian species are, in fact, placed in a group called the mammal-like reptiles. Some of these were jaguar-sized carnivores with huge sails on their backs, formed of soft tissue stretched between greatly elongated spinal processes. In mid-Permian time, the most advanced group of mammal-like reptiles evolved. These were the therapsids, which may have been at least partly endothermic ("warm-blooded") and which probably should not be classified with the Reptilia. By Late Permian time, although reptiles and amphibians were still present in modest numbers, the therapsids were the dominant group of large animals on the land. Their success can probably be attributed to their superior mechanisms for feeding and locomotion. Another possible advantage was their ability to sustain high levels of activity for long periods of time. More primitive reptiles and amphib-

Carnivorous therapsid mammal-like reptile (left). Animals of this type had highly differentiated teeth and a more upright posture than primitive reptiles. They suffered very heavy losses in the crisis that brought the Permian to a close. Reconstruction of a Carboniferous coal swamp (right). A fin-backed mammal-like reptile menaces other animals, and an early dragonfly of unusually large proportions hovers in the foreground.

ians, being unable to maintain high body temperatures through internal physiological mechanisms, can move rapidly even for brief periods only after absorbing heat from their environment. Lizards, for example, are only active when the weather is warm, and even then are only capable of short bursts of activity.

The shift of advanced animal life onto the continents during late Paleozoic time, culminating in the ascendancy of the therapsids, added a new dimension to mass extinction. The final biotic crisis of the Paleozoic Era, that of the Late Permian, struck not only in the oceans but also on the land.

THE BIGGEST MARINE CRISIS

The mass extinction of Late Permian time literally marked the end of an era. In its aftermath, the Mesozoic Era began. For the marine realm, the Permian crisis was the most severe of all time; it is estimated to have extirpated from 75 to 90 percent of all preexisting spe-

Late Paleozoic ammonoid. This specimen has the coiled outer shell worn away to reveal that the chambers between the wavy internal partitions are filled with sediment. Ammonoids flourished right up to the end of the era, but survived the terminal Permian crisis through the persistence of only a very few species.

cies. This number is, in a sense, meaningless because the crisis was spread over an interval of time in the order of 10 million years, and some new species were evolving even while it was in progress.

The primary marine victims included the single-celled fusulinaceans, none of which survived into the Triassic, the first period of the Mesozoic Era. No trilobites are found in Triassic rocks either, but the last trilobites are found in rocks much older than latest Permian; furthermore, because the group as a whole was on the decline before the period even began, its final demise cannot necessarily be attributed to the crisis. In fact, the crisis did not so much eliminate entire classes of animals as it cut a broad swath through many, leaving a generally impoverished fauna at the start of Triassic time. Suffering heavy losses were the corals (although they were not highly diversified even at the start of the Permian), crinoids, brachiopods, bryozoans, and ammonoids. In fact, the ammonoids seem barely to have scraped by, with just two or three genera (and not many more species) persisting into the Triassic Period. The tropical reef community was also decimated, as happened in both of the earlier Paleozoic crises.

The timing of the marine losses is of great importance with regard to our search for a cause. Extinction was not focused at the very end of the Permian Period, but was spread over the final two ages of Permian time, the Guadalupian Age and the Djulfian Age. In fact, heavy extinction for the brachiopods began even earlier; most Early Permian brachiopod genera failed to survive into Late Permian time. Only three families of fusulinaceans survived into Guadalupian time, and bryozoans as well as rugose corals were by this time restricted in variety and in geographic distribution. Philip Signor and Jere Lipps of the University of California at Davis have suggested that an imperfect fossil record may give us the false impression that a mass extinction was spread over a substantial interval of time. Their idea is that a group of taxa that actually disappeared simultaneously might appear to have died out sequentially because some of the taxa have poor fossil records. Could it be that very little of the Late Permian extinction took place before Djulfian time? This possibility appears to be ruled out by the fact that groups like the fusulinaceans and bryozoans produced vast numbers of minute skeletal remains that could hardly be overlooked in the Djulfian record.

Of great importance is the fact that by Djulfian time the remaining fusulinaceans, bryozoans, and rugose corals were all confined to the Tethyan geographic region. The Tethys was a sizeable embayment in the largest landmass of all time, the supercontinent known as Pangaea. Pangaea was assembled near the end of the Paleozoic Era by the attachment of Gondwanaland to a northern continent that included

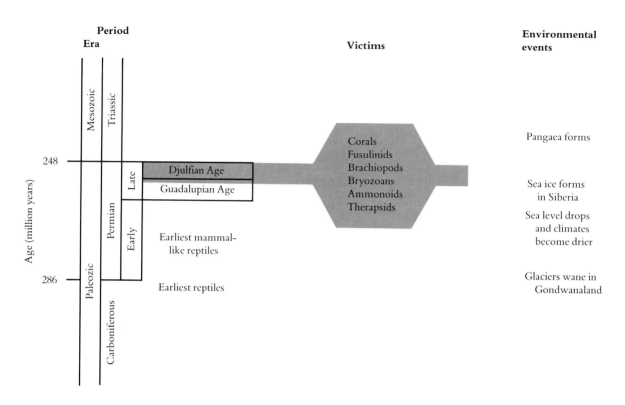

Major events of late Paleozoic time. The colored bar
represents a mass extinction.

North America, Europe, and most of Asia. The supercontinent thus
formed contained most of the landmasses of our modern world. The
Tethys, which seems to have been the last refuge of several important
Paleozoic groups, was a tropical sea in the region now occupied by the
Indian Ocean and eastern Mediterranean Sea. In considering possible
causes of the Late Permian crisis, we must ask why it was that the
Tethys served as a final refuge.

A CRISIS ON THE LAND

The Late Permian event was not only the first mass extinction to strike
terrestrial vertebrates, it was one of the most severe in this domain.
On the land, as in the sea, the crisis was protracted rather than instantaneous. Robert Sloan of the University of Minnesota has found that
several extinction events struck mammal-like reptiles during the sec-

Lystrosaurus, the mammal-like reptile that underwent a population explosion in Gondwanaland following the terminal Permian mass extinction. This tusked herbivore seems to have benefited from the dearth of large predators in the aftermath of the crisis.

ond half of the Permian. Each event was followed by renewed adaptive radiation. The last crisis may have been the most severe, however, because what remained was a markedly impoverished fauna of mammal-like reptiles in the earliest Triassic. This residual fauna has been named the *Lystrosaurus* fauna for its most abundant representative. *Lystrosaurus* was a squat, bulky herbivore whose remains have been found on many landmasses that are now widely separated but that in Triassic time were united within the supercontinent Pangaea: China, India, Africa, and Antarctica. It was the most abundant large animal of the community in which it lived, and the large size of its populations may have resulted from a dearth of large predators following the latest Permian extinctions.

For plants, the story is quite different. As Andrew Knoll of Harvard University has pointed out, terrestrial floras, throughout their history, have been largely immune to mass extinction. This trait may result from the fact that many plants can reproduce vegetatively, that is, by the survival and growth to maturity of a small portion of an individual. Many a tree that has been chopped down has sent new shoots up from its severed trunk. Plants have experienced periodic transformations, but these have occurred over substantial intervals of time. Plants seem not to have followed the pattern often seen in the animal world in which one group has suffered extinction and afterwards another has expanded to take its place. Instead, the expansion of the new plant group has occurred while the older one has been on the wane. Thus, late in the Paleozoic Era the coal swamp floras declined, in part because climates became more arid; gymnosperm floras, which included conifers, expanded in complementary fashion. In southern regions of Pangaea, it was the *Glossopteris* Flora that gave way to the Mesophytic Flora. Andrew Knoll has observed that the floral transition took place at different times in different places—during mid-Permian time in North America and Europe, for example, but not until about the end of the Permian Period in Asia and Australia.

PATTERN AND CAUSE

The mass extinction of animal life and biological developments that followed exhibited certain patterns that offer clues as to what may have caused the crisis. The most obvious of these patterns is temporal: As we have seen, devastation, both on the land and in the ocean, was spread over several million years and seems to have occurred in pulses. Robert Sloan has observed that among the vertebrates it was relatively small animals that survived each of the terrestrial extinction events; he has hypothesized that this pattern may have resulted from climatic oscillations that altered vegetation patterns and imposed food shortages on large animals. It is well known that the great glacial interval that began in the Southern Hemisphere during Late Devonian time continued into the mid-Permian. Just as glaciation had begun when the South American segment of Gondwanaland moved over the South Pole, it ended when Gondwanaland (at this time a part of Pangaea) finally migrated off the South Pole, with the margin of Antarctica having been the last in the polar position. During any long glacial interval, ice volume fluctuates and, correspondingly, climates alternately ameliorate and deteriorate and sea level rises and falls. Sloan has suggested that substantial climatic oscillations were associated with the expansion and contraction of glaciers in the Southern Hemisphere and that the continuation of pulses of vertebrate extinction into the latter part of Permian time resulted from post-glacial climatic oscillations.

Unfortunately, we do not have a picture of the geographic pattern of extinction of terrestrial vertebrates for latest Permian time, because fossils of this age are found only in South Africa and the western Soviet Union. For marine life, in contrast, the geographic pattern is rather well known. This and other features of both the marine crisis and the ecosystem that remained in its aftermath suggest that climatic changes were the primary agent of extinction.

One telling pattern was noted above: By the final age of the Permian (the Djulfian), the fusulinaceans, bryozoans, and rugose corals were restricted to the equatorial Tethyan region. Earlier in the Permian Period, these groups had enjoyed broader latitudinal distributions, and it is difficult to believe that the contraction of their collective geographic range could have resulted from anything other than climatic cooling.

Also highly significant is the nature of the marine ecosystem during Early Triassic time following the crisis of the Permian Period. It has long been recognized that taxa of Early Triassic seas tended to be unusually cosmopolitan in their distribution. The fossil record reveals that many species and genera occurred over broad regions of the globe. As for the crisis of the Late Ordovician and Late Devonian epochs, this pattern implies that the crisis interval was associated with global cooling.

There are other important pieces of evidence suggesting that relatively cool conditions continued into Early Triassic time. Two of

The supercontinent Pangaea in Late Permian time. The Late Permian was a unique interval in the Phanerozoic Eon, in that nearly all of the earth's continental crust was concentrated in this one landmass, which stretched from pole to pole, and sea level was depressed, leaving only small areas of shallow seas; furthermore, both poles were cold, as attested to by the presence of sea ice deposits in the Kolyma block, which lay somewhere in the Northern Hemisphere, and in Australia, which was no longer glaciated but received dropstones, probably from icebergs that originated in Antarctica.

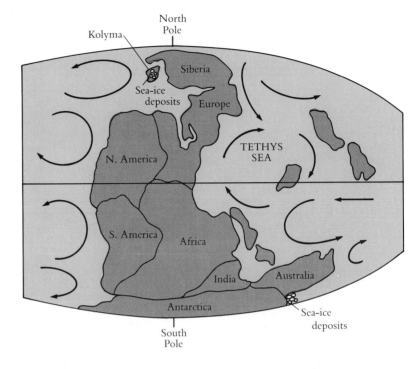

these, shared with the crises of the Late Ordovician and Late Devonian epochs, were that the mass extinction was followed by an interval of reduced limestone deposition and reef growth, both of which are largely restricted to warm seas. What is more, the most important builders of Permian reefs were calcareous algae and calcareous sponges, and after the interlude of no reef growth, the very members of these groups that had been major reef builders during Permian time recovered. Once again they began to build reefs. Remarkably, calcareous algae, which are restricted to warm habitats today, are virtually unknown from rocks of Early Triassic age. The recovery of the reef builders indicates that it was not extinction that terminated reef development. Some environmental condition suppressed the growth of calcareous algae and sponges for several million years before the recovery. Certainly temperature must be regarded as the most likely control.

Aerial view of the Permian reef complex of western
Texas and New Mexico. This is the most spectacularly
exposed reef of late Paleozoic age. Laid bare by the
erosion of soft rocks that once buried it, this structure
now stands above the surrounding terrain, as it did in
life. It was built by algae, sponges, and bryozoans of
types that are largely absent from rocks of Early Triassic age.

WORLD GEOGRAPHY

We have seen that the biotic crises of the Late Ordovician and Late
Devonian epochs each coincided with the inception of a glacial interval that was triggered by the passage of Gondwanaland over the South
Pole. It has long been recognized that the second glacial interval ended
in mid-Permian time, when the Gondwanaland segment of Pangaea
shifted off the South Pole. In fact, the south polar region remained
even in Late Permian time. Icebergs, probably broken from Antarctic
glaciers that reached the sea, dropped coarse sedimentary debris to
shallow sea floors in southern Australia. This forms part of the evi-

A Permian calcareous sponge of the genus *Girtyocoelia,* which was an important builder of Late Permian reefs, including the Permian reef complex of Texas. The holes in the bead-like skeleton are spouts from which water squirted after being relieved of digestible suspended particles. This genus is unknown from rocks of Early Triassic age but then reappears in rocks of Middle Triassic age, which suggests that adverse conditions—most likely low temperatures—suppressed its growth for an interval of time following the terminal Permian crisis.

dence that both poles of the Late Permian world were frigid. With so much attention having been paid to the history of glaciation in the Southern Hemisphere, little notice has been taken of a dramatic climatic change that occurred shortly thereafter in the Northern Hemisphere. Perhaps this oversight also reflects the fact that the evidence now lies in the northeastern region of Siberia.

As Pangaea shifted northward off the South Pole, this supercontinent, which was virtually as long as a meridian of the earth, encroached on the North Pole. By extrapolation from the earlier patterns of pole encounter and glaciation, we might predict the occurrence of a northern glacial interval, although the prediction should be regarded as tentative because it is not certain that Pangaea actually reached the North Pole before Triassic time. As it turns out, however, there is indeed evidence of glaciation in northeastern Siberia.

The Late Permian ice-deposited rocks of Siberia are dropstones—pebbles, cobbles, and boulders that were released by melting ice at the sea surface and then settled to the sea floor, where they became imbedded in muddy sediment. A small percentage of these rock fragments—called clasts—bear parallel grooves that attest to their previous position beneath moving glaciers. Fossils in sediments associated with the glacial marine deposits indicate both the marine nature of the depositional setting and a Late Permian time of accumulation. The glacial marine deposits are quite voluminous, covering some half million square kilometers (about 200,000 square miles) and attaining as much as a kilometer (about 0.6 mile) in stratigraphic thickness. Apparently a great deal of ice was reaching shallow seas. Another key piece of evidence is the occurrence of marine limestones stratigraphically beneath the glacial marine deposits. This unlikely juxtaposition testifies to a sudden and severe drop in temperatures from the warm conditions that typify regions of limestone deposition.

There is evidence that the terrain upon which the glacial deposits lie was not actually attached to Siberia during Late Permian time. This terrain, which has been named Kolyma, comprises ancient rocks that differ from the Siberian rocks with which it is now juxtaposed. Through plate-tectonic movements, Kolyma became sutured to Siberia late in the Mesozoic Era. During Late Permian time, when it was accumulating the glacial marine deposits, Kolyma must have been positioned at a high latitude near Pangaea.

When we recall that the Tethys was the final refuge for animal groups such as fusulinaceans, bryozoans, and corals that were noted for their adaptation to warm waters, the implication of sudden cooling

Dune deposits of Late Permian age that rim the Grand
Canyon of Arizona. The curved sets of layers in dune
deposits are known as cross beds. A single set of approximately parallel beds forms when several intervals
of strong wind deposit sediment on the steep leeward
slope of the dune. Another set, often truncating earlier
deposits, forms when the wind shifts.

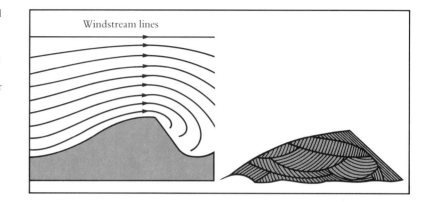

Windstream lines

of the Tethys in Late Permian time takes on great importance. What
the evidence points to is, first, a restriction of important tropical elements to the Tethys, which was equatorial in position, and then the
disappearance of these groups even from this final refuge. This is precisely the kind of pattern that would be expected to accompany a

cooling trend, as is an interlude in which reef growth is weak or absent—another feature that we have seen to have characterized the aftermath of the Permian extinction. It is in the Tethyan region that we have the earliest evidence of recovery of the reef ecosystem—a recovery that entailed the reexpansion of certain types of calcareous algae and sponges that had flourished in tropical seas during Late Permian time. Cooling would have been accentuated by the lowering of sea level that occurred during the latter part of the Permian Period. This recession of sea level drained shallow tropical seas that, because they were impounded, had remained warm. The west coast of Pangaea, like the west coast of the Americas today, must have been cooled throughout Permian time by the great oceanic gyres that the Coriolis force has always caused to flow toward the equator. (As a result of the earth's rotation, this apparent force causes air and water currents to flow clockwise in the Northern Hemisphere and counterclockwise in the Southern Hemisphere.) Early in Permian time, warm, shallow seas flooded substantial areas of western North America, but here too the lowering of sea level as the period progressed must have led to a dominance of cool oceanic currents. Thus, toward the end of Permian time, cool seas may have bordered both the east and west coasts of Pangaea.

The evidence that glaciation continued into Late Permian time after shifting to the Northern Hemisphere may explain why pulses of extinction, which Robert Sloan has attributed to climatic fluctuations, occurred throughout the Late Permian. Certainly climatic change has been widely viewed as important in the transition from the Paleophytic Flora to the Mesophytic Flora, which differed in timing from place to place but was concentrated between mid-Permian and earliest Triassic time.

The unusually widespread occurrence of dune deposits (deposits of wind-blown sand) and evaporite salts in stratigraphic sequences of Late Permian age has led some to suggest that terrestrial climates were unusually warm at this time. These sediments are indicative more of aridity than of extremely warm temperatures, however, and certainly their Late Permian abundance must in large part simply reflect the dry conditions that afflicted so large a continent as Pangaea when seas stood at an unusually low position. Under such circumstances, large land areas must have become interior deserts, in the manner of the modern Gobi. Furthermore, the unification of most landmasses into one huge continent from which the shallow seas had receded must have to some degree decoupled terrestrial climates from marine climates.

SHARED PATTERNS OF MASS EXTINCTION
SUGGEST A COMMON CAUSE

The number of traits that are shared by the mass extinctions of the Late Ordovician, Late Devonian, and Late Permian epochs is impressive. Many of these point to cooling as the primary cause of the three events. Movements of sea level, while they may have been partly linked to climatic change, did not follow a characteristic pattern. Although the seas were shrinking back from the continental surfaces during the Ordovician and Permian crises, much of the heavy extinction of the Late Devonian took place during a high stand of sea level.

One of the traits shared by the three crises and suggesting a prominent role for climatic cooling is the repeated pattern of heavy extinction in the tropics, an important aspect of which was the destruction of the tropical reef community. Also evident, at least for the crises of the Ordovician and Permian, is a progressive compression of the biotas of higher latitudes toward the tropical zone. In fact, each of the mass extinctions occupied several million years and probably occurred in several pulses.

The marine ecosystem that remained after each event was also unusual in that tropical reef growth was weak or absent and limestone deposition, which is also largely a tropical phenomenon, occurred in few areas. Each of the mass extinctions also took a heavy toll on calcareous algae of types restricted to warm seas. A reduction of tropical conditions is also suggested by the cosmopolitan distribution of the marine taxa that lived in the aftermath of each crisis: An unusual number of species and genera were able to occupy a wide range of latitudes. This biogeographic pattern might also be partly or entirely explained by the preferential survival of species tolerant of a wide range of temperature conditions. Both of these potential explanations imply that climates cooled.

Also remarkable is the fact that each of the three great Paleozoic extinctions took place at a time when one of three glacial intervals was getting underway. It is well known that the first two glacial episodes were continental in scale; their coarse deposits are spread over broad geographic areas. The third glaciation may have been more localized, perhaps being restricted to mountainous regions, but it nonetheless testifies to the cooling of previously warm seas; some of its sea ice moved into areas that had been sites of limestone deposition.

Finally, we can extend the apparent explanation to a more fundamental level. Each of the three extinctions and glacial episodes seem to
have coincided with one of the three times during the Paleozoic Era
when a huge continent encroached on one of the earth's poles, reflecting a high percentage of solar radiation and experiencing climatic
cooling.

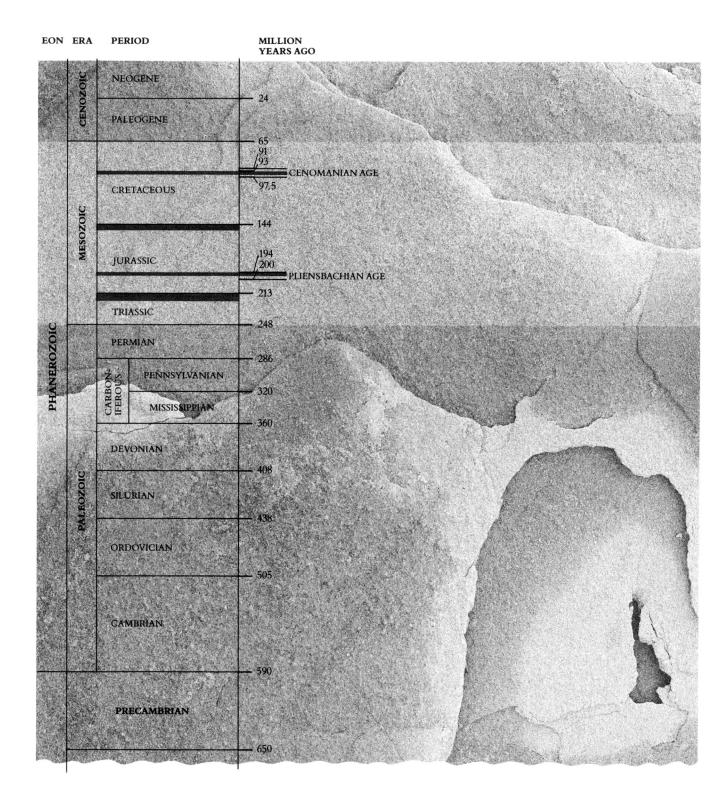

EON	ERA	PERIOD	MILLION YEARS AGO

PHANEROZOIC

CENOZOIC
- NEOGENE
- PALEOGENE

MESOZOIC
- CRETACEOUS
- JURASSIC
- TRIASSIC

PALEOZOIC
- PERMIAN
- CARBONIFEROUS
  - PENNSYLVANIAN
  - MISSISSIPPIAN
- DEVONIAN
- SILURIAN
- ORDOVICIAN
- CAMBRIAN

PRECAMBRIAN

24

65
91
93

CENOMANIAN AGE

97.5

144

194
200

PLIENSBACHIAN AGE

213

248

286

320

360

408

438

505

590

650

6 THE AGE OF DINOSAURS

The Mesozoic Era, while it has attracted much public attention for having witnessed the rise and fall of the dinosaurs, is of paleobiological interest for many additional reasons. This chapter will review not only the ascendancy of the dinosaurs, but also the Mesozoic histories of many other biological groups—histories that include the rise of the dominant modern groups of fish and land plants, the expansions of the major groups of phytoplankton, including one whose fossil skeletons formed vast deposits of chalk on Cretaceous sea floors, and the origin of a strange new group of reef-building bivalve mollusks that forced corals into a subordinate ecological role. We will also consider episodes of heavy extinction that took place long before the end of the era.

This great Mesozoic proliferation of new forms of life issued from modest beginnings; the Late Permian mass extinction, seemingly the most devastating of all time, had left impoverished communities of animals both on the land and in the sea. This chapter will review major developments in the history of Mesozoic life, setting the scene for the following chapter, which will deal with the demise of the dinosaurs and many of their contemporaries.

TRIASSIC RECOVERY

The previous chapter described how, after the terminal Permian crisis, life not only was sparse in earliest Triassic seas, but also included many species and genera that were cosmopolitan in distribution. Another trait of earliest Triassic marine life was the preponderance of mollusks, especially ammonoids. This might seem strange in light of the fact that the ammonoids were nearly wiped out by the Late Per-

Hexacorals of Triassic age (top). These are some of the earliest representatives of the group that includes the tropical reef-building corals of modern seas. Placodont reptile (bottom), a Triassic animal that lived in shallow seas and crushed shellfish with large, rounded molars.

mian mass extinction. Initially in the aftermath of this crisis the ammonoids were abundant but not rich in number of species. Apparently the few species that occupied earliest Triassic seas thrived because competition was weak: They had the world to themselves. Throughout their evolutionary history, however, when given the opportunity, ammonoids underwent rapid adaptive radiations. In the Early Triassic, just 5 or 6 million years after the Paleozoic–Mesozoic transition, their ranks had swollen to more than 150 species. Bivalve mollusks are the second most conspicuous group of marine life in rocks of Early Triassic age, although they are not truly abundant. A non-molluscan group, the brachiopods, probably rank third. These latter two animal groups resembled many others that survived into the Triassic in that many of their surviving genera are not known from rocks representing the oldest part of the Triassic System. Apparently what happened was that these genera made the transition to the new era by way of only a small number of species and thus left few fossil remains. In fact, other persisting groups, such as gastropods (snails), bryozoans, crinoids, sea urchins, sponges, and foraminiferans, are exceedingly rare in rocks of Early Triassic age.

As was noted in the previous chapter, the reef community of the Late Permian is unknown from rocks of Early Triassic age but is seen again in reefs of mid-Triassic age, perhaps because warm tropical seas reappeared. A new evolutionary event of major importance, however, soon resulted in the displacement of this reef system. This was the origin of the hexacorals—the group that forms the spectacular tropical reefs of the modern world. Before the end of the Triassic Period, the hexacorals were contributing to extensive reef tracts in southern Europe and other warm regions.

Through renewed adaptive radiation, many other groups of marine organisms that survived from Permian time joined the corals as major elements of the Mesozoic marine ecosystem. The mollusks, however, were the most successful of all. Their dominance in earliest Triassic seas foreshadowed their prominence throughout the Mesozoic Era—and, for that matter, right up to the present.

The most spectacular newcomers to the seas were not groups of mollusks or corals, however, but ocean-going reptiles that merit the informal appellation "sea monsters." Among these large swimmers were the placodonts, reptiles about the size of large seals with flattened, almost turtlelike bodies and huge, rounded teeth that were clearly adaptations for crushing shellfish—presumably mollusks and perhaps brachiopods. Probably the placodonts colonized the shore, periodically diving into the water to feed. Apparently living in somewhat the same fashion, but not fitted with shell-crushing dentition,

Ichthyosaur, a swimming reptile of early Mesozoic age. Ichthyosaurs were finned fish eaters that superficially resembled modern dolphins. Their streamlined shape reveals them to have been rapid swimmers, and the preservation of fossil embryo skeletons in the abdomens of some specimens shows that ichthyosaur young were born live; ichthyosaurs did not lay eggs.

were the nothosaurs. These were slenderer animals that used paddle-like limbs to pursue fish, which they captured with sharp teeth. A third reptilian group of great importance in the Triassic Period was the ichthyosaurs, whose name, meaning "fish lizard," is aptly descriptive. They were more highly adapted for swimming than the other two sea monster groups of the Triassic Period, being shaped very much like modern dolphins (which are mammals of the whale group). The fish upon which many of them fed were members of the Osteichthyes, the class that includes modern bony fish such as bass, pike, and tuna. Triassic representatives of this group, however, still possessed a number of primitive traits, including nonoverlapping, diamond-shaped scales and unsophisticated jaw mechanisms.

THE RISE OF THE DINOSAURS

Terrestrial habitats of the Triassic were, of course, characterized by gymnosperm plants of the Mesophytic Flora, which included conifers, cycads, and ginkgoes—groups that survive today, although only the conifers are abundant. Although very much on the decline, a fair variety of lycopods also persisted. The most diverse group of plants in the Triassic, however, was the ferns, which seem to have formed the undergrowth beneath trees belonging to the other groups.

It was in this vegetational context that the dinosaurs came into being, but they were not the first four-legged animals to dominate the Triassic landscape. Before the dinosaurs evolved, the therapsids held this position, having quickly rebounded from their severe losses in the terminal Permian crisis. This recovery was from very modest beginnings. The earliest Triassic fauna, dominated in many regions of Pangaea by the bulky herbivore *Lystrosaurus*, included very few therapsid species. Undoubtedly the great abundance of *Lystrosaurus* reflected the dearth of large carnivores capable of attacking it with success. This was especially the case toward the end of *Lystrosaurus's* reign on earth, when no predator larger than about a kilogram (2.2 pounds) is known to have existed. However, therapsids then diversified rapidly, just as they had after repeated extinctions in the Permian, and within just a few million years they were represented by numerous large herbivores and carnivores.

There also evolved during Early Triassic time the animals that were ancestral to the dinosaurs. These were the thecodonts, some of which were adapted for rapid two-legged running in the manner of ostriches, but all of which probably spent much time standing or walking on all fours. Most thecodonts were rather small animals, falling within the size range of domestic dogs, and were quite agile. This locomotory ability resulted in part from the positioning of the legs beneath the body, rather than in a sprawling posture, and it may well account for the evolution of some thecodonts to sizes in excess of 0.5 metric ton (about 0.5 U.S. ton). The dinosaurs evolved from thecodonts in mid-Triassic time. They were at first small, but before the end of Triassic time some species attained lengths of about 6 meters (about 20 feet).

Four other important vertebrate groups evolved during the Triassic Period—groups that would have longer tenures on earth than the dinosaurs. Two of these, the turtles and crocodilians, were reptilian groups, and a third was our own group, the mammals, which at this time were small and rodentlike. The fourth was an amphibian group whose members have remained diminutive to the present day: the frogs.

It is puzzling that the therapsid mammal-like reptiles had a considerable head start on the dinosaurs, and yet the dinosaurs expanded to dominate terrestrial habitats of the Mesozoic Era. Robert Bakker of The University of Colorado Natural History Museum has argued persuasively that this fact attests to the inherent superiority of the dinosaurs—and, in fact, of the thecodonts. These dinosaur ancestors, even before the dinosaurs themselves, seem to have begun to displace the therapsids. Even the early mammals were left behind, failing to undergo their great adaptive radiation until nearly 200 million years

Reconstruction of Late Triassic terrestrial life. The large animal is an early member of the crocodile group, and the smaller animals are thecodonts, diminutive members of the group ancestral to the dinosaurs.

later, after the dinosaurs' demise. Bakker has viewed the dinosaurs' ecological dominance as offering strong testimony that they were endothermic ("warm-blooded"). Reptiles, which depend on external sources of heat energy, are unable to sustain high levels of activity for long intervals of time, whereas mammals, with their continuously high metabolism, can remain active for hours. The question is, if dinosaurs were saddled with a reptilian physiology, how could they have maintained ecological superiority over mammals? Even stronger evidence that dinosaurs were to a considerable degree endothermic comes from predator/prey ratios. In a community of mammals, which are of course endothermic, there is a relatively small number of predators compared to the number of herbivores. The reason for this is that the predators, being endothermic, need a great deal of fuel to stoke their metabolic furnaces. An example is the small number of lions, cheetahs, hyenas, and wild dogs on an African savannah compared to the huge heards of wildebeests, zebras, gazelles, and other herbivores that serve as prey. In contrast, carnivorous reptiles tend to be relatively abundant within their communities. Being ectothermic, they require little food. Bakker has shown that in dinosaur communities, predator/prey ratios were consistently very low, resembling those of mammals—strong evidence that dinosaurs were endothermic.

It has been suggested that the small heads of some huge dinosaurs implies that these animals could not have chewed up enough food to

Dinosaur tracks preserved in mud that turned to rock. Series of left and right tracks of single animals are nearly aligned, showing that dinosaurs walked and ran adeptly with their legs positioned directly beneath their bodies, rather than splayed awkwardly to either side.

sustain an endothermic metabolism. Elephants, though much smaller animals, must nonetheless feed most of the time to support their bulk, and they have huge heads and massive, grinding teeth. In fact, this comparison is entirely unfounded, because giant dinosaurs used their heads only for taking in food. The much more difficult process of grinding it up for digestion was given over to the intestinal tract, where gizzard stones—rounded rocks that were swallowed—served as an enormous gastric mill. This structure is what permitted dinosaurs to become so much larger than the largest land mammals.

There is no question that dinosaurs have been widely underrated by members of the human species, who have pictured them as lumbering hulks that died out because they somehow became outmoded. Actually, some dinosaurs weighed only a few kilograms (about 5 pounds), but even without considering the biological features of dinosaurs, there is no reason that this negative appraisal should be correct. Extinction does not imply biological inferiority. The dinosaurs died out because of environmental changes, not because mammals suddenly developed superior traits. Late Cretaceous mammals, like those of earlier Mesozoic intervals, were small and, by modern standards, primitive. The trackways preserved in sedimentary rocks show dinosaur footprints to have been rather closely aligned, like those of mammals, and they also show that dinosaurs frequently moved quite rapidly. Groups of parallel trackways also reveal the presence of social behavior in dinosaurs: Some species, at least, travelled in herds. Duck-billed dinosaurs of Late Cretaceous age had tall, crested skulls that contained complex nasal chambers reminiscent of the coils of a brass musical instrument; these have been interpreted as resonating chambers employed in the production of trumpeting sounds, and their unique configuration in each species would then attest to species-specific sounds. In other words, it would appear that members of a single species called to each other.

Dinosaur fossils offer evidence of relatively advanced reproductive behavior as well. In Cretaceous rocks of Mongolia and the western United States, eggs can be found arrayed in rings, as if they were very precisely buried. The eggs were tapered toward one end, this end having been thrust into the ground by the mother. Even more revealing is the discovery by Jack Horner of the Museum of the Rockies and his coworkers of nests of baby dinosaurs in rocks of Late Cretaceous age in Montana. The first to be found was a cluster of skeletons, each about a meter (about 3 feet) long, surrounded by broken eggshells in a depression on top of an ancient hill. The nests demonstrate that dinosaurs cared for their young after they hatched.

Certainly Triassic dinosaurs did not possess all the traits that have

Reconstruction of duckbilled dinosaurs of Late Cretaceous age tending their nest. Nests, with skeletons of
juveniles, are preserved in Montana, revealing that
adults cared for their young.

been attributed to dinosaurs of later Mesozoic intervals. What is evident from trackways is that some Triassic species travelled in herds
and at high rates of speed. Also, some were of moderately large size,
even for dinosaurs. More generally, Triassic dinosaurs were proficient
enough at both feeding and locomotion to wrest from mammal-like
reptiles the dominant role in terrestrial ecosystems.

THE CRISIS OF THE LATE TRIASSIC

At times in the Mesozoic Era, long before the final event that swept
away the dinosaurs, global mass extinctions struck both in the ocean
and on the land. These episodes are for the most part rather poorly
understood, especially on the land, in part because the fossil record of
the dinosaurs is too incomplete to reveal exactly when and how
quickly one dinosaur fauna gave way to the next.

The first Mesozoic crisis took place near the end of the Triassic
Period, and it may have been a double crisis, with heavy extinction
occurring several million years earlier on the land than in the sea. It
eliminated the labyrinthodont amphibians, a group that had survived
from the Paleozoic Era, and almost all of the mammal-like reptiles.
Certain thecodont taxa also died out. It was following this crisis that
the dinosaurs, which had evolved somewhat earlier, came to monop-
olize terrestrial habitats.

The marine extinctions of latest Triassic time appear to have been even more devastating than those that later terminated the Mesozoic Era. About 20 percent of the preexisting families of marine invertebrates disappeared. Among the Triassic victims were the conodonts, which, having weathered all of the Paleozoic crises, finally died out. The ammonoids suffered major losses, and a less heavy toll was also taken on brachiopods and gastropod and bivalve mollusks. Anthony Hallam of the University of Birmingham has estimated that fewer than 10 percent of Late Triassic bivalve species survived into the Jurassic Period. The marine reptiles seem also to have been affected by this crisis, but their fossil record is too spotty to reveal exactly when Triassic groups died out; in any event, the ichthyosaurs were the only major group to persist into the succeeding Jurassic Period.

What happened to sea level at the end of Triassic time has been a matter of some controversy. It does appear that the sea surface fell relative to the level of the land in parts of Europe, but Cathryn Newton of Syracuse University has advanced stratigraphic evidence for a deepening of waters in most other areas, including western North America, and Peter Vail and his associates at Exxon Production Research Company have concluded that sea level was rising on a global scale during the Triassic–Jurassic transition.

The history of sea-level change is of particular importance with regard to the fate of the newly evolved coral reef community in southern Europe, where it produced large reef structures that now stand impressively exposed in the Alps, having been uplifted by mountain-building movements. These reefs grew along the northern margin of the Tethys Sea, which remained as a large embayment in Pangaea. During the Triassic Period, having formed not long before (in late Paleozoic time), Pangaea began to fragment in the area of the western Tethys. Reefs grew on blocks of the earth's crust that were shifting and moving up and down as Pangaea began to rift apart. The reef community here disappeared at the close of Triassic time. Some researchers have attributed this to a regional elevation of the land relative to the position of sea level. This suggestion is somewhat problematical, however, because we would expect that some of the many shifting crustal blocks would have stood at shallow depths even after a general change in the relative positions of land and sea in the Tethyan region. Other researchers have favored the idea that cooling of the Tethys exterminated the reef fauna.

The history of reef growth forms part of an interesting parallel between the Triassic crisis and the Paleozoic mass extinctions described in the previous chapter. Not only did reef growth virtually cease, at least in the Tethys where there is a good record of Late

Triassic reefs, but in the seas the rate of production of limestone and dolomite (a related carbonate rock) declined. This pattern is consistent with the idea that climatic cooling played a major role in the crisis. Nonetheless, we are hampered by gaps in the rock record. Because few continuous stratigraphic sections span the Triassic–Jurassic boundary, the terminal Triassic mass extinction in the marine realm has not been well studied, and no promising model has been advanced for its cause. The same is true for other less severe crises that occurred later in the Mesozoic Era but before the terminal Cretaceous event that ended the reign of the dinosaurs. The remainder of this chapter will be devoted to reviewing our meager information about these lesser events and to outlining the evolutionary development of the life that inhabited the earth at the time when extinction ended the Mesozoic Era.

JURASSIC LIFE

The marine biotas of Jurassic time were in many ways similar to those of the Triassic Period. The conodonts were gone, but other groups, although set back, had not been extirpated by the terminal Triassic crisis. Thus, mollusks—including ammonoids, bivalves, and gastropods—and the modern group of corals recovered to resume prominent roles in the marine ecosystem. Joining the ammonoids as important swimming predators were the belemnoids, which were also members of the molluscan class Cephalopoda. The belemnoids, however, were more squidlike in external form and possessed an internal skeleton with a cigar-shaped counterweight attached at the back. This structure, whose durability rendered it readily preservable in the fossil record, is a common feature of Jurassic sedimentary rocks. Belemnoids had existed before Jurassic time but, for unknown reasons, at relatively low diversities.

Other important new predatory groups also populated Jurassic seas. These were marine reptiles that replaced those that had died out at the end of the Triassic Period. Some ichthyosaurs lived through the crisis, but they gave rise to types different from those of the Triassic. Spectacular preservation of Jurassic ichthyosaurs in Germany sometimes reveals unborn fetuses in the abdominal cavities of female animals, showing that these reptiles, which probably lived far from both the shoreline and the sea floor (where eggs might have been laid) bore live offspring. Altogether new groups of marine reptiles also appeared in Jurassic seas. One of these was the marine crocodiles, which were equipped with eel-like tails for propulsion. These animals have been

Belemnoids, which were common cephalopods of Mesozoic seas. The reconstruction shows swimming animals, which resembled modern squids but possessed a gas-filled internal shell and a cigar-shaped counter-weight, or rostrum. The fossil photograph displays a rostrum.

found preserved in rocks with small clusters of pebbles positioned in the vicinity of their abdominal cavities; these were gizzard stones, like those of dinosaurs, that were used to grind up food. The plesiosaurs were a second group of swimming reptiles to emerge during the Jurassic Period. They were large animals, commonly 3 to 5 meters (about 10 to 16 feet) long in Jurassic time and attaining whale-like proportions [lengths of about 12 meters (about 40 feet)] during the Cretaceous.

On the land, the patchy fossil record of the dinosaurs leaves us with little information concerning the evolutionary history of the group about which we would most like to know. In fact, dinosaur fossils are relatively scarce throughout sedimentary rocks of Early Jurassic age. In sharp contrast, Late Jurassic rocks yield the most spectacular dinosaur fauna ever discovered; dinosaur remains are preserved in the Morrison Formation of the western United States and, displayed right in the rock, at Dinosaur National Monument, Utah.

The Morrison fauna includes species belonging to the dinosaur group of largest body size, the sauropods, of which the genus *Diplodocus* attained a length of more than 25 meters (about 80 feet). Preservational evidence appears to refute the old idea that the large sauropods, because of their bulk, must have been semiaquatic, stand-

The marine crocodile (above left) of Jurassic age was well adapted for aquatic life, with a finned tail for swimming and a narrow snout for catching fish. Plesiosaurs (above right) were important marine predators of the latter portion of the Mesozoic Era. These huge fish-eaters swam through the water in much the way that birds fly through the air. The Jurassic sauropod dinosaur *Mamenchisaurus* (below) was a member of the most gargantuan dinosaur group, some of which exceeded 30 meters (about 100 feet) in length.

ing partly submerged in lakes and rivers. The Morrison sauropods are found almost as frequently in flood plain and marsh deposits as in river-laid sediments. Living with the sauropods were other varieties of dinosaurs, including large predators that stood on their hind legs and stegosaurs, which had large triangular plates on their backs. The function of the stegosaur plates has been the subject of controversy; traditionally they have been thought to have served simply as protective

Fossil pterosaur. Long-winged, toothed, flying reptiles
of this type were abundant throughout most of the
Mesozoic Era but died out with the dinosaurs.

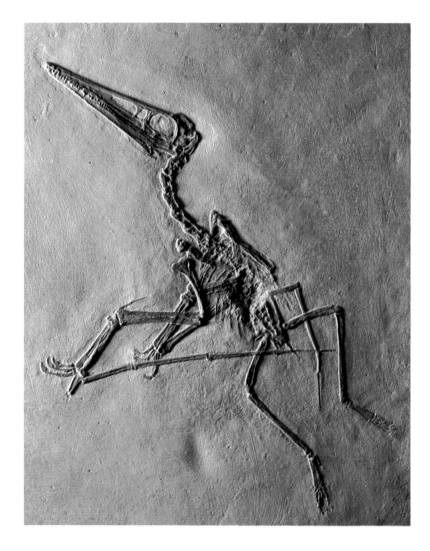

armor, but another hypothesis is that they functioned in thermoregu-
lation as absorbers and radiators of heat.

While dinosaur taxa flourished at body sizes ranging from that of a
small dog to that of the giant sauropods, mammals remained small
and comparatively inconspicuous. It is widely assumed that many
were nocturnal.

Vertebrate animals also colonized Jurassic skies. The pterosaurs,
flying reptiles that had evolved late in the Triassic Period, diversified

during the Jurassic. By Late Cretaceous time they included the gargantuan *Quetzalcoatlus* whose wingspan, estimated at more than 11 meters (about 36 feet), equalled that of a small airplane. Birds also appeared very late in Jurassic time, as evidenced by the famous fossil genus *Archaeopteryx,* a crow-sized animal whose preserved feathers betray its avian identity, despite its possession of teeth, a tail, and other skeletal features that closely resemble those of the dinosaurs. In fact, small dinosaurs are generally believed to have been the direct ancestors of *Archaeopteryx* and its descendants.

Anthony Hallam has identified two relatively minor events of marine extinction within the Jurassic Period. One of these, of Pliensbachian age, has been recognized in Europe, where the event eliminated more than 80 percent of marine bivalve species along with a variety of other shallow-sea species. Hallam has noted, however, that heavy Pliensbachian extinction was not global in scale, but was focused in western Europe where seas retreated and black muds accumulated under conditions of restricted water circulation and reduced oxygen concentration. It may be that hostile conditions here were unique. Hallam has shown, for example, that in the Andean region of South America and other Pacific areas there was no Pliensbachian crisis.

The second crisis of the Jurassic occurred near the close of the period, when bivalves suffered again along with ammonoids. The heavy ammonoid extinction did not occur suddenly, but was spread over the final several million years of Jurassic time. It is not clear when marine reptiles died out, but few marine crocodiles and ichthyosaurs survived the Jurassic. A drop in sea level during latest Jurassic time has been invoked to explain some of the heavy marine extinction, but this idea now seems inappropriate. Based on new data from extensive analysis of Jurassic strata, Peter Vail and coworkers at Exxon Production Research Company have concluded that global sea level underwent rapid but minor fluctuations as the Jurassic Period drew to a close, but remained at a moderately high position relative to the surfaces of major continents.

As evidenced by the large fauna of the Morrison Formation, dinosaurs also experienced heavy casualties at the end of the Jurassic Period. The stegosaurs and most groups of sauropods failed to make the transition into the Cretaceous Period. The cause of the heavy dinosaur losses remains no better understood than the extinctions in the ocean.

Thus, the terminal Jurassic event was of widespread importance with an impact both in the sea and on the land. Nonetheless, this crisis is not at all well understood. One point of interest, however, is that although sea level was once believed to have dropped substantially

Mosasaur consuming a swimming bird. Mosasaurs, which died out in the terminal Cretaceous crisis, evolved from nonmarine monitor lizards to become voracious marine predators of Cretaceous seas.

during the Jurassic–Cretaceous transition, this now appears not to have been the case.

CRETACEOUS MARINE LIFE

Once again the ecosystem recovered, and in early Cretaceous time life in the seas did not look drastically different from that of Jurassic time: Although groups of marine invertebrates had lost many species and some families, few higher taxonomic groups disappeared. Mollusks retained their prominent position, for example, and corals formed reefs as they had before. As the Cretacous Period progressed, however, marine life underwent important transformations, some of which caused it to look increasingly like that of the modern world.

A drastic change occurred in the nature of marine vertebrate faunas. Although plesiosaurs survived, ichthyosaurs and swimming crocodiles were rare, and huge swimming monitor lizards, the mosasaurs, were now on the scene. With large heads and body lengths as great as 15 meters (about 50 feet), they probably pursued larger prey than those of even the biggest ichthyosaurs. Turtles also invaded the seas on a grand scale. Of the several types that evolved, the largest attained lengths of nearly 4 meters (13 feet). Another important development

Groups of single-celled phytoplankton that played important roles in Mesozoic seas and that remain as the most important groups of the modern world. These are dinoflagellates (A); diatoms, which secrete box-like skeletons of silica (B); and calcareous nannoplankton, which secrete tiny plates that armor their cells (C).

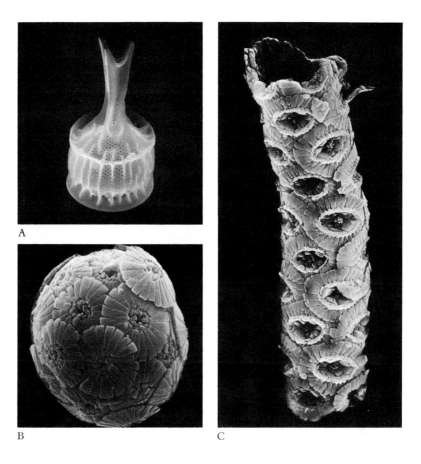

A

B

C

as the Cretaceous progressed was the origin and adaptive radiation of the teleost fish, the group that has thrived to the present day, comprising nearly all of the sport fishes in modern seas, rivers, and lakes. Predecessors of the teleosts broadly resembled them, but had less advanced fins and jaws and were thus less adept in both locomotion and feeding. Teleosts feed not only on floating or swimming life, but also on organisms of the sea floor. Their adaptive radiation during the Cretaceous must have had a severe impact on bottom-dwelling animals, and a similar effect resulted from the adaptive radiations of two carnivorous invertebrate groups that radiated at the same time: crabs and predaceous gastropods (snails).

At the base of the marine food web there were also important evolutionary developments. Three groups of single-celled planktonic algae that account for most of the photosynthesis in modern seas ex-

A scanning electron micrograph of Cretaceous chalk, showing that it is a mass of loosely attached nannoplankton fossils.

panded to assume their prominent modern role. All of these may have evolved earlier in the Mesozoic Era. Certainly one did—the dinoflagellates, whose fossil record extends back to the Late Triassic. Each of these unicellular algae has a thick cell wall and two whiplike flagella. A second group, the diatoms, may have existed as early as Jurassic time, but the record is not clear. These unicellular algae are housed in solid structures resembling pillboxes and composed of silica. Both dinoflagellates and diatoms are especially productive in nontropical seas today, and this was probably true in Mesozoic times as well. The third algal group was the calcareous nannoplankton (meaning "minute plankton"); these forms, which are best represented in warm seas today, secrete minute shields of calcium carbonate (the primary component of limestone), which in life cover their nearly spherical cell wall but in death are liberated and descend to the sea floor. The calcareous nannoplankton played an especially significant geological role during the latter part of the Cretaceous Period, when they rained down on the sea floor in such quantities at many localities that they formed the white, fine-grained form of limestone known as chalk. The White Cliffs of Dover are the most famous deposits of Late Cretaceous chalk, but similar rocks occur from Denmark to France, and in the western interior of the United States from the Gulf Coast to the vicinity of the Canadian border. In all of these localities, the chalk accumulated in seas that spread over continental surfaces; the Late Cretaceous was a time when the seas stood substantially higher relative to continental surfaces then they do today.

Also coming into their own, after a modest beginning earlier in Mesozoic time, were the planktonic foraminiferans. These protozoans are rather well represented in the modern oceans, where their calcareous skeletons settle in great enough abundance to constitute the dominant component of fine-grained sediments over large areas of the deep sea floor. As the following chapter will describe, these foraminiferans and the calcareous nannoplankton were among the groups of organisms most heavily devastated by the extinction at the end of the Mesozoic Era.

The reef community was another segment of the marine ecosystem that was reshaped in mid-Cretaceous time. Early in the period, corals retained their dominant position, but then the evolutionary development of a totally different group of animals, the rudist bivalves, forced the corals into a subordinate reef-building role. The rudists were coral-like in skeletal form, having a conical lower valve (shell), which was covered by the second valve, which was cap-shaped. This group of bivalves evolved earlier in the Mesozoic Era, but through the evo-

Rudist bivalves. These remarkable animals monopo-
lized the reef environment during the latter part of the
Cretaceous Period before their demise at the period's
end.

lution of new modes of skeletal growth became superb at reef building
only in mid-Cretaceous time. We can trace the rudists' history back to
large Paleozoic clams that burrowed in the sediment. These gave rise
to early Mesozoic animals whose preservation in life position (the
position assumed by a living organism) reveals that they lived only
partly buried in the sediment, in an overturned posture. This life position almost certainly evolved to expose symbiotic algae, like those of
corals, to sunlight for efficient photosynthesis. The algae were housed
in the tissue of the mantle, a sheetlike organ that protruded between
the two halves of the shell. It was this association with algae that
endowed rudists with the capacity for rapid growth that is a requisite
for success in the reef environment, where competition for space is
severe. Significant in this light is the fact that the so-called "man-
eating clam," *Tridacna,* shells of which are sometimes used to form
bird baths, is the largest bivalve in the modern world, and it owes its
great size to the presence of symbiotic algae in tissues that protrude
through the gap between its shells. Like the ancestors of rudists, it
lives upside-down relative to orientation for normal bivalves. The
replacement of corals by bivalves during the Cretaceous Period is one

Cretaceous angiosperm, or flowering plant, with a double-lobed leaf. Veins are clearly visible in the fossil.

of the most clear-cut examples of wholesale competitive displacement of one group by another in the history of life. In effect, nature conducted a test of the competition hypothesis when the rudists died out with the dinosaurs—an event to be discussed in the next chapter. With these bizarre but eminently successful bivalves out of the way, the corals reexpanded during the Mesozoic Era to reclaim their dominant position within the reef community.

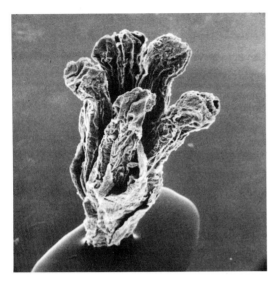

Scanning electron micrographs of a Cretaceous fossil flower (left) and a porous grain of its pollen (right). Pollen, being durable, is plentiful in the fossil record, whereas flowers, being fragile, are extraordinarily rare. This small flower offers direct evidence of the presence of flowering plants during the latter portion of Cretaceous time.

FLOWERING PLANTS AND THE LAST DINOSAURS

To an outside observer of the Mesozoic world, the terrestrial ecosystem would have seemed to change much more radically in mid-Cretaceous time than the marine ecosystem, owing to the transformation of the landscape when a new group of plants rose to dominance. At this time angiosperms, known informally as flowering plants, began their great adaptive radiation. The angiosperms include not only plants with showy flowers, but also hardwood trees, grasses, and weeds. We cannot be certain exactly when the first flowering plants evolved—the fossil record of this group is spotty because leaves are fragile—but it may not have been much earlier. Grasses and the most successful groups of weeds did not evolve until the Cenozoic Era was well under way, yet the adaptive radiation of the angiosperms during the latter part of the Cretaceous Period was nonetheless spectacular. In the Atlantic coastal plain between Baltimore and the District of Columbia, fossil leaves and pollen record substantial diversification during an interval of just a few million years. During this interval, both pollen and leaves increased in variety and in average level of morpho-

Map of the Late Cretaceous world, showing the tropical Tethyan seaway, where heavy extinction occurred, and also the great seaway that extended the length of North America, from the Gulf Coast to the Arctic.

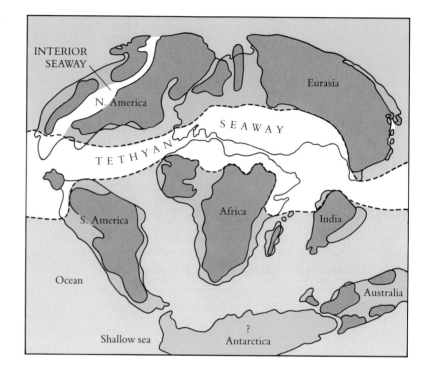

logical complexity. By the end of the Cretaceous Period, the angiosperms were the dominant terrestrial plants. It appears that, through competition for light and nutrients, they displaced conifers and other gymnosperms, which were thus relegated to the subordinate ecological status that they retain today.

The dinosaurs must in some way have felt the impact of the great floral change, but it is not clear exactly what problems it may have posed or what opportunities it may have provided. What is apparent is that sometime near the transition from Early to Late Cretaceous time (roughly 100 million years ago) the dinosaurs experienced pronounced evolutionary turnover.

This turnover, which has been noted by Robert Bakker, may have been part of a global mass extinction that also brought destruction to marine life. It is well documented that heavy extinction occurred in the marine realm during the Cenomanian Age of the Cretaceous Period, more than 90 million years ago. Like so many other crises, this one was protracted in nature. Ammonoids experienced their heaviest

Skull of the Late Cretaceous *Tyrannosaurus,* which may have been the largest carnivorous dinosaur of all time.

losses early in Cenomanian time. Erle Kauffman and coworkers at the University of Colorado have also studied a series of extinction pulses that occurred close to the end of the age within the great interior seaway that spread from the Gulf Coast to Alaska. Standing in front of the active mountain chain that was the predecessor of the modern Rockies and their counterparts to the north and south, this seaway was cooler than the tropical waters to the south that connected the Atlantic and Pacific oceans in the vicinity of the present Gulf of Mexico and Caribbean Sea. A geographic occurrence that deserves mention is the encroachment of Antarctica on the South Pole, which remained attached to Australia and South America after the partial fragmentation of Gondwanaland. Reconstructions of plate positions show the encounter of the pole taking place at about the start of the Cenomanian Age. There is at present no record of ice cap development at this time, but in light of the repeated Paleozoic pattern of polar encounter and glaciation, we must wonder whether some degree of climatic cooling may have been triggered by the new configuration.

The Late Cretaceous recovery of marine life that followed the Cenomanian crisis produced few pronounced changes. Few major groups of animals had disappeared in the crisis, and the lower taxonomic ranks were simply replenished. On the land, the faunal turnover was apparently more severe (if we can attribute it to the same crisis, because the timing remains uncertain). The most important dinosaur groups to diversify during Late Cretaceous time were the predatory tyrannosaurs and the herbivorous ceratopsians and duckbills (hadrosaurs). These animals roamed the American west, leaving an especially impressive fossil record in Montana and Alberta, where the fauna that they constituted might be compared to the mammalian fauna of modern-day African grasslands and open woodlands, though with a scaling up of body sizes. The ceratopsians, ancient analogs of the rhinoceroses, were massive creatures equipped with nasal horns. The duckbills, which were the dinosaurs that seem to have trumpeted signals to one another through convoluted nasal passages, were clearly fast runners like today's antelopes and wildebeests; the duckbills' webbed feet indicate, however, that they were good swimmers as well. The tyrannosaurs were the largest terrestrial predators of all time, attaining lengths as great as 15 meters (about 50 feet). They were the "lions" of the Late Cretaceous—but they were not alone. Also preying on dinosaurs were great terrestrial crocodiles that grew to the incredible length of 15 meters (about 50 feet) with heads about 2 meters (about 7 feet) long. In the skies above were the airplane-sized flying reptiles such as *Quetzalcoatlus.* It has been speculated that these

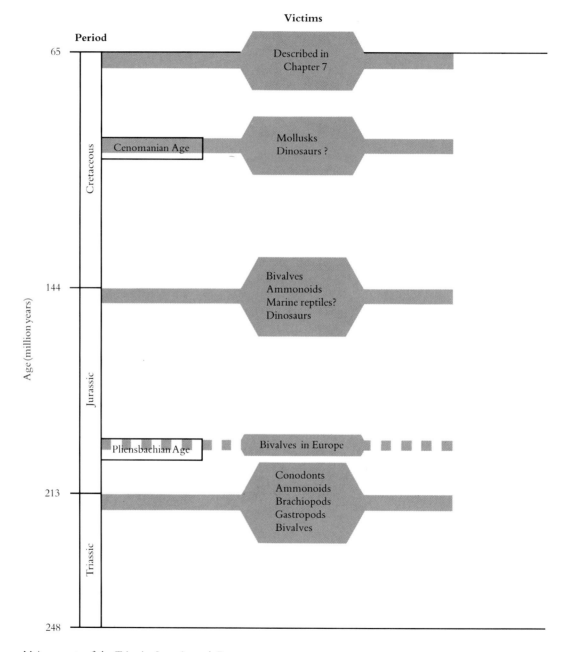

Victims

Period

65

Cretaceous

Cenomanian Age

Described in
Chapter 7

Mollusks
Dinosaurs ?

144

Bivalves
Ammonoids
Marine reptiles?
Dinosaurs

Jurassic

Age (million years)

Pliensbachian Age

Bivalves in Europe

Conodonts
Ammonoids
Brachiopods
Gastropods
Bivalves

213

Triassic

248

Major events of the Triassic, Jurassic, and Cretaceous
periods. Colored bars represent mass extinctions.

animals swooped down to scavenge on the carcasses of dead dinosaurs—a mode of life for which their size was appropriately scaled.

The development of this remarkable terrestrial fauna and of the
Late Cretaceous marine ecosystem, with its ammonoids, rudist reefs,
and swimming and flying reptiles, set the stage for the infamous biotic
crisis that brought the Age of Dinosaurs to a close.

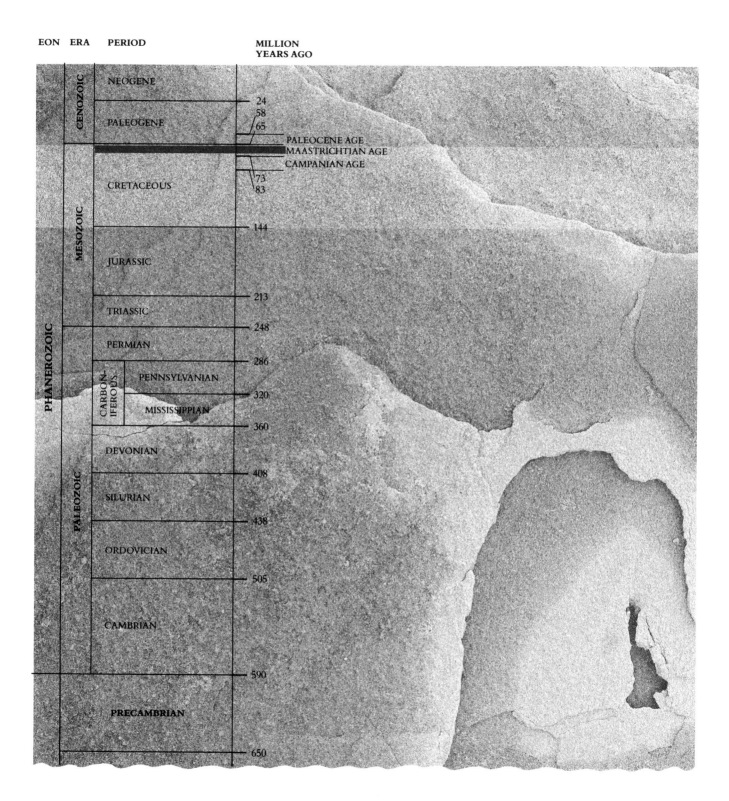

EON	ERA	PERIOD		MILLION YEARS AGO

PHANEROZOIC

CENOZOIC
— NEOGENE
— 24
— 58
PALEOGENE
— 65

PALEOCENE AGE
MAASTRICHTIAN AGE
CAMPANIAN AGE

MESOZOIC
CRETACEOUS
— 73
— 83
— 144

JURASSIC
— 213

TRIASSIC
— 248

PALEOZOIC
PERMIAN
— 286

CARBON-IFEROUS
PENNSYLVANIAN
— 320
MISSISSIPPIAN
— 360

DEVONIAN
— 408

SILURIAN
— 438

ORDOVICIAN
— 505

CAMBRIAN
— 590

PRECAMBRIAN
— 650

7 HOW THE MESOZOIC ERA CAME TO AN END

The mass extinction that terminated the Mesozoic Era has always attracted more interest than any other, originally because the ever-intriguing dinosaurs were among its victims, and more recently because evidence has been advanced that it may have resulted from a fatal collision between the earth and a meteor or comet. This event holds additional interest for us humans because had the dinosaurs not died out, mammals would never have come to dominate terrestrial environments and we would never have evolved. All of these factors have led us to overrate the terminal Cretaceous crisis. In fact, its effects in the ocean were far less devastating than those of the terminal Permian event, which eliminated more than twice as large a percentage of marine families.

Whether the impact on earth of a large extraterrestrial body caused the extinction of the dinosaurs and contemporary life is a question to be considered later in this chapter. Nonetheless, in order to provide a frame of reference in which to discuss patterns of extinction, it will be useful at the outset to provide a brief review of the basic evidence that has been invoked to support this idea of an extraterrestrial cause. This evidence is the presence in uppermost Cretaceous rocks in many parts of the world of an anomalously high concentration of the element iridium, a metal of the platinum group that is extremely rare in the earth's crust. A group of scientists at the University of California at Berkeley—including the physicist Luis Alvarez, his geologist son Walter Alvarez, and the chemists Frank Asaro and Helen Michel—made the discovery by means of neutron activation analysis. At some locations, the iridium anomaly is positioned within a thin layer of fine-grained sediment known as the boundary clay. Recognizing that iridium is relatively abundant in stony meteorites, the Berkeley group proposed that it was distributed over the surface of the earth as fallout,

The coin rests on the terminal Cretaceous boundary
clay at Gubbio, Italy. This clay layer, which was tilted
with the surrounding sedimentary rocks when the
Apennine Mountains were uplifted, harbors the
iridium anomaly.

following the explosive arrival of a meteorite that had a diameter in
the order of 10 kilometers (about 6.5 miles).

Evidence bearing on the cause of the Late Cretaceous crisis has been
surfacing at such a rapid rate that any report on the subject runs the
risk of being outdated almost before it appears in print. Nonetheless, a
number of patterns have come well enough into focus to provide at
least a partial picture of what happened.

Time divisions of the Cenozoic Era. Epochs are shown in the central column. This book employs the newer Paleogene–Neogene classification, rather than the traditional Tertiary–Quaternary classification.

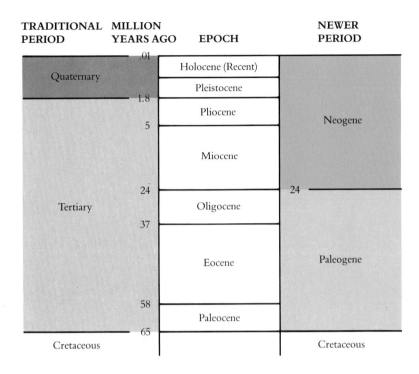

TRADITIONAL PERIOD	MILLION YEARS AGO	EPOCH	NEWER PERIOD
Quaternary	.01	Holocene (Recent)	
		Pleistocene	
	1.8	Pliocene	Neogene
	5		
		Miocene	
Tertiary	24	Oligocene	24
	37		
		Eocene	Paleogene
	58		
		Paleocene	
Cretaceous	65		Cretaceous

The upper boundary of the Cretaceous is commonly termed the Cretaceous–Tertiary boundary, with reference to the geologic period that followed. Division of the Cenozoic Era into the Tertiary and Quaternary periods has fallen into disfavor in recent years, however, and with good reason. The problem with this division is that the Tertiary, which encompasses the Paleocene, Eocene, Oligocene, Miocene, and Pliocene epochs, dwarfs the Quaternary, which includes only the Pleistocene and Recent, or Holocene, epochs. (The Pleistocene has traditionally been thought of as the recent Ice Age, but we now know that continental glaciers began to expand in mid-Pliocene time). The temporal disparity between the Tertiary and Quaternary is enormous, with the first interval spanning some 63 or 64 million years and the second, less than 2 million years. Far more reasonable is the scheme that divides the Cenozoic into the Paleogene and Neogene periods, with the division falling between the Oligocene and Miocene epochs, about 24 million years before the present. This newer scheme will be followed here, and the boundary between the Mesozoic and Cenozoic eras will be referred to as the Cretaceous–Paleocene boundary. Although this pairs a period with an epoch, which is of lower rank in the geological time scale, the Cenozoic record, resting on top

A section of a deep-sea core from the Pacific Ocean containing the Cretaceous–Neogene boundary (about half way up). Just above the boundary is the so-called boundary layer, which, because of the extinction event, is characterized by a reduced concentration of white calcareous nannofossils.

of older deposits, presents us with such widespread and well-preserved sediments that we often treat Cenozoic epochs as if they were periods.

The stratigraphic record representing Late Cretaceous time offers certain advantages for study when compared to the record for earlier intervals of mass extinction. In the first place, stratigraphic sections spanning the Cretaceous–Paleocene boundary often consist of soft sediment rather than hard rock. We can collect fossils more easily from the soft sediment, and the fossils are also normally in better condition than ones embedded in solid rock; microfossils are especially easy to collect. Even strata representing the Jurassic Period, the one preceding the Cretaceous, are old enough that virtually all that occur on continents have been lithified—that is, turned into rock.

The presence of vast expanses of Cretaceous sediment beneath the sea floor in the ocean basins, where it can be sampled from ships by coring procedures, also adds an important dimension to the study of Cretaceous fossils. Here, in the protection of the deep sea, sequences of fine-grained sediment offer a relatively complete record not only of deep-sea life with preservable hard parts, but also of similarly endowed phytoplankton and zooplankton. Here, too, we find the iridium anomaly in a thin boundary clay. Again, sediments of Jurassic age do not provide the same opportunity for fossil discovery, and they are also much less widespread. Deep-sea sediments of Paleozoic age, in fact, are absent altogether from the ocean basins, being preserved for study only where they have been uplifted by earth movements. The reason for their absence is that the crust of the earth beneath the oceans and the sediments that blanket it are constantly disappearing into the earth's mantle along deep-sea trenches. At the same time, new crust is forming along midocean ridges and moving laterally over the deep layer of the earth's mantle known as the asthenosphere toward the zones where it is consumed. The resulting "conveyor belt" motion renews the entire crust of a large ocean basin every 200 million years or so, leaving no sea floor sediment appreciably older than this.

Finally, Late Cretaceous sediments on the continents harbor fossils of flowering plants, sometimes referred to as thermometers of the past. As we shall see later in this chapter, both the leaf shapes and the taxonomic identities of these advanced plants reveal important information about ancient climates.

One of the most important questions about the Late Cretaceous mass extinction concerns its timing. The iridium-rich layer that has been taken to mark the very end of the Cretaceous is 65 or 66 million years old. Some important Late Cretaceous extinctions appear to have occurred at the very time when the iridium layer accumulated. On the

DECLINE AND EXTINCTION

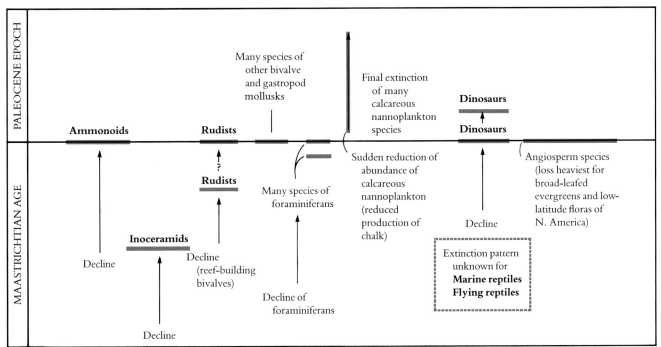

Patterns of extinction during late Maastrichtian time. Several groups declined or disappeared well before the end of the Maastrichtian, and many species of calcareous nannoplankton declined in abundance at the boundary but did not die out altogether until Paleocene time. It is uncertain whether some species of dinosaurs may have survived into the Paleocene.

other hand, some groups of animals began to dwindle several million years earlier, losing species until none remained at the end of the period; declines of this type took place during the Maastrichtian Age, the final epoch of the Cretaceous, which spanned about 8 million years, but some declines began even earlier, during the preceding Campanian Age, which lasted about 10 million years. These patterns reveal that the terminal Cretaceous crisis was a complex event, in which a long interval of heavy extinction was capped by a final pulse of especially heavy losses. There is evidence that climatic changes played a primary role in these events, as in earlier crises.

Paralleling the experience of the dinosaurs on the land, large vertebrates in the ocean failed to make the transition to the Cenozoic Era. Most important was the disappearance of the mosasaur and plesiosaur reptiles and of the largest marine turtles. The state of Kansas has yielded magnificent fossil specimens of these "sea monsters" from deposits of the great interior seaway that stretched northward from the Gulf Coast, but unfortunately their record is in general too spotty to reveal the temporal and geographic patterns of their demise.

Marine invertebrates and plankton, because of their greater abundance, provide a much clearer picture of patterns of extinction. Some of the marine groups that were victimized by the Late Cretaceous event underwent geologically instantaneous extinction. Many groups, however, declined toward their final extinction through intervals of Late Cretaceous time in excess of a million years. Among the latter were groups whose last survivors died out suddenly, after a decline, at the close of Cretaceous time.

Despite the utility of fossil plants and the special interest attracted by the dinosaurs' demise, we will begin our analysis of the terminal Cretaceous crisis with a review of what happened in the oceans. It is here that the fossil record is richest and most revealing.

GRADUAL IMPOVERISHMENT ON THE SEA FLOOR

Marine mollusks, which rose to great prominence during the Mesozoic Era, included several groups that dwindled over the course of several million years before finally disappearing at or slightly before the end of the Cretaceous Period. One such group is the inoceramid family of bivalves, whose membership included some species that reached a diameter of about 1 meter (about 3 feet). The inoceramids for the most part lived on the surface of the sediment, sieving food from the surrounding water in the manner of an oyster or scallop. Some were attached to the substratum by an array of threads. During Late Cretaceous time, the inoceramid family was represented by many species living at many depths in the ocean, ranging from shallow sea floors to the deep sea. The shells of inoceramids were composed of fibrous crystals that, when remaining in the sediment after death and shell decomposition, are diagnostic for recognition of the family, although they cannot be identified to the level of species. Annie Dhondt of the Belgian Royal Institute of Natural History has reviewed the Late Cretaceous fossil record of the inoceramids on a worldwide scale. Her analysis shows the family declining gradually during the final two ages of the Cretaceous, the Campanian and Maastrichtian. The number of species dwindled after mid-Campanian time, and of the four or so genera making their way into the Maastrichtian (the precise number is a matter of taxonomic judgment), none survived into the latter part of the interval. In fact, no normal inoceramid species is known from this final Cretaceous interval; there was only a very small number of species that perhaps do not even belong within the family, and only one of these is known to exist in latest Cretaceous strata.

Confirmation of this pattern of extinction for the inoceramids comes from a different kind of study altogether—the evaluation of a remarkably continuous sequence of deep-sea sediments that has been uplifted by mountain-building movements so that it can now be studied along the coast of Spain. Here Peter Ward of the University of Washington has found that fossil inoceramids decline in diversity upward toward the Cretaceous–Paleocene boundary, and disappear altogether at a level representing a time some 1.5 million years before the end of Cretaceous time.

Working with Philip Signor of the University of California at Davis, Ward has also made general observations about the periodic mass extinction of ammonoids. These were animals that experienced heavy extinction during the Late Devonian crisis, then barely survived the terminal Permian event, and went on to suffer repeatedly in the Mesozoic mass extinctions that preceded the one now under discussion. In other words, the ammonoids, throughout their history, were prone to mass extinction. Ward and Signor noted, however, that the ammonoid groups that survived the earlier Mesozoic crises were of a particular type. They consisted of forms that possessed an especially thick siphuncle (the siphuncle was an internal tube running the length of the coiled shell). The functional reason for this pattern of extinction remains a mystery. The exceptional thing about the terminal Cretaceous extinction was that it eliminated all the ammonoids—even the types that had survived the previous Mesozoic mass extinctions.

At Zumaya, along the coast of Spain, where Peter Ward has uncovered the gradual nature of inoceramid extinction, he and Jost Wiedmann of the University of Tubingen have found much the same pattern for the ammonoids. Here the final decline of the ammonoids can be seen to have begun approximately at the boundary between early and late Maastrichtian time, about 4 or 5 million years before the end of the Cretaceous. A plot of diversity shows that the ammonoids declined gradually from about 10 species in earliest late Maastrichtian time to their final disappearance. The last ammonoid has been found about 12 meters (about 40 feet) below the terminal Cretaceous boundary, in rocks that are estimated to have been deposited about 100,000 years before the end of Cretaceous time.

The rudist bivalves are another group of marine invertebrates that experienced attrition before the end of the Cretaceous Period. As described in the preceding chapter, these were the remarkable animals that evolved large, conical shells and won over the reef habitat from

Gradual decline in diversity of ammonoid species in
Maastrichtian rocks at Zumaya, Spain. The last ammonoid fossil found thus far was positioned several
meters below the Maastrichtian–Paloeocene boundary.

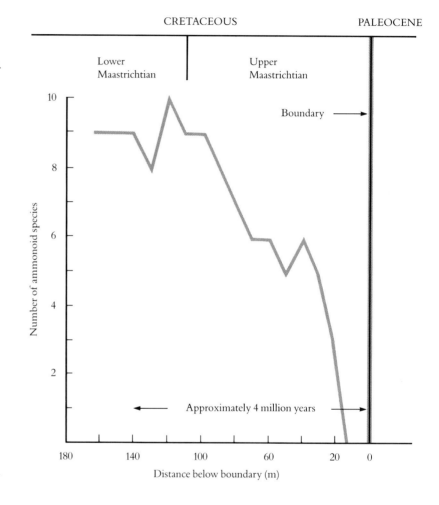

the corals. Early in the Cretaceous Period, when warm temperatures
extended to high latitudes, tropical rudist reefs flourished in shallow
waters from the Gulf of Mexico to the areas now positioned offshore
from New Jersey, where they are encountered today in submarine
drilling operations. According to the evaluation of Erle Kauffman of
the University of Colorado, the rudists were then decimated near the
beginning of late Maastrichtian time, as seen in areas of excellent reef

Four species of single-celled planktonic foraminiferans of Late Cretaceous age.

preservation, such as Jamaica and the Pyrenees. In regions such as Holland, where rudists survived more-or-less to the end of Cretaceous time, they existed at very low diversities and formed only small mounds rather than substantial reefs. This shrinkage of rudist reefs is reminiscent of the repeated collapse of the reef community during the Paleozoic Era—and, by analogy, we must suspect a role for climatic cooling in the rudists' decline.

PLANKTONIC FORAMINIFERANS

In contrast to the patterns of long-term decline for the ammonoids and other marine groups was the geologically sudden extinction of some components of the marine biota at the very end of the Cretaceous Period. Some of these were the last survivors of groups that had previously declined, so that the temporal pattern of extinction for these groups is a combination of gradual and sudden losses. The planktonic foraminiferans provide the best example of this complex kind of pattern. As oceanic floaters, planktonic species have always tended to occur over broad areas, so that the extinction of a large group of these organisms can be taken to signal the occurrence of a large-scale catastrophe.

Sequences of deep-sea sediments spanning the Cretaceous–Paleocene boundary and bearing abundant fossil remains of planktonic life that settled to the sea floor have been studied in several areas. Some of these boundary sequences have been sampled by coring the floor of the deep sea and others by collecting from land areas that have been uplifted by mountain building or exposed by lowering of sea level.

PLANKTON

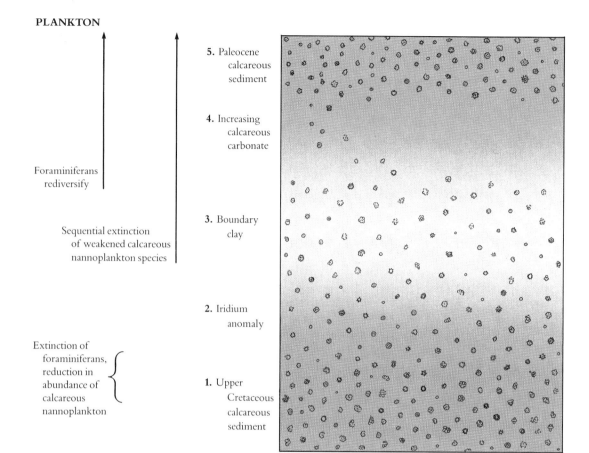

Foraminiferans
rediversify

Sequential extinction
of weakened calcareous
nannoplankton species

Extinction of
foraminiferans,
reduction in
abundance of
calcareous
nannoplankton

5. Paleocene
   calcareous
   sediment

4. Increasing
   calcareous
   carbonate

3. Boundary
   clay

2. Iridium
   anomaly

1. Upper
   Cretaceous
   calcareous
   sediment

Typical sequence in a deep-sea core spanning the Cretaceous–Paleocene boundary at low latitudes, where
calcareous nannoplankton are abundant.

The terrestrial geological sections, as they are called, include the previously described stratigraphic sequence at Zumaya on the northern
coast of Spain, and others at Caravaca, which is near the Mediterranean coast of Spain, several locations in Denmark, and El Kef, near
the coast of Tunisia. The quality of the fossil record of extinction
varies from locality to locality. At Zumaya, fossil foraminiferans are
poorly preserved, for example, and in cores from the deep sea the
layering is typically disturbed slightly by drilling. In addition, some
sections display an incomplete record, owing to discontinuous sedimentation and sometimes even removal of sediment by the scouring
action of bottom currents.

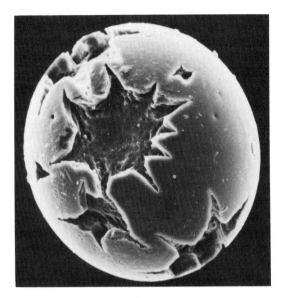

Microtektites, which are small, glassy, spheroidal particles that probably formed when an extraterrestrial object struck the earth with great enough force to melt earth materials.

Approximate ideas of rates of deposition of particular deep sea sequences come from two sources. First, they come from estimates of the geological durations of the fossil species that are found within the sequences. The planktonic species fossilized in deep-sea deposits are especially useful here because many such species, when they first come into being, spread rapidly across large oceanic areas and then, much later, die out quite suddenly. Second, estimates of rates of deposition come from knowledge of the time represented by packages of sediment that were deposited during particular intervals of normal or reversed polarity of the earth's magnetic field. Radioactive dating, often carried out far from an area of current interest, provides the actual date for the appearance or disappearance of a particular species or for a particular reversal of the earth's magnetic field.

Jan Smit of Amsterdam and A. J. T. Romein of Utrecht have observed that most deep-sea sequences exhibit a particular vertical sequence of sediment layering and fossil occurrences across the boundary. At the base is the normal Upper Cretaceous sequence of calcareous sediments and fossils; in fact it is the fossils—primarily planktonic foraminiferans and nannoplankton—that make the sediments calcareous. Above this is a layer that displays the primary iridium anomaly. The anomaly has been smeared vertically over at least 20 centimeters (about 8 inches) in every section by animal burrowing and other disruptive processes, but may originally have been confined to an interval of half a centimeter (about 0.2 inches) or so. The location of this primary iridium-rich layer is normally represented by the peak iridium concentration today. Occurring with the iridium anomaly and normally most abundant at the level of the iridium peak are minute round or dumbbell-shaped grains that have been interpreted as altered microtektites. Microtektites are glassy entities the size of a sand grain or smaller that have formed when silicate material of the earth's crust has been fragmented and melted by the impact of an extraterrestrial object and the resulting droplets have then cooled quickly. The rapid thermal quenching produces the glassy texture of tektites by preventing microscopically visible crystals from growing within them. In their lower content of water, tektites differ in composition from volcanically produced glass such as obsidian. The spherules at the Cretaceous–Paleocene boundary have been described as "microtektite-like" because they are not glassy in texture but consist of more coarsely crystalline materials. They have been interpreted to be the products of chemical alteration of microtektites, but the case that they are the products of an impact remains unproven. In addition, Gerta Keller of Princeton University and her student W. R. Chi have failed to discover these structures at the El Kef section in Tunisia,

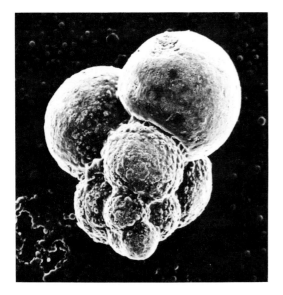

Guembelitria cretacea, a species of planktonic foraminiferan that survived from Cretaceous into Paleocene time.

where they instead have found only spherules of pyrite (fool's gold) that clearly grew within the sediment. In any event, this second layer has been referred to as the extinction layer because it has been taken to represent the time when one or more extraterrestrial objects struck the earth and altered the environment.

Third in the sequence is a unit termed the boundary clay. In the deep-sea sections, this is dominated by clay particles, and the abundance of calcium carbonate ranges from only about 20 to 40 percent. The Cretaceous sediments below contain the same kinds of clay particles, but they are less abundant than particles of calcium carbonate contributed by the death and decay of planktonic organisms. The boundary clay grades into the fourth unit, which is marked by an increased percentage of calcium carbonate because it represents a time when planktonic foraminiferans were rediversifying after the disaster. The fourth unit, in turn, grades into the fifth, which represents a time when new Paleocene foraminiferans were becoming fully established; except for the character of its fauna, this unit closely resembles the initial, pre-disaster unit of Late Cretaceous age.

The stratigraphic section at El Kef offers the most complete picture of the crisis for planktonic foraminiferans. This excellent record is the product of unusually rapid deposition, which apparently resulted from proximity to the margin of the Mediterranean Sea; this setting provided an abundance of detrital clay from the land and a plentiful supply of carbonate skeletons from a rich planktonic biota. At El Kef the boundary clay is unusually thick—about 1 meter (about 3 feet) from top to bottom—and several species of planktonic foraminiferans terminate abruptly at the sharp contact between this unit and the underlying sediment. It was once thought that the earliest Paleocene sediments at El Kef harbored only one fossil species, which was regarded as the sole Cretaceous survivor. Ironically, although this species persisted into Paleocene time, it has been named *Guembelitria cretacea,* as if it somehow symbolized the former interval. Having examined finer sievings than those normally studied by micropaleontologists, who by convention disregard material that passes through a 150-micrometer mesh, Gerta Keller and her student Steven D'Hondt have found that at least five other species accompanied *Guembelitria cretacea* on its passage into the Paleocene Epoch. Thus, the terminal Cretaceous crisis was less severe than was once believed.

As it turns out, the overall crisis was also less sudden. The details are as follows: Many species of planktonic foraminiferans disappear from the record—almost certainly as a result of their extinction—about 20 centimeters (about 8 inches) below the base of the boundary clay. *Guembelitria cretacea* is the most abundant species in the lower part of the boundary clay, although it is rare in the latest Cretaceous sediments below this interval. This species seems to have been especially well adapted to the environmental conditions of the crisis interval, during which the boundary clay was beginning to accumulate. The several other species that survived into this interval of time resembled *Guembelitria cretacea* in having been the smallest planktonic foraminiferans of latest Cretaceous time. In the boundary clay, perhaps because of environmental stress, they are even smaller than normal. New species of Paleocene planktonic foraminiferans evolved while the boundary clay was accumulating. The first of these appear about 20 centimeters (about 8 inches) above the base of the boundary clay. We have no way of estimating accurately the intervals of time represented by these episodes, but in all likelihood a few thousand years separated the extinction event recorded at the base of the boundary clay from the one recorded 20 centimeters lower in the El Kef section.

Taking a broader view of the Late Cretaceous record of planktonic foraminiferans, we can observe that this group began to decline millions of years before the end of the Maastrichtian Age, long before all of the extinctions described above. Keller and D'Hondt have, in fact, shown that the extinction followed a stepwise pattern during Maastrichtian time. In effect, the terminal event at the base of the boundary clay was the last of these steps.

In contrast, species of foraminiferans that occupied the deep-sea floor were little affected by the terminal Cretaceous crisis. Apparently their location deep below the ocean surface in some way protected them against the agent or agents of extinction. The dwindling of the planktonic species before the sudden pulses of extinction at the very end of Cretaceous time suggests that during a relatively long interval the planktonic fauna was undergoing heavy extinction at the hands of some agent that was quite distinct from the one that wrought the terminal Cretaceous crisis. In other words, the final crisis may have constituted a final blow to an already weakened and depleted ecosystem.

THE NANNOPLANKTON

Also preserved in deep-sea sediments is the fossil record of the Cretaceous–Paleocene transition of the calcareous nannoplankton. A general decline in the abundance of this group during this interval is illustrated by the global reduction in the rate of deposition of chalk, a sediment composed primarily of the skeletal plates of nannoplankton. It is not clear, however, that the nannoplankton suffered heavy extinction at this time. One detailed study of the pattern has been conducted by Stephen Percival in his graduate studies at Princeton University, in conjunction with his advisor Alfred Fischer. These workers found that in the Zumaya section in Spain, several species that are abundant in the latest Cretaceous sediments become rarer in the boundary clay (which here has been lithified to shale). The pattern of occurrence of these affected species is quite different from that for foraminiferans, however. The nannoplankton species do not disappear right at the base of the boundary clay. Rather, they persist, in reduced abundance, upward through several meters of Paleocene sediment; different species make their last appearances at different levels. The sediments that record this total interval of decline—intervals 4 and 5 in the diagram on page 142—represent about a million years of deposition. There has been much disagreement as to whether this fossil record, which is crudely mimicked in other stratigraphic sections, can be taken at face value. Did the calcareous nannoplankton decline over a span of time that extended well into the Paleocene Epoch, or did they suffer heavy extinction right at the end of the Cretaceous and then have their skeletal remains reworked by bottom currents and perhaps by animals that burrowed through deep-sea sediments? Possibly these activities artificially smeared the record of extinction over a great thickness of sediment.

A test of the two hypotheses has been devised by Katharina Perch-Nielsen and Judith McKenzie of the Swiss Federal Institute of Technology and Qiziang He of the People's Republic of China. This test involves the recognition that, in all sections where it has been measured, the isotopic ratio between carbon 13 and carbon 12 in all fossil groups decreases sharply from below the terminal Cretaceous boundary to above it. This change is generally believed to reflect a reduction of photosynthesis that elevated the level of the lighter isotope in the upper ocean. This happened because during photosynthesis phytoplankton preferentially remove the lighter isotope from surface waters. When phytoplankton flourish for a long interval, the settlement of their skeletons to the deep sea after death depletes the surface waters of carbon 12. Nannoplankton had thrived in latest Cretaceous time, but then declined in productivity with the onset of the Paleocene. Had the nannoplankton fossils found above the boundary been reworked from below the boundary by currents or burrowing animals, they would exhibit the characteristic carbon isotope ratio for the Late Cretaceous. The fact that they instead display the characteristic ratio for the early Paleocene indicates that they actually lived at this time.

Braarudisphaera bigelowi, a species of nannoplankton that not only survived the terminal Cretaceous crisis but underwent a pronounced bloom in the aftermath. This long-lived species survives today.

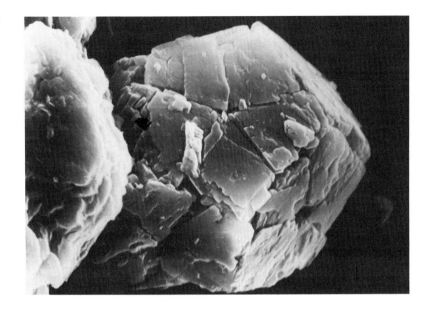

Also of great interest is the fact that a large percentage of the earliest Paleocene nannoplankton fossils belong to a small number of species that survived from the Cretaceous but did not dwindle and then disappear. Instead, after the mass extinction they suddenly flourished—or, in the jargon of phytoplankton ecology, they bloomed. It appears that different species bloomed in different areas, perhaps by chance or perhaps because each was favored by different environmental conditions. This pattern was first recognized by Alfred Fischer and his student Michael Arthur, who also noted that one of the species that bloomed after the Cretaceous crisis was *Braarudosphaera bigelowi.* This hardy species, which survives even to the present day, seems now not generally to flourish in the open sea so much as in bays and lagoons, from which brackish conditions exclude most other species. As Fischer and Arthur have pointed out, this and the other "disaster forms" seem to be ecological opportunists—species that are tolerant of adverse conditions and that persistently wait in the wings to take over the depopulated oceans at times of crisis. Within a million years after the terminal Cretaceous crisis, a number of other species that were weakened by the event had died out, but the flourishing disaster forms had been joined by newly evolved species, and in time the disaster forms returned to their normal, less conspicuous roles.

THE PLANKTON AND CLIMATE

A number of changes in planktonic life at the end of the Cretaceous reveal the geographic pattern observed for so many other groups of organisms: a preferential extinction of tropical species. While warm-adapted calcareous nannoplankton suffered profoundly, dinoflagellates, which were for the most part denizens of higher latitudes, were only weakly affected. A more detailed picture of how climatic change may have altered planktonic life before, during, and after the terminal event comes from the El Kef section and from a deep-sea site in the central Pacific, not far from the equator. The latter site is labeled Deep Sea Drilling Project Hole 577, and the investigators are Jennifer Gerstal and Robert Thunell of the University of South Carolina and James Zachos and Michael Arthur of the University of Rhode Island. Like Gerta Keller in her evaluation of the El Kef section, these investigators have uncovered evidence that major environmental changes began before the time of the terminal crisis. First, they have taken note of the previously recognized fact that planktonic foraminiferan species of the simplest form—the so-called globigerine shape—were the ones that survived the Cretaceous crisis and later crises as well. Richard Cifelli of the Smithsonian Institution pointed this out in 1969, along with the other side of the story: Species with ornate skeletons were annihilated in the mass extinctions. An important aspect of this pattern is the fact that species of the globigerine shape tend to be adapted to cool waters or to a wide range of temperature conditions. *Guembelitria cretacea,* for example, was cosmopolitan in distribution, which attests to a broad thermal tolerance. Species with ornate skeletons are for the most part restricted to tropical water masses in modern oceans today, and all forms of this type were annihilated in the Cretaceous extinctions. Thus, the pattern of extinction suggests that climatic cooling may have played a dominant role.

Site 577 also reveals interesting temporal patterns. First, the quality of preservation of microfossils improves suddenly at a level estimated to represent a time about 50,000 years before the end of the Cretaceous. This appears to indicate a major change in the physical–chemical conditions of the deep sea. The record then shows that about 20,000 years later there was a decline in the relative abundance of the family Globotruncanidae, which were almost exclusively tropical in distribution; increasing simultaneously were the Heterohelicidae, which are recognized to have enjoyed a more temperate distribution. Still later, about 15,000 years before the boundary event, the genus *Hedbergella,* which had previously been restricted to cool water masses at high latitudes, migrated into the low-latitude region of site 577. All of these changes occurred too early to be attributed to the impact of an extraterrestrial object at the very close of Cretaceous time. Also to be accounted for is the reduced fraction of carbon 13 in surface waters that was noted earlier. Its initial reduction at the boundary can be attributed to reduced productivity of plankton, but carbon 13—and presumably productivity—remained at a depressed level for several hundred thousand years. It is difficult to explain this in terms of the impact of an extraterrestrial object. It could, however, be attributed to a sustained interval of reduced temperature. The pattern observed at site 577 suggests that a pulse of cooling accentuated a climatic trend that was already underway. If this scenario is correct, an extraterrestrial event or group of events could have been the final blow in a long interval of devastation. How the pulse of extinction a few thousand years before the final event, recently noted by Gerta Keller and W. R. Chi, may fit into this picture remains to be explained.

SUDDEN EXTINCTIONS ON THE SEA FLOOR

In contrast to the gradual dwindling of some groups that inhabited Late Cretaceous sea floors was the sudden demise of many species at the very end of the period. A catastrophic pattern of extinction such as this can only be documented in a local area where the rock record is nearly complete—where there is no major gap at the Cretaceous–Paleocene boundary. Unfortunately, areas that offer such excellent records for the crucial interval of time are quite rare.

The precipitous decline of some of the bottom-dwelling bivalves and brachiopods at the very end of the Cretaceous Period may have been linked to the sudden decimation of the phytoplankton, and the fate of both of these groups has been claimed to support the idea that the impact of an extraterrestrial body was responsible. Denmark is the region that first attracted attention here to the possibility of sudden extinction. Although most Maastrichtian chalk deposits accumulated in relatively deep water, at one famous Danish locality called Stevns Klint, they were deposited in shallow seas near the margin of the basin of deposition, which was an inland sea that spread eastward from the Atlantic. Stevns Klint is a beautifully exposed sea cliff, about 40 kilometers (about 25 miles) south of Copenhagen. Here the white chalk bears a rich fauna of bryozoans, which over the course of many generations built low mounds on the sea floor. On top of the chalk is a darker group of beds known collectively as the Fish Clay because they contain the fossilized teeth and scales of fish. Detailed study by Alan

Stevns Klint, Denmark, a cliff of Cretaceous chalk.
The Fish Clay, which constitutes the boundary clay in
this area, is positioned about halfway up the cliff.
Below are scanning electron micrographs of nannofossil species that characterize Late Cretaceous sediments
below the boundary. Above are similar pictures of
species found in Paleocene sediments, above the
boundary.

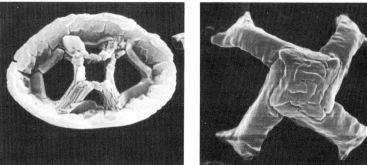

Vertical bars show stratigraphic ranges of species of brachiopods found in chalk deposits of Denmark. Many species disappear right at the Cretaceous–Paleocene boundary, perhaps because the reduction of chalk deposition left them living in clay, which clogged their feeding apparatuses. Only a few of the species reappeared early in Paleocene time, when new species also evolved.

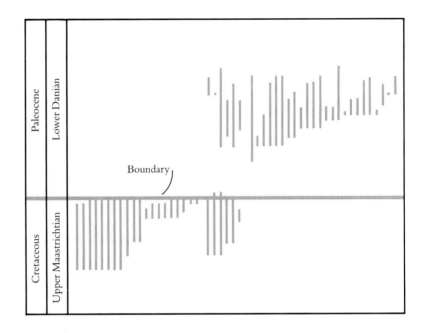

Ekdale of the University of Utah and his Danish coworker Richard Bromley reveal that the Fish Clay has been condensed by the dissolution of calcium carbonate. The fossil content of the Fish Clay, though severely diminished by the condensation, reveals that this unit is of Paleocene age. In addition, the Fish Clay contains a large iridium anomaly. These features pose problems for interpretation. Perhaps the iridium is of latest Cretaceous age and has been secondarily united with Paleocene fossils by the condensation of the section and mobility of the iridium. In any event, the evidence that the latest Maastrichtian sediments have disappeared in the condensation of the lower part of the fish clay means that the apparently abrupt disappearance of a number of invertebrate species below the fish clay cannot be taken necessarily to indicate sudden disappearance in geological time.

Small brachiopods were one group of animals that probably did die out rather suddenly in the region of Denmark with the cessation of chalk deposition, even though chalk was deposited again later in Paleocene time. The history of the brachiopods has been studied in great detail by the Danish workers Finn Surlyk and Marianne Johansen. Although brachiopods were no longer diverse on a global scale by Cretaceous time, the sea floor upon which chalk accumulated was colonized by many brachiopod species that were only a few millimeters (1 millimeter = 0.039 inch) in adult length. Most of these were ones that attached to minute hard substrates by means of a pedicle—

the fleshy stalk that is present in most brachiopods. The fossil record of these animals is remarkably good; their shells were resistant to destruction in the chalk sediment and can be extracted by procedures that involve repeatedly soaking the chalk in salt solution and freezing it.

To study the fates of brachiopod species, Surlyk and Johansen focused their efforts on the Nye Klov section, in northwestern Denmark. The chalk accumulated in a deeper depositional setting at this locality than at Stevns Klint, and here there is not the same condensed sequence seen in the Fish Clay at Stevns Klint. Rather, the boundary is marked by a transition from pure chalk to marl, which is a soft mixture of clay and chalk, and this marl is riddled with a profusion of small, flattened burrows. At about this level, the vertical ranges of about 20 of 26 known late Maastrichtian brachiopod species come to an end. The six other species disappear from the record here as well, but only temporarily. One by one, they reappear a few meters higher in the section, within an interval in which the marl gives way to chalk. The initial disappearance of the chalk apparently reflects reduced productivity of calcareous nannoplankton during the terminal Cretaceous crisis, and its return reflects a partial recovery. The brachiopods were apparently unable to cope with the marl substratum, perhaps because its clay clogged their feeding structures, and they disappeared from the area during the cessation of chalk deposition. By the time they were able once again to colonize the sea floor, only six of the original species survived. It may be that all the rest died out precisely when chalk deposition ceased—right at the end of the Cretaceous—but the possibility remains that some of these species survived for a time, perhaps in the same unknown location that served as a refuge for the six species that returned.

Exhibiting the sudden extinction of a greater variety of animals are sections along the Brazos River in Texas, where relatively continuous deposition and good preservation have permitted Thor Hansen of Western Washington University and students at the University of Texas to uncover important patterns of biotic change for marine invertebrates. One of their principal conclusions is that animals that relied on planktonic organisms for food died out suddenly when the planktonic community collapsed at the very end of Cretaceous time. The Brazos River sections include outcrops along the banks and bed of the river. The sediments that they comprise accumulated at a depth of several tens of meters on the continental shelf at a time when sea level stood higher than its position today, and shallow seas in the area now occupied by the Gulf of Mexico spread over part of Texas. At the base of the Upper Cretaceous section here are clays that accumulated under

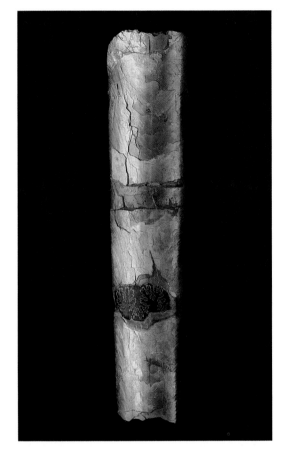

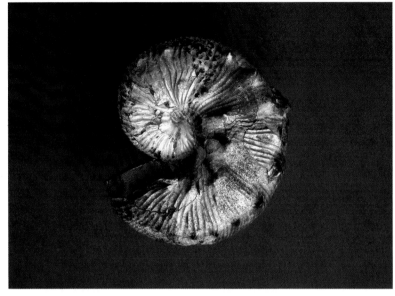

Two genera of ammonoids that survived to, or very close to, the end of Cretaceous time. Part of the outer shell of the straight-shelled form *(Baculites)* has been removed to reveal the convoluted pattern of the internal partitions. The coiled form is *Scaphites.*

relatively quiet conditions. These contain a rich fauna of fossil mollusks, including cockles, oysters, and arc shells that are not greatly different from modern bivalves of these groups, and also snails that generally resemble living forms. Only two genera of ammonoids are present, *Baculites,* a straight-shelled form, and *Scaphites,* which had a loosely coiled shell. Occurring with these mollusks is a great variety of planktonic foraminiferans and calcareous nannoplankton.

Within a narrow stratigraphic interval of about 3 centimeters (about 1 inch) right at the Cretaceous–Paleocene boundary, this fauna becomes depauperate, both in abundance and in diversity of species. The precise thickness of the interval is unimportant because many of the molluscan fossils are themselves 1 or 2 centimeters (about 0.4 to 0.8 inch) in vertical dimension when resting in the sediment. In this same narrow interval, the level of iridium in the sediment rises markedly, and there is a profusion of calcareous nannoplankton belonging to the genera that represent the disaster flora—genera such as *Braarudosphaera* and *Thoracosphaera* that evidently bloomed here, just as they did elsewhere in the oceans when the terminal Cretaceous crisis struck. While a number of the gastropod and bivalve mollusk species survived the crisis, no ammonoid made the transition to the Paleocene Epoch. The last fragments of *Baculites,* perhaps reworked from sediments a few centimeters lower in the section by waves or burrowing animals, are found 2 or 3 centimeters above the 3-centimeter interval that appears to mark the mass extinction. These were certainly among the very last ammonoids on earth.

For an interval of about 10 centimeters (about 4 inches) above the narrow zone marking the crisis, there is an impoverished fauna. The dominant forms are small bivalve species that were deposit feeders—animals that ingested sediment and extracted organic matter from it. Hansen and his coworkers have noted that in the aftermath of the mass extinction there was a dearth of suspension feeders—animals that sieve phytoplankton and organic debris from the water. Their hypothesis is that for at least a brief time after the crisis, the seas were depleted of phytoplankton because of the impact of the event on the nannoplankton and perhaps other groups of floating algae as well. The same hypothesis has been advanced by Michael Arthur and James Zachos of the University of Rhode Island working in conjunction with Douglas Jones of the Florida State Museum, based in part on the evidence of carbon isotopes that plankton productivity dropped precipitously during the Cretaceous–Tertiary transition.

Despite the drop in productivity, it is notable that in Texas, as in Denmark and Spain, few nannoplankton species have fossil records that actually terminate right at the Cretaceous–Paleocene boundary. Many become sparse at this level but nonetheless continue upward for a few meters. Ming-Jung Jiang and Stefan Gartner of Texas A&M University, who have documented this pattern, propose that the fossils have been reworked upward after the species that they represent became extinct. Running counter to this idea is the previously cited evidence, found in a number of regions, that the individuals found in Paleocene sediments must actually have lived in Paleocene seas because they display a low concentration of carbon 13, which seems to reflect the isotopic composition of shallow waters of Paleocene seas.

Also complicating the picture of sudden extinction in Texas is the fact that there are relatively few ammonoid species in the stratigraphic interval below the crisis level. In fact, for the entire world fewer than 20 genera of late Maastrichtian age are known, and many of these include only one species. About twice as many genera are known from early Maastrichtian strata, and still higher diversities are recorded for earlier Cretaceous intervals. In other words, the demise of the ammonoids seems to have occurred through a general decline over a period of several million years, followed by the final extinction of a small number of persisting groups at the very end of Cretaceous time. Thus, the pattern of extinction for the ammonoids typified that for marine life in general. Major losses in the course of Maastrichtian time

Albertosaurus (left), a huge carnivorous dinosaur of Late Cretaceous time, pursuing a juvenile duckbilled form. *Albertosaurus* was one of the last of the dinosaurs. *Monoclonius* (right), a genus of Late Cretaceous dinosaurs. This horned animal was an herbivore.

depleted the ecosystem, and then a sudden pulse of extinction at the very end brought the mass extinction to its climax.

TERRESTRIAL CHANGES: THE PLANTS' TESTIMONY

The information about dinosaurs provided in the previous chapter should dispel the time-honored but misguided notion that the dinosaurs died out because they became in some way outmoded. These fascinating creatures proved their mettle by clinging to their dominant position in the terrestrial ecosystem in the face of competition from mammals and mammal-like reptiles. Mass extinction represents failure to adjust to drastic environmental change, not failure to flourish under normal circumstances. Recognizing that dinosaurs thrived for more than a hundred million years and only failed—along with many other forms of life—during a much briefer biotic catastrophe, we must agree with their most ardent champion, Robert Bakker, that they were ecologically adept, even by the standards of modern mammals. To address the question of what reversed the dinosaurs' fortunes, it is appropriate to consider first the fate of terrestrial plants, not only because they formed the base of the dinosaurs' food web but because their history reveals important evidence as to the nature of environmental change during the Cretaceous–Paleocene transition.

As has been their tendency throughout Phanerozoic time, higher plants on the land experienced only modest losses during the Late Cretaceous crisis. It appears that the heaviest land plant extinctions were in the region known as the *Aquilapollenites* botanical province. Named for a prominent genus of flowering plants, this province stretched from northern Asia through Siberia to the western United States. In North America the *Aquilapollenites* province essentially co-incided with the elongate land area lying to the west of the great narrow seaway that extended from the Gulf of Mexico to the Arctic Ocean bordering Alaska. Forming the spine of this long body of land was an active mountain chain that included the peaks that were ancestral to the modern Rockies. This region is especially important for the study of Cretaceous dinosaurs, having yielded the largest faunas known. In fact, the taxonomic diversity of the dinosaurs was greater here in Late Cretaceous time, before their final decline, than in any region at any earlier time. They lived in marshy areas fringing the great interior seaway and farther west in lowland areas bordering the mountain chain. Late Cretaceous dinosaur fossils representing these habitats are recovered in moderate numbers from New Mexico, but are most plentiful in Wyoming, Montana, and Alberta.

The floras of this so-called western interior region underwent a sudden change right at the Cretaceous–Paleocene boundary—a change that has been taken to reflect climatic cooling. What happened was that the latest Cretaceous flora, which had been dominated by seed-bearing plants (angiosperms—flowering plants—and conifers) suddenly gave way to one in which ferns prevailed. This pattern has been especially well studied in the Raton Basin of northern New Mexico, where the iridium anomaly is situated in a boundary clay that ranges in thickness from about 1 to 3 centimeters (about 0.4 to 1 inch) and is overlain by a thin bed of coal. These deposits as well as muddy and sandy sediments below them were laid down in a freshwater swamp. At the top of the boundary clay four types of pollen abruptly disappear, and this termination, which constituted total extinction (the disappearance was permanent), has long been taken to mark the end of the Cretaceous. The extinction was accompanied by a major change in floral abundances. Below the top of the boundary clay, horizons yielding plant microfossils contain only 15 to 30 percent as many fern spores as pollen grains of seed-bearing plants. Above the boundary clay, about 99 percent of the microfossils are fern spores. Then, within 10 to 15 centimeters (about 4 to 6 inches) above the boundary, pollen returns to its original, much higher percentage. What this indicates is a brief interlude in which higher plants declined greatly in abundance, while ferns dominated the landscape, and then higher plants recovered. The same brief ecological explosion of ferns

Graph showing the sudden, temporary increase in the concentration of fern spores relative to the concentration of the pollen of seed plants at the position of the iridium anomaly in northern New Mexico.

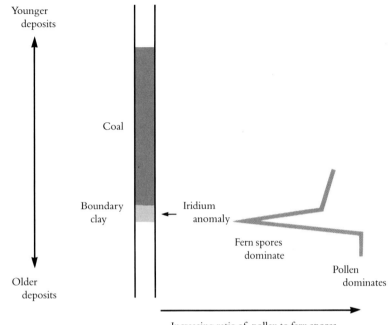

has been documented in the sedimentary record farther north in the western United States and Canada. It is reminiscent of the opportunistic spread of ferns over the barren surface of a new volcano in the modern world. Ferns are good invaders, but in time give way to higher plants that are better competitors for space, light, and nutrients. It has, of course, seemed appropriate to associate the abrupt floral change with whatever catastrophe was responsible also for the iridium anomaly.

Jack Wolfe and Garland Upchurch of the U.S. Geological Survey have documented in detail the recovery of the flora after the "fern event" in the Raton Basin. Above the high concentration of fern spores in the rock record is an interval of about 10 meters (about 33 feet) in which fossils of higher plants, though present, are of restricted variety; they represent the kinds of plants that rapidly colonize weakly vegetated areas—river banks and terrains recently laid bare by forest fires. How long this flora prevailed cannot be estimated accurately,

Graph showing decrease in the percentage of flowering plant leaves with entire, or smooth, margins during the transition from Cretaceous to Paleocene time in Wyoming.

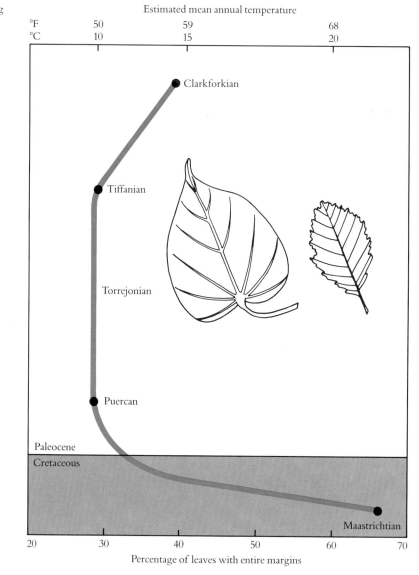

Estimated mean annual temperature

°F   50   59   68
°C   10   15   20

Clarkforkian

Tiffanian

Torrejonian

Puercan

Paleocene
Cretaceous

Maastrichtian

20   30   40   50   60   70

Percentage of leaves with entire margins

but it was only a brief geological interval. Next came a richer flora, and then a still richer one that constituted a rain forest.

Wolfe and Upchurch have also determined that the abrupt extinction that preceded the fern event was much more severe in the south than in the north. It removed some three-quarters of the species in northern New Mexico, about half in Wyoming, and perhaps a quarter in central Alberta. This latitudinal extinction gradient may manifest a climatic cause for the crisis, because the narrowly adapted tropical Late Cretaceous flora of New Mexico would have been more vulnerable to cooling than the temperate fauna farther north. For many years, the fossil record of leaves and pollen in Wyoming and neighboring areas has, in fact, been interpreted as revealing a cooling of climates here from subtropical in Maastrichtian time to temperate in Paleocene time. Recently, Leo Hickey of Yale University has made more quantitative estimates of the transition by means of leaf margin analysis. This technique was perfected by Jack Wolfe, who showed that for modern floras of the Asian continent, which spans a broad range of latitudes, the percentage of flowering plant species whose leaves have entire margins increases linearly with mean annual temperature. An entire margin is simply a smooth one, as opposed to the type of jagged or sawtoothed margin that characterizes the leaf of an oak, maple, or elm. Hickey has estimated that near the Wyoming-Montana border, the percentage of species with entire margins decreased from about 65 to 40 percent during the Cretaceous–Paleocene transition, which should reflect a drop in mean annual temperature from approximately 20°C to not much above 10°. Needless to say, this would have represented a major climatic deterioration. Moreover, the new flora, which included many deciduous trees resembling those of modern temperate forests, persisted through several million years of Paleocene time.

Despite the presence of so much general evidence, the details of terminal Cretaceous cooling in western North America remain controversial. Hickey has taken the leaf margin data for Wyoming at face value. His interpretation is that the persistence well into Paleocene time of floras containing relatively few species with entire margins implies that temperatures remained low for a few million years. Wolfe and Upchurch, in contrast, have suggested that temperatures quickly returned to their Maastrichtian levels but that floras failed to recover quickly. Their proposal is based in part on the presence in Paleocene sediments of fossils representing warm-adapted reptiles such as alligators and turtles. Howard Hutchison of the University of California at Berkeley has noted, however, that large reptiles are far less tolerant of cold winters than are small ones, and that the one large Cretaceous turtle species of the Wyoming area died out in the crisis. Wolfe and Upchurch have advanced the rather unorthodox proposal that, even though the climate ameliorated after a brief pulse of cooling, the floras of Wyoming for several million years failed to rebound by the evolution of new evergreen species and by the immigration of such plants from other areas.

Perhaps a compromise is in order. It seems reasonable to propose that climates in Wyoming remained cool well into Paleocene time, as the Paleocene floras testify. On the other hand, climates may never have cooled quite as much as the leaf margin analyses have suggested, remaining warm enough for many reptiles to survive into and through Paleocene time.

THE FALL OF THE DINOSAURS

It is interesting to note that the history of land plants in western North America offers a picture of biotic change analogous to that in the oceans—a long-term transformation of the ecosystem that was interrupted by a pulse of more sudden change. This same pattern is evident for the last of the dinosaurs, whose fate is also best studied in the North American region to the west of the great interior seaway where, as noted previously, the dinosaur fossil record is of unusually high quality.

Sites in Montana have provided new data that may be of enormous importance to our understanding of the final dinosaur extinction. These data and others acquired over the course of many years by field work in Montana and southern Alberta have been interpreted by a team consisting of Robert Sloan of the University of Minnesota, Keith Rigby of the University of Notre Dame, Leigh Van Valen of the University of Chicago, and Diane Gabriel of the Milwaukee Public Museum. These workers have documented a decline of dinosaur diversity and abundance that took place over the course of some 6 million years. A maximum diversity of 30 genera is recorded for a fauna that existed between 76 and 73 million years ago, just before the start of Maastrichtian time; this, in fact, appears to be the most diverse dinosaur fauna of all time. Most dinosaur genera consist of but a single species, so this and other generic numbers that follow approximate numbers of species. Two faunas dated at about 70 and 69 million years in age include 23 and 22 genera, respectively. Finally, the uppermost 16 meters (about 53 feet) of the Hell Creek Formation in Montana, representing latest Cretaceous time, have yielded only 13 genera.

It would be a remarkable accident if the progressive decline of dinosaurs near the Montana-Wyoming boundary were an artifact of preservation. Sloan and his coworkers make a strong case that the decline is real. They and others before them have employed a wide variety of collecting techniques, retrieving isolated bones as well as articulated specimens—ones in which the bones are still joined together—and also sieving isolated teeth from large volumes of sediment. Furthermore, there is much more outcrop available for prospecting in the upper 30 meters (about 100 feet) of the stratigraphic section than at lower levels. Thus, the bias of preservation is against the observed pattern of progressive impoverishment upward in the rock record.

Quantitative collecting has revealed that the abundance of fossils also declines gradually upward in the section, suggesting that not only number of species but also number of individuals was on the wane. This powerful case for long-term decline reduces the significance of the argument between two Berkeley scientists as to whether dinosaurs died out right at the Cretaceous–Paleocene boundary. Arguing for a slightly earlier disappearance has been William Clemens, a paleontologist, and favoring sudden extirpation at the boundary has been Luis Alvarez, the physicist coauthor of the extraterrestrial impact scenario. Alvarez's case has been based on an argument that the failure to discover dinosaur bones right at the boundary does not mean that dinosaurs were extinct in latest Cretaceous time. His point is that dinosaur bones are uncommon and scattered in their occurrence throughout the Mesozoic record. Presence or absence is not all that matters, however. The evident decline of the dinosaurs in both abundance and diversity renders less important any event right at the boundary.

Van Valen and Sloan have asserted that while the dinosaurs were declining, mammals were diversifying. This conclusion is based on evidence that several sites assigned to the Hell Creek Formation are Late Cretaceous rather than Paleocene in age. These sites reveal that mammals, probably from Asia, invaded the dwindling community of dinosaurs and then diversified during latest Cretaceous time, even before the last of the dinosaurs had died out. The idea is that the entire ecosystem was undergoing a transformation well before the end of the Cretaceous because the flora was declining in diversity along with the dinosaurs while mammals were beginning to expand.

The progressive decline from 30 dinosaur genera to 13 during the final 10 million years of Cretaceous time in Montana and southern Alberta indicates that most dinosaur losses preceded the terminal Cretaceous event. Sloan and his fellow workers suggest an even smaller role than this implies for the terminal event, arguing that nine of the 13 genera actually lived through it into the Paleocene Epoch. Their case, which would be of momentous importance if true, is based on the occurrence of dinosaur fossils in deposits of unquestioned Paleocene age. These fossils, mostly teeth, are from the sediments of a stream channel at the Ferguson Ranch locality in Montana. A Paleocene age is established for these sediments by the fact that, along with the dinosaur fossils, they harbor Paleocene pollen and mammal fossils. In addition, the channel, which migrated laterally when it was active, in places eroded away a unit known as the lower Z coal, where the terminal Cretaceous iridium anomaly is found in this area. This, too, shows the channel to be post-Cretaceous in age. The question is whether the dinosaur fossils were originally preserved in Cretaceous sediments through which the channel cut, and then, as the stream

Reconstruction of a Late Cretaceous mammal. After the dinosaurs were gone, small, inconspicuous creatures of this type soon gave rise to a wide variety of mammal groups, some of large body size.

eroded its bed, were washed out and redeposited in Paleocene sediment. Sloan and his fellow workers argue against this possibility, primarily on the basis of two lines of evidence. First, the teeth are in excellent condition, bearing sharp edges; they have not suffered the kind of wear that one normally associates with the abrasion against sand and gravel that comes with travel along a stream bed. Second, dinosaur remains are less common than mammalian fossils in the Cretaceous sediments through which the channel cut, yet no Cretaceous mammal fossils whatever have been found with dinosaur remains in the Paleocene channel deposits.

Certainly the arguments for a Paleocene dinosaur fauna are suggestive. In the vicinity of Montana it is possible that at least nine species of dinosaurs survived into the Age of Mammals. If so, the terminal Cretaceous event that left the telltale iridium trace could account for the disappearance of no more than four species. Still, skepticism will remain as long as the only dinosaur remains in unquestioned Paleocene deposits come from a channel deposit that cuts through Cretaceous units. The discovery of dinosaur remains in other kinds of sedimentary environments of earliest Paleocene age would solidify the case. Possible finds of this type have been reported from many areas, including New Mexico, South America, India, and China, but they remain to be substantiated.

In any event, Sloan and his coworkers attribute the dwindling of the dinosaurs during the final 10 million years of Cretaceous time to climatic changes—not only the cooling trend indicated by floral transformations, but also a drying of climates that resulted from the lowering of sea level during the final few million years of Cretaceous time. Here, unfortunately, the paleobotanical evidence is weak because there are few Early Maastrichtian floras to be compared to Late Maastrichtian floras. It does appear, however, that vegetation from Wyoming northward became substantially more deciduous during Maastrichtian time. It may be that climatic changes did not cause the demise of dinosaur species directly, but rather indirectly, through its effects on plants. While land plants did not suffer extremely heavy extinction during Late Cretaceous time, at least in some regions their populations—the fodder of herbivorous dinosaurs—underwent significant changes. Van Valen and Sloan have even raised the possibility that the invading and diversifying mammals may have defeated dinosaurs in competition for food. Such an idea is difficult to disentangle from the likelihood that the dinosaurs' problem was that they were inherently poorly adapted to new forms of vegetation. Herbivorous mammals, being smaller, may have sustained themselves on more diminutive plant offerings, including seeds and nuts.

A CATASTROPHIC END OF AN ERA?

Whether the impact on earth of an extraterrestrial object caused mass extinction in latest Cretaceous time is really a double question. The first part of the question is, did an impact occur? The second is, if an impact did occur, how much extinction did it cause? In a recent survey of scientists, Antoni Hoffman of Columbia University and Matthew Nitecki of the Field Museum of Natural History found that a majority of American paleontologists believed that an impact occurred at the end of the Cretaceous, but the large majority of these opposed the idea that it caused the mass extinction. (Some other groups of geoscientists voted somewhat differently.) One problem with the poll is that it failed to offer respondents the option of believing in an impact but attributing to it only a modest percentage of the Late Cretaceous extinctions.

First, let us address the question of the reality of an extraterrestrial event or group of events. Here we can note that an iridium anomaly of latest Cretaceous age has been found in many areas of the world and in both terrestrial and marine strata. Peak concentrations range from a few parts per billion to more than 40, in contrast to background concentrations that are about 10,000 times smaller. The most serious challenge to the idea that the higher levels require an extraterrestrial source has come from the discovery that some volcanoes emit iridium in relatively high concentrations as well. A recent eruption of Kilauea, in Hawaii, yielded anomalously high levels in airborne particles, for example. Especially significant in this light is the fact that the Deccan traps, which are volcanic rocks covering a large fraction of the Indian peninsula, were produced by great outpourings of lava during a brief geological interval beginning at or very close to the Cretaceous–Paleocene transition. Other areas were also sites of intensive volcanism at roughly the same time: the western United States, Great Britain, eastern Greenland, the Hawaiian region, and areas of the western Pacific Ocean.

Additional questions also remain to be resolved. Charles Officer and Charles Drake of Dartmouth College, the most persistent critics of the impact scenario, have questioned whether the geologically instantaneous accumulation of iridium could lead to anomalies that are spread through thicknesses of deep-sea sediment in excess of 30 or 40 centimeters (about 12 or 16 inches). These skeptics maintain that neither burrowing animals nor physical processes could disperse the iridium to this degree, whereas intense volcanism over a period of one or two hundred thousand years could account for the thick iridium-rich interval by producing a fallout of iridium while many centimeters of

Recent eruption of the volcano Kilauea, in Hawaii.

Scanning electron micrograph of a shocked quartz grain from the Cretaceous–Paleocene boundary clay in Garfield County, Montana. The planar fractures have been accentuated by etching with hydrofluoric acid.

sediment were accumulating. Officer and Drake also point out that in some areas the iridium layer is remarkably rich in antimony and arsenic, elements that are so rare in extraterrestrial objects that their high concentrations would seem necessarily to be of volcanic origin; this is taken to imply that the associated iridium enrichment is also the product of volcanism.

Geologists of the U.S. Geological Survey, led by Bruce Bohor and Glen Izett, have employed a new kind of evidence, however, to make a case that the excess iridium came from an impact rather than from earthly volcanism. This evidence takes the form of shocked mineral grains that have been discovered within the iridium-rich boundary clay, first in Montana and later in New Mexico and Europe. The shock features of these grains are sets of nearly parallel planar fractures of a type formed only by the rapid application of very high pressures such as those generated when a large extraterrestrial object strikes the earth.

In response to these arguments, Officer and Drake have joined forces with Neville Carter of Texas A&M University, an expert on shock fracturing of minerals, and Joseph Devine of Brown University, an expert on volcanism. To investigate whether explosive volcanism can shock minerals in the fashion of meteorite impacts, these workers have begun to examine mineral grains formed by massive eruptions of the Indonesian volcano Toba, whose crater is 50 times larger in areal extent than the nearby crater of the famous volcano Krakatoa. Toba has experienced at least three major eruptions during the past half million years, the most recent having occurred just 75,000 years ago. The search for shocked grains has thus far yielded equivocal results. Shocked features have been discovered, but, especially in quartz grains, they are not as complex or as well delineated as those observed in grains from the Cretaceous boundary interval. A possible reason is that the grains studied thus far are ones that accumulated in volcanic flows at temperatures of nearly 700°C. It may be that these high temperatures healed many shock fractures after they formed.

The question of whether shocked mineral grains like those from the Cretaceous boundary interval can form volcanically is pivotal to the impact controversy. If volcanism can produce the shock features, then there is a strong possibility that heavy volcanism produced the shocked grains at the boundary, as well as the high concentrations of iridium and other metallic elements. As will be discussed later in this chapter, heavy volcanic emissions might also be expected to cause climatic changes harmful to life. Study of volcanic ash spewed from Toba, which forms a layer in the sedimentary record of the deep sea nearby, may soon reveal whether Toba produced shocked minerals like those found at the Cretaceous boundary.

Complicating the controversy is possible evidence, just now emerging, of more than one iridium anomaly at some Cretaceous boundary sections. For example, the Berkeley group that first discovered the iridium anomaly at the Cretaceous–Paleocene boundary has now found a second peak about 40 centimeters (about 16 inches) below the boundary peak east of Japan at Site 577B of the Deep Sea Drilling Project. This lower peak is an order of magnitude smaller than the boundary peak, but is nonetheless substantial and demands interpretation. Until informal communications of other double or multiple anomalies are published as reports available for public scrutiny, there is no way of assessing the facts here, but there remains a possibility that more than one impact or burst of volcanism occurred close to the end of Cretaceous time.

THE IMPACT SCENARIO

Where a terminal Cretaceous impact might have occurred remains a mystery. The mineralogy of the shocked grains, if they were formed by an impact, would indicate a terrestrial landing: these grains include quartz and feldspar—mineral species that are extremely abundant in continental crust but poorly represented in the ocean basins. Some of the shocked particles in New Mexico are the size of small sand grains, whose resistance to atmospheric transport would perhaps require a not-too-distant location for an impact. One site proposed as a possible candidate by Bevan French of Washington, D.C. is a crater near the town of Manson, in north-central Iowa. This crater has been identified from well drilling, which has revealed the anomalous presence of fragmented igneous and metamorphic rocks (rocks formed at high temperatures) in a region that is characterized by sedimentary bedrock. The igneous and metamorphic rocks were once exposed at the surface but now lie shallowly buried beneath glacial deposits of the recent Ice Age. They apparently rose to the surface from deep within the earth following the penetration of a meteorite. The impact deformed and depressed sedimentary rocks throughout a circular area about 25 kilometers (about 16 miles) in diameter. The Manson impact was of great regional significance, and it penetrated Cretaceous rocks, suggesting that it may be of the right age to qualify as the terminal Cretaceous event. On the other hand, it appears to have been too small an event to have wrought the effects seen in the global stratigraphic record. The diameter of its crater is an order of magnitude smaller than was envisioned in the Alvarez group's original impact scenario. The search continues.

Another arresting report, by Wendy Wolbach, Roy Lewis, and Edward Anders of the University of Chicago, is of a high concentra-

Meteor crater, Arizona. This structure remains as a distinct topographic feature because it was produced by the arrival of a meteorite only a few thousand years ago.

tion of sootlike carbon particles from the terminal Cretaceous boundary clay at many localities around the world. Some of the particles formed clusters that are only known to develop in a hot gas or flame. The only hypothesis that the Chicago group finds acceptable is that wildfires ignited by the impact swept over a broad continental area, sending vast quantities of soot into the atmosphere. There is now a need to search higher and lower in the stratigraphic record to determine whether the newly discovered concentration of carbon particles is indeed unique. Critics of the wildfire hypothesis have already noted, however, that charcoal is not uncommon in Late Cretaceous terrestrial sediments at many levels. Critics have further observed that the carbon-bearing boundary clay in areas such as Denmark represents a long interval of time, not a geological "instant" during which a fire might have spread.

Even the general effects of the impact of a bolide (large extraterrestrial object) are widely debated. The Alvarez group originally estimated that the size of the iridium anomaly would have required a bolide diameter in the order of 10 kilometers (about 6 miles), which would have left a crater about twenty times wider. Among the chemical effects that have been imputed to such an impact event are poison-

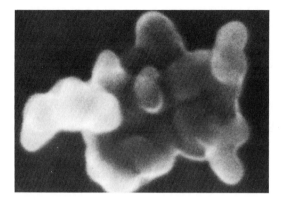

A minute carbon particle from the terminal Cretaceous boundary clay at Caravaca, Spain.

ing of life by hydrogen cyanide and damaging of the atmospheric ozone layer by the generation of nitrous oxide. Specifically, it has been postulated that hydrogen cyanide would have issued from the nucleus of an impacting comet, as opposed to a meteor, and it has been suggested that the nitrous oxide would have formed by oxidation of nitrogen as a descending bolide of either type heated the atmosphere. It is not clear, however, that comets contain high concentrations of iridium. Physical models invoking a continental impact site have predicted that dust injected into the atmosphere should have screened out sunlight, refrigerating the earth's surface in a manner analogous to the now famous "nuclear winter" aftermath of an artificial holocaust. The concept of a nuclear winter, in fact, has its origins in the idea that the purported impact at the close of the Cretaceous Period should have darkened the skies and cooled the earth.

Patterns of phytoplankton extinction may accord with the idea of a virtual shutdown of photosynthesis. First, it is notable that the dinoflagellates, which during Cretaceous time, as today, were most successful outside the tropics, survived the Cretaceous crisis with only modest losses. Dinoflagellate fossils are generally resting stages—cystlike structures that promote survival at times of ecological stress, including the onset of winter conditions. Calcareous nannoplankton, which were decimated by the terminal Cretaceous crisis, for the most part lack such resting stages; accordingly, we would predict that they should be especially vulnerable to an interval of darkness. A parallel argument has been offered for diatoms by Jennifer Kitchell of the University of Michigan and her collaborators David Clark of the University of Wisconsin and Andrew Gombos of Exxon Production Research Company. It turns out that centric diatoms, which formed an important component of the phytoplankton at high latitudes in Cretaceous seas, were able to form resting spores under stressful conditions, just as they do today; their high incidence of survival may reflect their ability to weather intervals of darkness. These patterns might in part explain why extinction of marine animals was heaviest in tropical seas: calcareous nannoplankton, which sustained heavy losses, are concentrated here, whereas dinoflagellates and diatoms prevail at high latitudes.

A VOLCANIC SCENARIO

Officer, Drake, and Devine have painted an alternative picture, reflecting their opinion that the geological record points to massive volcanism as the cause of extinction. These authors note that volcanoes

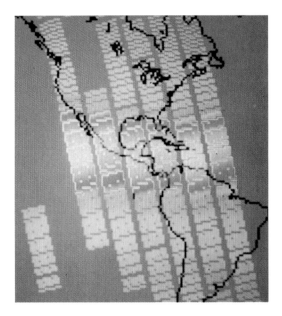

Infrared satellite image of a cloud of volcanic aerosols produced by the 1982 eruption of El Chichon. In this view, the cloud appears as a bright horizontal band above Latin America.

that have erupted during the past few decades have ejected not only rock dust high into the atmosphere, but also aerosols—minute droplets of liquid, primarily sulfuric acid. The residence time for the aerosols in the stratosphere is 1 to 2 years, compared to only a few months for the dust. Sulfuric acid aerosols, which issue in especially large quantities from volcanoes that produce dark, dense lava, reduce global temperatures by screening some sunlight from the earth. Massive volcanic activity in latest Cretaceous time might, then, have depressed global temperatures by as much as 4 or 5°C. Other authors had previously concluded that volcanism should tend to raise global temperatures by enhancing the greenhouse effect through emissions of carbon dioxide, but it now appears that this factor is minor compared to the cooling effects of aerosols.

Sulfuric acid would return to earth as acid rain, which might also be expected to damage life in a variety of ways. Officer and his colleagues estimate that the influx of acid would substantially reduce the alkalinity of the oceans, perhaps to the level of neutrality (the boundary between alkaline and acid conditions). Interestingly, studies of modern plankton reveal that calcareous nannoplankton, which suffered their heaviest extinction after the heavy pulse of foraminiferan losses, can survive at lower alkalinities than foraminiferans. This could be explained by a decline in alkalinity over an interval of several thousand years. Similarly, it is known that modern planktonic foraminiferan species of small size tolerate lower alkalinities than do species of large size—and diminutive species preferentially survived the crisis. As noted earlier, however, these patterns and others also match our predictions for extinction by climatic cooling.

Officer and his colleagues also point to the effects expected from the volcanic emission of hydrogen chloride into the atmosphere. This compound attacks the ozone layer of the upper atmosphere, which normally screens out a large percentage of incident ultraviolet radiation. A major increase in the intensity of this radiation would damage animal life.

A COMPOUND CRISIS

Many patterns described earlier in this chapter suggest that even if a bolide impact or burst of volcanic activity occurred at the end of Cretaceous time, the event can account for only one pulse of extinction within an interval of more general biotic attrition that lasted for several million years. Recall that the planktonic foraminiferans experienced major losses well before the end of Cretaceous time. Also, many calcareous nannoplankton species declined abruptly in population size right at the boundary but then persisted for substantial periods of time; something delayed this group's recovery for more than a million years. Similarly, the ammonoids dwindled markedly over an interval measured in millions of years, and in areas such as Spain they seem to have disappeared altogether before the terminal crisis. For two major groups of bivalve mollusks, the inoceramids and the reef-building rudists, the gradual decline proceeded to the point of total or near-total global extinction in advance of the final event. Nonetheless, marine invertebrates, like single-celled planktonic life, were also struck by a pulse of extinction in the final crisis; this has been most convincingly demonstrated for mollusks in the Brazos River section of Texas, where the preextinction fauna is preserved in abundance and there is neither an erosional surface nor a condensed section at the boundary.

It cannot be overemphasized that the terrestrial biota exhibits a parallel history. Long-term floral changes in Late Cretaceous time have been recognized for many years, yet we now also have evidence of a sudden change at the boundary, with ferns colonizing large areas of western North America. Similarly, a protracted diminution of the dinosaur fauna in the American west is now well established. How large a role the terminal Cretaceous event played in the dinosaurs' decline depends on whether nine or more species actually made their way into the Age of Mammals; but even if this possibility is removed, a cogent assessment of the numbers indicates that most of the huge Late Cretaceous fauna was gone before latest Cretaceous time.

What caused the long interval of general biotic deterioration? Many lines of evidence summarized earlier in this chapter point to climatic change as the primary agent. In the terrestrial realm, the case for this is especially strong because of the testimony of flowering plants. A reduction of mean annual temperature between Campanian and Maastrichtian time in the vicinity of Wyoming exemplifies the trend. The linkage between large terrestrial animals and vegetation is so strong that it is natural to seek to explain the dinosaurs' decline in terms of the floral, and hence, climatic change.

The marine record provides similar testimony. Ratios of oxygen isotopes in fossils offer evidence of ancient ocean temperatures because as temperatures decline, organisms assimilate an increased ratio of oxygen 18 to oxygen 16. Unfortunately, the isotopic record is imperfect because preserved skeletons are commonly altered in the course of geological time. Nonetheless, plots of oxygen isotope ratios for skeletons of foraminiferans that lived on the deep-sea floor and also for skeletons of planktonic foraminiferans and calcareous nannoplankton

Estimates of temperatures in the tropical Pacific Ocean during the Cretaceous Period, showing a decline near the end. Estimates for surface waters have been derived from the analyses of oxygen isotopes in planktonic foraminiferans and calcareous nannoplankton, and estimates for bottom waters have been derived from similar analyses applied to deep-sea foraminiferans.

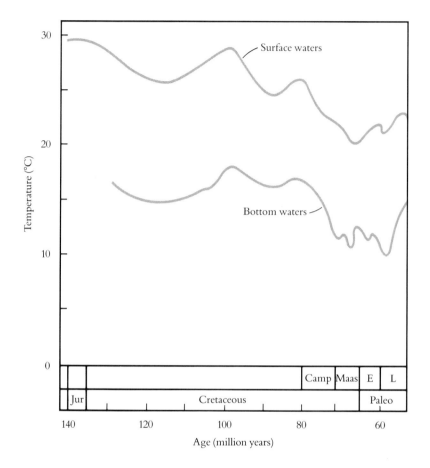

reveal a major cooling trend in the marine realm, culminating in Maastrichtian time. This cooling may well have been responsible for the general decline of life before the final pulse of extinction at the very close of Cretaceous time. Both the isotopic record and the history of land plants have been interpreted, however, to indicate one or more brief pulses of warming in late Maastrichtian time before the final crisis.

The idea of extinction via climatic change has sometimes been subordinated to the notion that a lowering of sea level decimated faunas by reducing living space for animals of shallow sea floors. One problem with this second idea is that it cannot apply to the heavy extinction of the plankton, which range over the surface water of vast oceans. Another is that although sea level did fall toward the end of

Cretaceous time, its lowest position relative to continental surfaces approximated that of the present day. As one example of the weak effect that this change had, lowered sea level eliminated the great North American interior seaway but left a sizable embayment along the Gulf Coast, and this was a place where unusually heavy extinction of marine life occurred. We have shown elsewhere in this book that several other dramatic episodes of sea level lowering failed to cause mass extinction.

The severity of losses in the Gulf of Mexico and Caribbean Sea formed part of a general picture of latitudinal bias in the pattern of the Late Cretaceous extinctions. There were, in general, much heavier losses in warm climatic regimes than in cool ones. In North America, for example, the reef-building rudists and other tropical elements died out in the south, whereas there was remarkably little extinction of marine bivalves in the vicinity of North Dakota. For this northern region, it has been shown that about 60 percent of the bivalve species in the Cannonball Sea, an arm of the ocean that spread down from Canada during the Paleocene Epoch, were survivors from Late Cretaceous time. Recall that the extinction of plants was also much heavier in New Mexico than to the north. Similarly, we have seen that warm-adapted planktonic life, in particular, was decimated and that cool-adapted foraminiferans migrated toward the equator before the very end of the Cretaceous, as tropical species died out. Supporting evidence comes from the record of the marine gastropods (snails), as analyzed by Heinz Kollmann of Vienna. Kollmann has found that tropical gastropod faunas of northern Africa disappeared at the end of Cretaceous time and were replaced by ones adapted to cool conditions and previously restricted to northern regions such as Greenland. There could hardly be firmer evidence of biotically significant cooling in the marine realm. Thus, once again we see played out the familiar theme of heavier losses in tropical regions than in the temperate zone— a theme consistent with the idea that climatic cooling played a dominant role, leaving warm-adapted species of low latitudes without refuge.

Unfortunately, we do not know what caused thermal vicissitudes during the final several million years of Late Cretaceous time. Certainly, changes in the intensity of volcanism, operating through its production of sun-blocking aerosols, may have been an important variable.

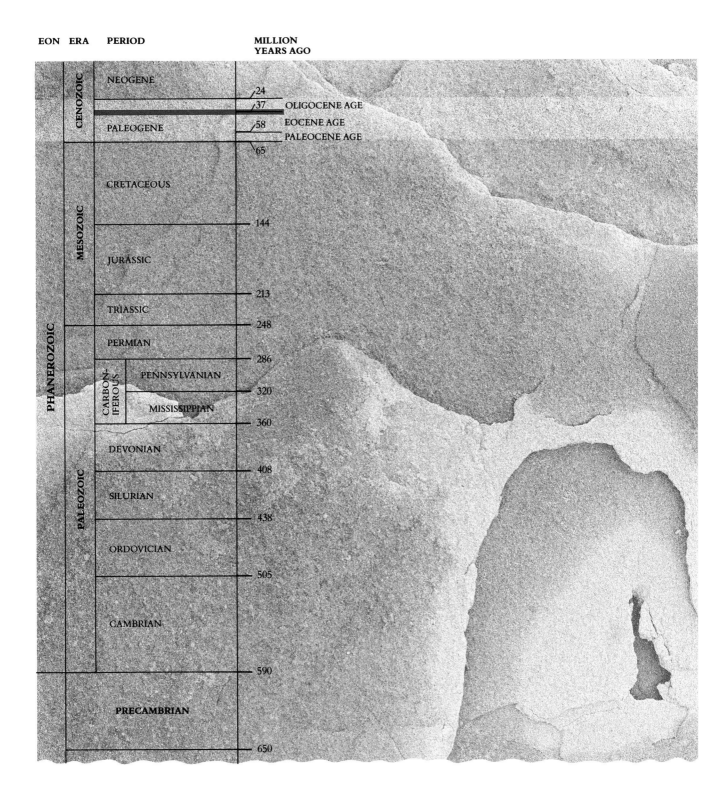

EON	ERA	PERIOD	MILLION YEARS AGO
PHANEROZOIC	CENOZOIC	NEOGENE	24
			37 — OLIGOCENE AGE
		PALEOGENE	58 — EOCENE AGE
			PALEOCENE AGE
			65
	MESOZOIC	CRETACEOUS	
			144
		JURASSIC	
			213
		TRIASSIC	
			248
	PALEOZOIC	PERMIAN	
			286
		CARBON-IFEROUS PENNSYLVANIAN	
			320
		MISSISSIPPIAN	
			360
		DEVONIAN	
			408
		SILURIAN	
			438
		ORDOVICIAN	
			505
		CAMBRIAN	
			590
		PRECAMBRIAN	
			650

8 THE PALEOGENE: RECOVERY, THEN CRISIS

The most dramatic change with the dawning of the Cenozoic Era was, of course, the immediate rise of the mammals to terrestrial dominance. At first, this was a matter of ecological victory by default—the dinosaurs having retired from the field of play—and mammalian species remained small and somewhat rodent like. Given the opportunity, however, the mammals soon did just what we would expect: They underwent a spectacular adaptive radiation. Within the first 10 million years of Paleogene time, the ranks of the Mammalia expanded to include a wide variety of creatures—such forms as ancestral horses and rodents, and even primitive primates (members of the human order) and such anatomically and ecologically divergent animals as bats and whales.

The evolution of birds early in the Cenozoic Era was not so spectacular. Having fragile, hollow bones and a mode of life that is not generally conducive to the formation of fossils, these animals have left a relatively meager fossil record throughout their history. The record is nonetheless adequate to show that the great adaptive radiation of songbirds, which constitute by far the largest avian group in the modern world, did not commence until midway through the era. In fact, during the Paleogene Period, the most numerous groups of birds were apparently long-legged waders—groups that in form and habit broadly resemble cranes and herons.

At the close of Cretaceous time, the vegetation that supported life on the land was still dominated by the flowering plants, and during the Paleogene Period these in many ways assumed a modern character. By 10 or 12 million years after the start of the period, about half of the existing genera of flowering plants were ones that are represented in the modern world. Slow to originate and expand, however, were the grasses. These appeared early in Paleogene time but did not prevail over large geographic areas until near the end of the period. In part,

Fossil bat of Eocene age. The origin of the bats from terrestrial mammals early in the Cenozoic Era exemplifies the great rapidity of the mammals' adaptive radiation following the demise of the dinosaurs.

their delayed expansion resulted from global climatic changes, which because they also caused widespread extinction will be a major focus of this chapter.

As a result of the Late Cretaceous crisis, several major Mesozoic groups were conspicuous by their absence from early Cenozoic oceans. These included the ammonoids, the rudists, and the large swimming reptiles. Marine life at the start of the Cenozoic Era was thus a residual biota, but it was nonetheless generally similar to that of modern seas. In other words, the biota of today has developed from Mesozoic survivors not so much by major evolutionary transformations as by the evolution of new species, genera, and occasionally families—within previously established higher taxa, orders and classes. Thus, at the base of the early Paleogene food web were phytoplankton groups that survived from the Mesozoic Era, the most important being groups that retain their dominant role today—calcareous nannoplankton (which were temporarily set back by the terminal Mesozoic extinctions), diatoms, and dinoflagellates. Similarly, the most prominent groups that fed upon these unicellular algae and other algae that colonized the sea floor included sea urchins, foraminiferans, and mollusks in the form of gastropods (snails) and bivalves.

Corals of the type that build reefs today got a second chance at the start of the Paleogene Period. Having lost their dominant position to the rudists in mid-Cretaceous time, they were once again unchallenged in the reef habitat. It is therefore of interest that fossil coral reefs are not well represented in the sedimentary record representing the first epoch of the Paleogene Period, the Paleocene Epoch, which lasted about 8 million years. Thus, the corals' recovery was delayed for a substantial interval of geological time. A diverse variety of corals survived the Late Cretaceous crisis, so this event cannot account for the slow ecological rebound. One possibility is that tropical seas remained relatively cool for the first few million years of Paleogene time.

Also already well established, in terms of taxonomic diversity, when the Paleogene Period began were the dominant modern groups of large-bodied marine predators—carnivorous snails, crabs, and teleost fish. The whales evolved after a few million years, although the subgroup that we informally term dolphins did not appear until close to the end of Paleogene time. The whales have in part been the ecological successors of the reptilian sea monsters of the Mesozoic Era, the chief exceptions being the baleen whales, which strain vast quantities of zooplankton from the ocean with bony, toothlike sieves.

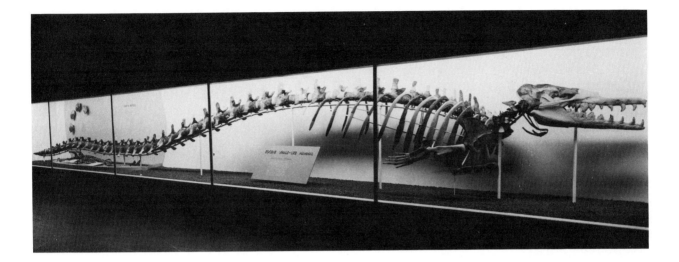

An Eocene whale belonging to a species that reached a length of about 14 meters (about 55 feet). The rapid origin of the whales, like that of the bats, illustrates how dramatically mammals diversified early in the Cenozoic Era.

This chapter will focus on the fates of many of these groups, not in a major mass extinction but in one of second rank. There are special reasons for focusing on this Paleogene event, even though its impact was not nearly as dramatic as that of the Cretaceous crisis. The Paleogene event took place during an interval of several million years that spanned the boundary between the Eocene and Oligocene epochs. Because its occurrence was fairly recent in geologic time, the record of what happened is especially well documented, even with respect to causation. A wide variety of evidence, coming from sedimentary deposits of both marine and terrestrial origin, indicates that the prevailing cause was cooling that may have resulted indirectly from movements of the earth's crust.

EXTINCTIONS IN THE OCEAN

Sea-floor life underwent substantial changes during the latter part of the Eocene Epoch, the second epoch of the Cenozoic Era. These changes were not so much a matter of extinctions of families and orders, but rather entailed the disappearance of large numbers of species and genera. It has long been recognized that heavy extinction of this type occurred in Europe, where the primary victims were species

Late Eocene gastropod mollusk from the Gulf Coast that suffered extinction, along with many other species, at a time when we know the climate was cooling in this region and many others.

of warm-water affinities, that is, species that had close relatives in subtropical and tropical regions. Carole Hickman of the University of California at Berkeley has observed the same pattern for approximately contemporaneous molluscan faunas along the Pacific coast of Oregon. In these examples we see the same bias observed in earlier mass extinctions—a bias against species adapted to warm conditions.

For molluscan faunas of roughly the same age, William Zinsmeister of Purdue University has observed heavy extinction in the vicinity of Antarctica and New Zealand, and David Dockery of the Mississippi Bureau of Geology and Thor Hansen of Western Washington University have documented heavy extinction along the northern margin of the Gulf of Mexico. In this latter region, the sedimentary record of the molluscan losses is relatively complete because sediments have been accumulating here almost continuously as they have been carried to the sea by the Mississippi and other smaller rivers. The crisis here came in pulses, and Hansen has found that it began late in middle Eocene time and continued through late Eocene time into the early part of the Oligocene, thus spanning approximately 7 or 8 million years.

The Gulf Coast extinctions parallel earlier biotic crises in their protracted and pulsatile temporal pattern and also in another feature: according to Hansen's analysis, the individual episodes of extinction did not coincide with events of sea level lowering that punctuated the general crisis interval. Hansen has concluded that the extinctions must have resulted not from sea level changes but from episodes of climatic cooling, which, as will be explained shortly, are known to have occurred during the same interval.

The Eocene–Oligocene extinction interval has been best studied for the planktonic realm. Here it was first recognized through the study of foraminiferans, which suffered losses over a period of several million years. Richard Cifelli of the Smithsonian Institution, who seems first to have noted this protracted event, showed that it was followed by an adaptive radiation that produced a set of species that in gross form closely resembled those that had lived before. This striking example of iterative evolution seems to illustrate how constraints on the ways that organisms develop tend to restrict the evolutionary potential of a group of organisms. Cifelli also noted that the survivors of the crisis— the species that gave rise to the adaptive radiation that ensued— belonged to the groups known as the globigerines, a group that today comprises most species able to live in cold seas.

Since Cifelli's seminal contribution, other workers have reconstructed a much more detailed picture of the Eocene–Oligocene extinctions, not only for the planktonic foraminiferans but also for other

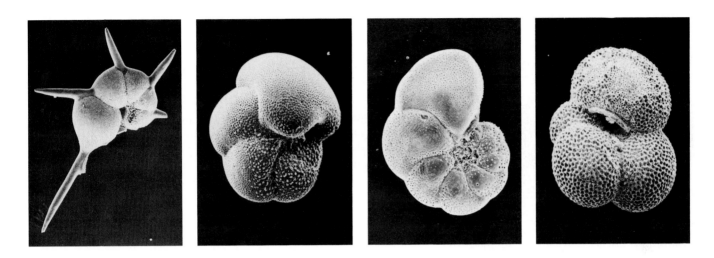

Paleogene foraminiferans illustrating the range of forms
that existed before the heavy extinction of Late Eocene
and Oligocene time. Species with similar shapes
evolved during the foraminiferan's Neogene recovery.

members of the plankton. The data here have come primarily from
cores of deep-sea sediments obtained by the global Deep Sea Drilling
Project. Part of the key evidence from the cores is the occurrence of
microfossils themselves and part is isotopic data derived from these
minute skeletons, especially from planktonic foraminiferans. We
know that during the Cenozoic Era, continental glaciers grew somewhat fitfully to the large dimensions that they attained during the
recent Ice Age. As we have seen, when glaciers expand, the associated
cooling of sea temperatures causes most organisms that secrete calcium carbonate to incorporate oxygen with an increased ratio of oxygen 18 to oxygen 16. The effect is exaggerated, however, by the tendency for the lighter oxygen 16 isotope to evaporate from sea water at
a higher rate and thus preferentially end up in the precipitation that
becomes locked into glaciers and thus removed from the global hydrological cycle. There is much evidence that most events of widespread climatic cooling during the Cenozoic Era have been associated
with glacial expansion near one or both of the earth's poles. Given this
linkage, we are faced with a problem: how much of any rise in the
oxygen18/oxygen 16 ratio in Cenozoic fossils should be attributed to
glacial growth, and how much to cooling? Nonetheless, we can at
least conclude that some degree of cooling occurred.

It has been found that small hiatuses in the deep-sea sedimentary
record commonly represent times of oceanic cooling during the Cenozoic Era. In other words, the deep-sea floor has been scoured

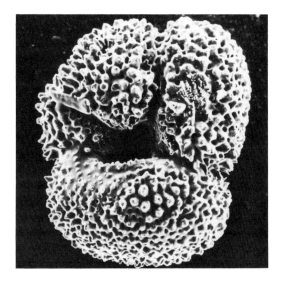

Spiny foraminiferan of Late Eocene age. This is typical of the tropical types that failed to survive into the Oligocene.

slightly rather than having received fine-grained sediment at a very slow rate, as it normally does. The explanation seems to lie in the way in which currents are driven along the deep-sea floor. At any time in the earth's history, the coldest waters at the earth's surface sink to the bottom and spread laterally, forming the water mass that occupies the lowest zone of the ocean basins. Today, when polar regions are quite cold, the deep sea is only slightly above freezing, and the rapid descent of large volumes of frigid water produces relatively strong currents. Presumably hiatuses in deep-sea cores represent past times when one or both poles became cooler.

There was, in fact, a major elevation in the oxygen 18 level in planktonic foraminiferan tests during the latter part of the Eocene Epoch and the early part of the Oligocene. While this general trend is evident, the details are unclear, owing to the imperfect preservation of original isotopic ratios and the minor mixing of sediment and microfossils by burrowing animals.

Microfossils provide a record of extinction with a much finer scale of resolution than has been attained in the study of larger marine organisms. Among micropaleontologists who have examined this record, there is universal agreement that it reveals not a sudden disaster, but a series of pulses of extinction; these perturbations, like those that affected shallow-water mollusks, were spread over several million years, beginning long before the end of the Eocene Epoch.

Gerta Keller of Princeton University has provided a synthesis of data from several oceanic regions that reveal five pulses of extinction for planktonic foraminiferans during the Eocene–Oligocene interval. The first pulse occurred at the boundary between middle and late Eocene time, about 40 million years ago. The extinctions at this time manifest an interesting pattern very much like that of the terminal Cretaceous crisis: they eliminated species that possessed spiny skeletons, and these skeletons were characteristic of groups that were adapted to warm conditions—conditions that apparently ceased to exist, at least over many broad areas. (Most of the nonspiny early Eocene species that survived this event died out during the four subsequent pulses of extinction.) The preceding transition from early to middle Eocene time had been marked by the migration of cool-adapted species from middle latitudes to low latitudes. This is a sign of global cooling during the interval leading up to the first pulse. Another sign of cooling is the presence of a widespread hiatus in the sedimentary record of the deep sea precisely at the boundary where the extinction occurred. This hiatus represents so little geological time that it cannot create the false appearance of sudden extinction; the extinction event probably spanned no more than a million years, and perhaps much less. Keller has also noted a pattern that suggests a transition from an ocean that exhibited a relatively weak vertical temperature gradient, because the deep sea was relatively warm, to one with a strong gradient that developed when surface waters cooled but the deep sea cooled even more. The evidence of planktonic foraminiferans takes the form of a differentiation of the fauna into subgroups adapted to shallow, intermediate, and deep-water masses. These are of course preserved together because all rained down on the deep-sea floor, but their differing depth (and temperature) preferences can be deduced from the differing ratios of oxygen isotopes in their skeletons.

Slightly more than 38 million years ago, a second event caused the extinction of a small number of species and severe reductions in the abundance of others that soon led to their extinction as well. Most of the species affected at this time were members of the genus *Globigerapsis*. Noting that this event roughly coincided with the accumulation of a microtektite layer over a broad zone from the Caribbean Sea to the Indian Ocean, Keller has suggested that the planktonic community may have been perturbed by a comet shower or some other impact of extraterrestrial origin. Edward Petuch of Florida International University has suggested that the depression now occupied by the Florida Everglades formed when a meteor landed at the end of Eocene time. This novel hypothesis remains to be tested.

The third event, dated at about 37.5 million years before present, is evidenced, first, by the final extinction of species that had begun their decline several hundred million years earlier and, second, by the expansion of other species. This faunal turnover is recorded in cores below the level of two microtektite layers; there is no basis for relating it to an extraterrestrial event, and an abundance of hiatuses in deep-sea cores suggests that this too was a time of general global cooling. According to studies of Annika Sanfilippo of the Scripps Institution of Oceanography and three coworkers, the lower microtektite layer is, however, positioned at the level of disappearance of five radiolarian species. Although others would apply the label "microtektite" to the glassy spherules found at this level, the Sanfilippo group withholds this label because the structures differ from standard microtektites in containing the heavy mineral clinopyroxene. This is only a matter of semantics, however. There is general agreement that the spherules resulted from the impact of one or more asteroids or comets and that these may have led to a very small number of extinctions of radiolarians, if not of foraminiferans.

It was once believed by some that the heavy extinction in the vicinity of the Eocene–Oligocene boundary took place precisely at the boundary. Although this fourth crisis is now seen as a complex event spread over several million years, it is also evident that a few species of planktonic foraminiferans did die out right at the boundary. Gerta Keller has nonetheless shown that their loss was not a dramatic event: The species that disappeared had become relatively rare long before their disappearance. Two facts suggest that the Eocene–Oligocene transition was a time of global cooling. First, it was a time when cool-water species expanded in population size whereas warm-water species declined in abundance. Second, the earliest Oligocene is represented by deep-sea hiatuses in a number of regions, which again suggests the presence of relatively strong, temperature-driven currents close to the ocean floor.

Heavy extinction continued well into Oligocene time, with the final pulse occurring 31 or 32 million years before the present. It is interesting that this event, which eliminated most Eocene survivors and a few new Oligocene species as well, followed an interval of biotic stability. Keller's data suggest that just one species became extinct during a 3-million-year interval ending about 32.5 million years ago. The extinctions that then struck the fauna coincided with a drop in sea level that Peter Vail and his coworkers at Exxon Production Research Company consider to have been the most severe during the past 100 million years and perhaps during all of Phanerozoic time. Sea level and cooling, though interrelated, are not tightly coupled, and some workers have argued that the drop in sea level was much more severe in late Oligocene time than the drop in temperature.

Marie-Pierre Aubry of the Woods Hole Oceanographic Institution has found the history of the calcareous nannoplankton to parallel that of the planktonic foraminiferans for Eocene and early Oligocene time. There were, however, fewer replacements of the nannoplankton species that disappeared—a situation that can presumably be attributed to the fact that this group of phytoplankton is adapted primarily to warm conditions. Between late middle Eocene time and the end of the Eocene, an interval of perhaps 7 million years, there was a reduction in the number of calcareous nannoplankton species throughout the world by about 70 percent—a decline from about 120 species to less than 40. It is notable that for this group, as for planktonic foraminiferans, heavy extinction began and, in fact, struck with greatest impact at the end of middle Eocene time, about 40 million years ago. For the calcareous nannoplankton, the crisis seems not to have continued into Oligocene time. Aubry also reports, however, that high latitude floras

Scanning electron micrograph of a deep-sea ostracod of Oligocene age. This is one of the many species that occupied the newly refrigerated waters of the deep sea.

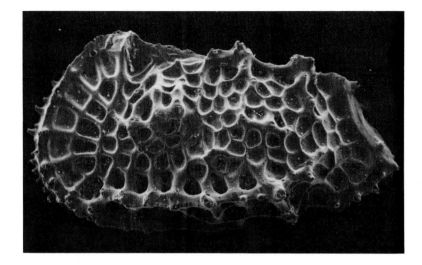

of this group, in response to cooling, migrated equatorward during the latter part of Eocene time and also the early part of the Oligocene.

We can readily explain the previously noted fact that oxygen isotope curves indicate a more pronounced cooling in the deep sea, as reflected in the skeletal composition of bottom-dwelling foraminiferans, than nearer the surface, as reflected in planktonic skeletons. This divergence of temperatures reflects the way in which the general thermal structure of the oceans changed, very close to the end of the Eocene Epoch. This was the time of origin of the psychrosphere—the cold layer of bottom water in the oceans that is produced by the polar submergence of dense, refrigerated waters. In the 1970s, by noting changes in the composition of faunas of deep-sea ostracods (ostracods are small, bivalved crustaceans that have left an excellent fossil record), Richard Benson of the Smithsonian Institution deduced that the psychrosphere came into being during the Eocene–Oligocene transition. Foraminiferans of the deep-sea floor also changed at this time, but not markedly; apparently they were relatively tolerant of the temperature change.

The reason that cooling of ocean surface waters was less pronounced than cooling of the deep sea is that the cause of the cooling was climatic deterioration near the South Pole, and frigid water from this region sank and spread over the entire deep-sea floor. As they do

Estimates of surface and bottom water temperatures for the tropical Pacific Ocean during the Cenozoic Era, based on oxygen isotope data for fossils representing planktonic and bottom-dwelling microorganisms. Cooling is evident at both water levels during the Eocene–Oligocene transition.

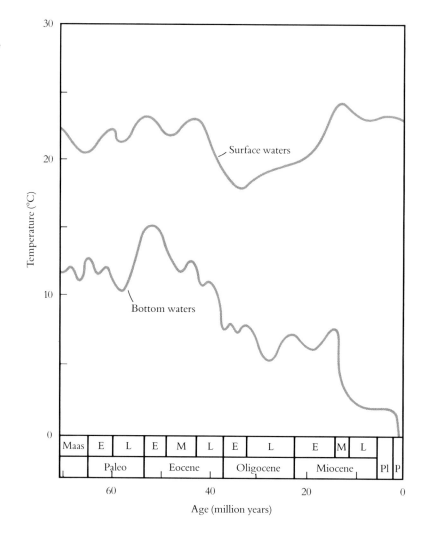

today, cool polar waters found their way to the shallow seas at low latitudes only where major surface currents carried them equatorward or where they were dragged upward from great depths in areas of upwelling. Even so, the histories outlined above—of shallow-water mollusks, of planktonic life, and of oxygen isotope ratios—all testify to significant drops in temperature for large masses of shallow water during the latter portion of Eocene time and the early portion of Oligocene time. This picture is paralleled by patterns of biotic change on the land, where extinctions were also severe in the animal world.

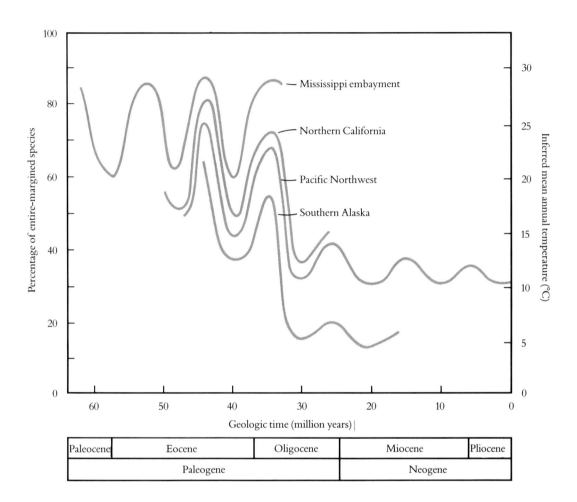

Climatic changes in North America during Eocene and Oligocene time. These curves, which show the same pattern for four areas, are based on the percentages of flowering plant species with leaves having entire-margins.

COOLING AND CRISES ON THE LAND

Evidence of climatic cooling in terrestrial habitats during the Eocene and Oligocene epochs comes chiefly from changes in flowering plants. For western North America from California to Alaska and also for the Gulf Coast, Jack Wolfe of the United States Geological Survey has documented dramatic declines in the percentage of fossil species with entire (or smooth) margins. These declines, signalling episodes of reduced mean annual temperature, were episodic, beginning in

Badlands of South Dakota, formed by the erosion of
Oligocene sediments harboring a rich fossil mammal
fauna that records the heavy extinction of mid-
Oligocene time.

mid–Eocene time and continuing into the Oligocene. The last major
cooling episode took place slightly more than 30 million years ago,
apparently at the time when the last pulse of extinction occurred and
when sea level dropped to its lowest Cenozoic position. The timing of
these events is especially well known for the Pacific Northwest, where
volcanic rocks associated with fossil leaves have been dated radio-
metrically. Here and also in the Gulf Coast, fossil floras reveal cooling that is temporally associated with regional marine mass extinctions described earlier.

In Great Britain, climates seem to have deteriorated a bit earlier.
Margaret Collinson of Kings College in London and her coworkers

have studied the fate of the flora of the London Clay in southern England that, quite remarkably, in early Eocene time was tropical, or nearly so. Many of the families represented here are primarily of tropical distribution today, and the flora has been compared to that of the modern Malaysian jungle. The London Clay and younger deposits superimposed on it form a virtually complete record of deposition from early Eocene into Oligocene time. Their fossil floras, which consist of seeds, fruits, pollen, and spores, reveal that temperatures dropped in latest early Eocene time, causing many tropical and subtropical species to disappear. Another episode of climatic change in this region came in late Eocene time.

Possibly pulses of cooling on the land generally coincided with those in the ocean, but the fact that major changes in England seem to have begun earlier than the onset of marine extinction suggests that the global pattern of cooling was variable in space as well as in time.

Mammals on the land also suffered the effects of climatic deterioration, as analyzed by Donald Prothero of Occidental College in Los Angeles. North American faunas preserved in terrain west of the Mississippi, such as the Badlands of South Dakota, experienced two intervals of heavy turnover, one in late Eocene time and the other in late Oligocene time. The second interval occurred slightly more than 30 million years ago, when, as we have seen, sea level dropped dramatically and terrestrial floras were transformed. The first change in mammalian faunas entailed the elimination of many species and also a modest number of genera, most of which were already on the decline—remnants of groups that were well past their prime. At the same time, many new groups originated. In Prothero's view, these changes resulted in large part from faunal interchanges between North America and Asia. The route of migration was the Bering Strait, which may have connected Siberia and Alaska during times of sea level lowering, or Greenland, which was still largely connected to both the Old and New Worlds.

The Oligocene event included fewer extinctions. Among its victims were the titanotheres—huge rhinoceros-like animals with blunt horns. Preservation and dating are good enough that Prothero has been able to estimate that the interval of extinction did not exceed 200,000 years. Ancient soils in the Badlands seem clearly to implicate climate. Here Gregory Retallack of the University of Indiana has found that at the time of the faunal transformation, soils of the type formed in subhumid, open woodlands gave rise to soils of semiarid woodlands and grasslands. This indication of drying is not unexpected. The lowering of sea level would have left inland areas extremely far from oceans, the ultimate source of atmospheric moisture.

The Oligocene mammal fauna of Western North America that lived before the mid-Oligocene crisis. Titanotheres, the large rhinoceros-like animals, disappeared from the earth at this time.

Thus, both a cooling and a drying of climates seem to have contributed to floral changes, which probably in turn led to the demise of certain species of mammals that were heavily dependent on particular kinds of plants for food.

THE ANTARCTIC SEPARATION: A MODEL FOR GLOBAL COOLING

The preceding discussion describes evidence of climatic deterioration at a time of major biotic turnover, but does not address the question of how cooling came about. The strongest hint of causation comes from the evidence that the oceanic psychrosphere formed at the time of the Eocene–Oligocene transition. This major thermal event leads us back to the poles of the earth, the source of the deep sea's frigid waters, and in particular to the South Pole, because deep-sea cores from near Antarctica reveal that cold-water plankton began to flourish here at about the time when the psychrosphere came into being.

James Kennett and Margaret Murphy of the University of Rhode Island have advanced a plate tectonic model for the inception of the psychrosphere that has been well received. Today the waters around Antarctica are caught up in the circumantarctic current, a clockwise gyre formed by the southern extremities of the great counterclockwise

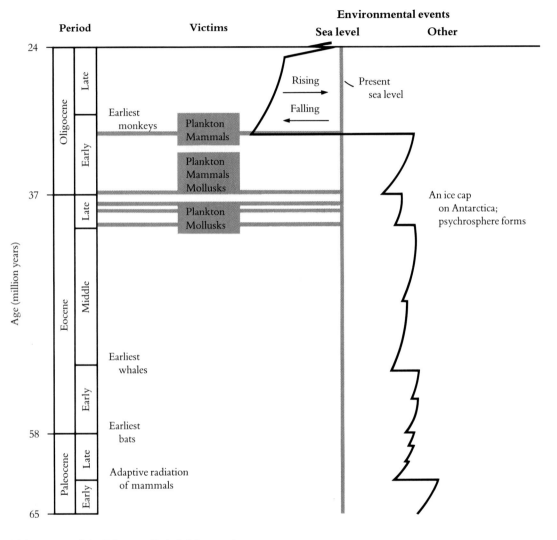

Major events of the Paleogene Period. Many extinctions preceded the dramatic drop in sea level of the Oligocene Epoch.

gyres of the southern Atlantic, Pacific, and Indian oceans. Thus, the circumantarctic gyre is like a single gear turned by three others, and it serves as a cooling machine for the deep sea, trapping water from higher latitudes, which is thus forced to cool markedly and then sink to great depths, where it spreads toward the equator.

Before the end of the Eocene Epoch, Antarctica remained attached to both South America and Australia, and consequently there was no

Separation of Australia from Antarctica during Eocene and Oligocene time. These are fragments of Gondwan-aland, and their parting caused a cold ocean current to deflect a warm current that had previously affected Antarctica. Antarctica cooled markedly, and cold water trapped in its vicinity began to descend to the deep sea.

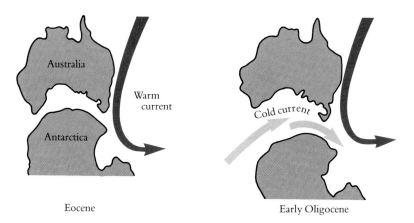

Eocene   Early Oligocene

circumantarctic current. Kennett has noted that at the end of Eocene time Australia separated from Antarctica, allowing a cold current to flow between the two as the first segment of the circumantarctic current to form. Before this separation, the warm South Pacific gyre had swept southward against Antarctica, but the new cold current deflected this current northward before it reached the polar continent. South America remained attached to Antarctica for millions of years after Australia made a clean break, but the separation of Australia was enough to allow sea ice to form and cold water to sink to the deep sea, producing the psychrosphere.

In mid-Oligocene time, about 33 million years ago, the strait between Antarctica and Australia deepened and the cold current grew stronger. This was reflected in the growth of glaciers on Antarctica and the expansion in the seas around this continent of diatoms— cold-adapted phytoplankton whose silica skeletons settle to leave a fossil record in the deep sea.

Precise patterns of climatic change for the Eocene Epoch are not known, but it appears that the widespread extinctions of Late Eocene time described in this chapter coincided with the initiation of cooling in Antarctica. The final pulse of extinction in mid-Oligocene time appears to have taken place when the cold current between Antarctica and Australia grew stronger. The various extinctions apparently took place in pulses, as cool temperatures were transmitted to lower latitudes by winds, by ocean currents that pulled waters from the circumantarctic gyre, and by upwelling of cold waters from the deep sea. Through these events, the climatic history of the earth experienced profound and lasting change that, as we shall see in the following chapter, culminated in the recent glacial age that has episodically spread ice sheets over large areas of the Northern Hemisphere.

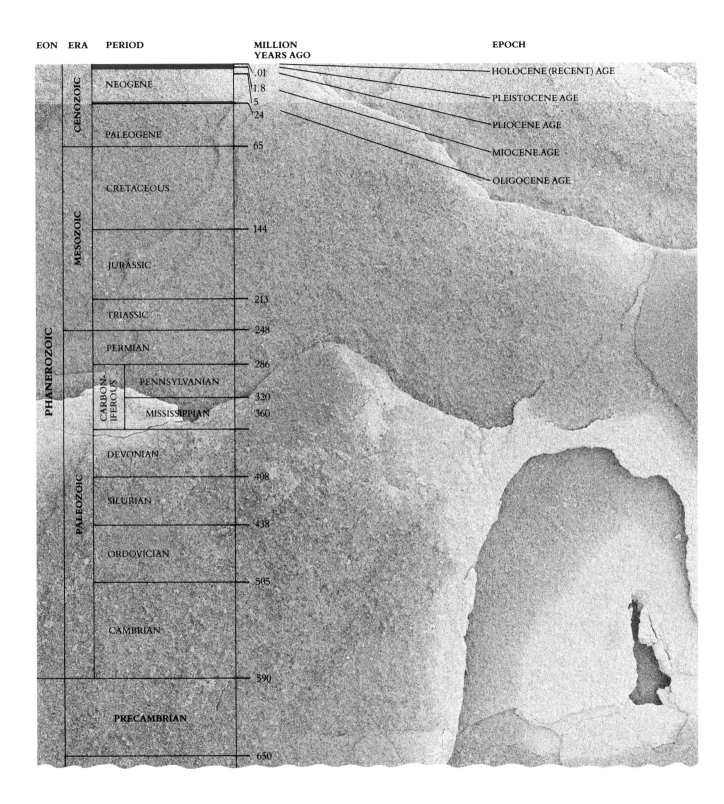

EON	ERA	PERIOD		MILLION YEARS AGO	EPOCH
PHANEROZOIC	CENOZOIC	NEOGENE		.01	HOLOCENE (RECENT) AGE
				1.8	PLEISTOCENE AGE
				5	PLIOCENE AGE
		PALEOGENE		24	MIOCENE AGE
				65	OLIGOCENE AGE
	MESOZOIC	CRETACEOUS			
				144	
		JURASSIC			
				213	
		TRIASSIC			
				248	
	PALEOZOIC	PERMIAN			
				286	
		CARBON-IFEROUS	PENNSYLVANIAN		
				320	
			MISSISSIPPIAN	360	
		DEVONIAN			
				408	
		SILURIAN			
				438	
		ORDOVICIAN			
				505	
		CAMBRIAN			
				590	
		PRECAMBRIAN			
				650	

9 NEOGENE EXTINCTIONS: OUR RECENT HERITAGE

The Neogene Period, which has spanned the last 24 million years or so, includes the Miocene Epoch, a relatively long subdivision that ended only 5 million years ago, and the progressively shorter epochs labeled the Pliocene, Pleistocene, and Recent (Holocene). We tend to think of the Pleistocene as the modern interval of glaciation in the Northern Hemisphere, but actually Cenozoic continental glaciers first expanded here in mid-Pliocene time, about 3 million years ago. Furthermore, the glacial interval has not yet ended. The "Recent" is a name that we use for convenience to label the interval of 10,000 years or so since the latest withdrawal of continental glaciers. The human species lived through most or all of the most recent cold spell. Today we are enjoying a geologically brief respite, in the form of an interglacial age, but the established pattern serves warning that in a few tens of thousands of years the glaciers almost certainly will expand again.

Climatic change has, in fact, exerted a dominant control over changes in the ecosystem throughout Neogene time. The net trend has been one of sporadic deterioration of climates, and this has represented a continuation of the changes that began during the Eocene Epoch. Global climates have never again been as warm as they were during Early Eocene time, when a tropical or near-tropical jungle occupied southern England and temperate forests cloaked much of Alaska.

There were few changes in the general composition of marine life during the Neogene Period, perhaps the most conspicuous being the diversification of the whale family, in part through the adaptive radiation of the dolphins. On the land the situation was quite different. Because of their great sensitivity to climatic conditions, terrestrial floras underwent widespread alterations during Neogene time—alterations that had their beginnings in Oligocene time. Among the most conspicuous of floral changes was the expansion of grasslands at

Tallgrass prairie in Iowa, a remnant of natural grass-
land of the type that expanded in North America during the climatic changes of Neogene time.

the expense of forests. As evidenced by the prairies of North America
and the savannahs of Africa, moderately dry conditions favor grasses.
Grasses had evolved early in Paleocene time, but initially played a
relatively minor ecological role. The dry habitats that have favored
their expansion spread over large areas as climates cooled. Also of
great significance was the Neogene adaptive radiation and ecological
expansion of the flowering plants known as herbaceous plants; these
are plants that die back to the ground after releasing their seeds. The
largest modern family of these, the Compositae, contains some 10,000
species, including the daisies, asters, sunflowers, and diverse groups
that we loosely describe as "weeds." Weeds are poor at holding down
territory—they are weak competitors for space and nutrients—but
they excel at invading vacant terrain. It is largely for this reason that
they have expanded during Neogene time, when climatic severity and
instability have offered them excellent opportunities to flourish in
their characteristically transient fashion. Possessing a dormant stage,
they thrive in strongly seasonal climates, and being efficient at dis-
persing and occupying bare ground, they flourish when other vegetation is suddenly exterminated.

Animal life on the land also responded to climatic deterioration,
primarily through adjustments to vegetational change. Rats, mice,
songbirds, and snakes have been among the groups of animals to undergo the most dramatic Neogene adaptive radiations. Their success
cannot be attributed entirely to the expansion of grasses and herbs, but

Fossil horse teeth of the high-crowned (left) and low-crowned (right) types. A high-crowned tooth, which characterizes all living members of the horse family, is adapted for grinding harsh grasses and grows continuously to offset the constant wear. A low-crowned tooth is adapted for chewing soft, leafy vegetation.

it is notable that rats, mice, and many songbirds feed heavily on the seeds of these plants, and snakes, in turn, consume large numbers of rats, mice, and birds' eggs. Among the other groups of mammals that evolved or radiated markedly during Neogene time, the Bovidae (cattle, antelopes, sheep, and their relatives) have clearly owed much of their success to the spread of grasslands and the expansion of weeds. During Oligocene and Miocene time, before the Bovidae were so prominent, the horse family underwent changes that have been attributed to the vegetational shift. Species of horses with high-crowned cheek teeth that were well adapted to grinding harsh grasses diversified, while there was an attrition of types having low-crowned molars, useful only for browsing rather than grazing—that is, for chewing softer leaves. All living members of the horse family, including zebras and asses, are grazers.

As these climatically driven events have transpired, there has been no biotic crisis that would qualify as a mass extinction by the standards of the great catastrophes of the more distant past. It appears that the shock of the initial climatic changes during the latter part of the Eocene and first part of the Oligocene restructured the ecosystem to such a degree that the residual biotas were for the most part resistant to later events of the new climatic regime. Various biotic elements have suffered extinction in particular regions at particular times during the Neogene Period, but there has been no major crisis on a global scale. Even the Eocene–Oligocene losses added up to only a weak mass extinction.

Although Neogene extinction events have not been spectacular, they arouse great interest for two reasons. First, they are readily accessible for study, being recorded in still-soft sediments via fossils that consist of skeletal remains and other features that are often remarkably well preserved. Second, the Neogene events are, on a geological scale of time, part of our recent history, so that from our perspective they have an immediacy not shared by episodes of the more remote past.

THE MIOCENE EPOCH:
A TIME OF MILD EXTINCTION

A significant restructuring of the oceans took place during middle Miocene time, roughly 14 million years ago. Changes of oxygen isotope ratios in the fossil skeletons of foraminiferans that lived on the deep-sea floor suggest a drop in deep-sea temperatures of perhaps 7 or 8°C. The figure is imprecise because of our perennial problem of not

Rings of glacial debris and diatomaceous sediments on
the sea floor around Antarctica today. Diatoms are especially well adapted to the cool waters adjacent to this
polar continent.

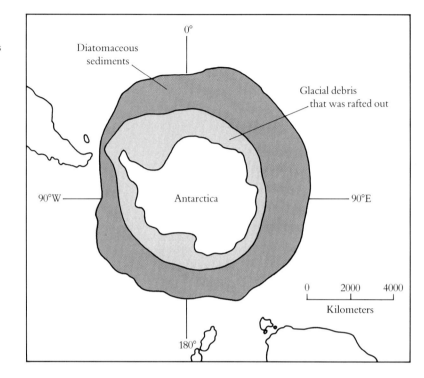

knowing how much of an increase in the oxygen 18 fraction to attribute to cooling and how much to the growth of ice sheets on the land.
Indeed, we know that the east Antarctic ice sheet did expand at this
time, because debris rafted out to sea by glacial ice suddenly appeared
farther from Antarctica than it had previously been carried. This
change signalled a spalling off of more icebergs than before, as more
glacial lobes reached the Antarctic coast. With a greater flux of cold
Antarctic water to the deep sea, there was also an increase in the upwelling of cool water far from the poles. This is manifested in the
fossil record of diatoms, which bloomed in areas like the coastal zone
of California. Shifts in the isotopic and taxonomic composition of
plankton reveal that seas did not cool everywhere, however. At low
latitudes, surface temperatures seem to have increased somewhat.
Thus, there was a steepening of temperature gradients from the poles
to the equator, especially in the Southern Hemisphere. In fact, ice
sheets had not yet expanded in the arctic region of the Northern
Hemisphere. This general pattern of change, in which cooling was not
effectively transmitted to shallow seas (or, presumably, terrestrial cli-

mates) at low latitudes, did not yield generally heavy extinction except in the deep sea, where the changes were, of course, pervasive because Antarctic waters spread across the entire deep-sea floor. Thus, the middle Miocene events were nothing like the great extinctions of earlier times, which almost universally wrought heavy destruction of life in shallow tropical seas.

Cores taken from the deep-sea floor reveal that at the very end of the Miocene Epoch, between 5 and 6 million years ago, there was another expansion of the Antarctic ice cap, as evidenced by a northward spread of the belt of siliceous deep-sea sediments that surrounds Antarctica. This belt results from the great abundance of planktonic diatoms that occupy the cold waters of this region and, upon death, release their siliceous skeletons. The expansion of these sediments at the close of the Miocene Epoch reflects an enlargement of the body of cold water encircling Antarctica, which, in turn, points to an expansion of the Antarctic ice cap. The resulting drop in sea level had an especially profound effect on the Mediterranean Sea, which actually dried up for a geologically brief interval. Apparently what happened was that the connection between the Mediterranean and the Atlantic Ocean disappeared when sea level fell below the sill over which that narrow connection—the Straits of Gibralter—had been (and is again today) maintained. Evidence that the isolated Mediterranean then became desiccated is provided by salt deposits in the center of its basin beneath younger sediments. These were precipitated from the saline waters above as they evaporated and were replenished by only a weak inflow of new water, perhaps much of it from nearby land areas. Deep valleys, cut when the Mediterranean stood at a very low level, have also been discovered beneath large modern rivers such as the Rhone, the Po, and the Nile; in studying the footing for the Aswan Dam, Soviet geologists found a declivity buried beneath the Nile that they judged to rival the Grand Canyon in size.

There appears to have been a minor episode of cooling in the oceans when the Antarctic ice cap expanded at the end of the Miocene, and there appears also to have been some extinction in shallow seas. At this time, however, as during the similar mid-Miocene event, neither life of the sea floor nor plankton experienced heavy losses at the genus or family level. The same can be said for the terrestrial biota. The fluvial (river) deposits of northern Pakistan offer the best evidence here. Having been deposited at the foot of the newly forming Himalayas, where erosion has been rampant, these sediments are remarkably thick and provide a stratigraphic section with only minor gaps. A team led by John Barry of Harvard has traced the occurrence of fossil mammal species through these deposits, finding that there were inter-

Coarse Neogene sediments derived from erosion of the rising Himalayas and deposited in front of these enormous mountains. An excellent fossil record of Miocene mammals is preserved in this region.

vals of rather heavy faunal turnover in early and late Miocene time. These did not constitute major crises, however, and even less extinction took place during the middle Miocene and at the very end of the epoch—the times for which we have evidence of ice cap expansion in Antarctica. In other words, neither the events in Antarctica nor any others during Miocene time were destructive enough on a global scale to cause extinctions of land mammals nearly as severe as those of the Late Eocene and mid-Oligocene crises described in the previous chapter.

THE PLIOCENE EPOCH: THE CALM AND THEN THE STORM

The early Pliocene was an interval of relatively high sea level and warm climates—two conditions that seem to reflect a modest melting back of glaciers. At this time, about 4 million years ago, shallow seas lapped up over parts of southeastern England and in the eastern United States spread inland south of Richmond, Virginia and inundated most of the Florida peninsula. The high sea level and relatively equable climates caused waters harboring temperate molluscan faunas to spread across the Arctic, allowing a number of Pacific species to

Mollusks representing the spectacular early Pliocene molluscan fauna of southern Florida. Most of the species shown here, and most species of the fauna as a whole, died out when the North Atlantic cooled down in the early phases of the modern Ice Age.

migrate into the Atlantic. Temperate faunas recording this biogeographic shift are fossilized in Iceland. The equable conditions are also reflected in a fossil record displaying enormous early Pliocene molluscan faunas along the Atlantic coastal plain and on Caribbean islands. Waters adjacent to the eastern United States alone probably accommodated in the neighborhood of 3000 species. New species are constantly being discovered, and even of those species that have been collected not all have yet been named and described. The number of molluscan species living along the coast of eastern North America during early Pliocene time was considerably larger than the number living here today.

The decline in molluscan diversity since early Pliocene time in both the western Atlantic and Caribbean received little notice until recently. Part of the problem was that early Pliocene faunas included so few species that survive today—about 20 percent—that, in the absence of good dating techniques, they were thought to be of Miocene age or even older. More accurate dating has been achieved by the discovery in western Atlantic sediments of fossil plankton species that occur in other regions where they have been precisely dated and also by the use of radiometric dating of well-preserved corals. Recognizing the early Pliocene age of these faunas, we must now contemplate the remarkable fact that their 20 percent survivorship to the present is far below the survivorship in California and Japan of perhaps 63 percent of early Pliocene bivalve species. Working with Lyle Campbell of the University of South Carolina at Spartanburg, I have concluded that the western Atlantic fauna suffered a severe regional extinction. As evidenced by the faunas of California and Japan, we expect some extinction to occur even in the absence of catastrophic environmental change. Taking the similar histories of California and Japan to represent the incidence of normal losses—background extinction—we can calculate the amount of excessive extinction in the western Atlantic, which is the amount attributable to the sudden pulse of heavy extinction. This method of estimation indicates that this regional crisis eliminated about 66 percent of the early Pliocene bivalve fauna, and similar data reveal that the gastropod fauna was similarly decimated.

Study of the western Atlantic crisis is facilitated by the remarkably complete record of the Pliocene faunas (certainly the great majority of species left a record in the Atlantic coastal plain from Virginia to Florida) and also by the excellent state of preservation of many individual shells—a condition that enhances the quality of taxonomic work. Many of these fossil seashells remain shiny, and a few even display original color patterns.

Focusing on the bivalve species, which are considerably less numerous and more readily identified than the gastropods, I have analyzed the regional crisis in detail. Unfortunately, we lack continuous, or even nearly continuous, stratigraphic sequences in which to discern the precise temporal pattern of extinction. Rather, what we have are fossiliferous formations representing a few intervals between the early Pliocene and the present. These are exposed in stream cuts and artificial pits. Their position above sea level, in the coastal plain, reflects the fact that each was deposited during a high stand of sea level like the one during which the early Pliocene formations came into being. The faunas preserved in these units reveal a progressive impoverishment of the bivalve fauna. A few new species have been added, but in general each successive fauna is a subset of the previous one. In Florida, workers who have studied the 4-million-year-old early Pliocene fauna as well as faunas about 2 million, 1 million, and 125,000 years old have found this kind of progressive impoverishment. The two youngest faunas represent interglacial intervals of the Pleistocene, an epoch when episodes of glacial advance took place about every 100,000 years; as currently defined, the Pleistocene Epoch began about 1.8 million years ago.

The heavy extinction in the western Atlantic had ended by the time of the last interglacial interval, about 125,000 years ago; faunas of this age consist almost exclusively of still-living species. We can conclude that whatever agent or agents caused the heavy extinction had ceased to operate by this time or that the remaining species were somehow immune to their effects. The latter hypothesis is favored by the fact that the timing of the extinctions points strongly to a cause associated with continental glaciation in the Northern Hemisphere. Not only did the Ice Age begin at the end of early Pliocene time—about the time of the first wave of heavy extinction—but the most recent glacial interval, called the Wisconsin in North America and the Riss-Würm in Europe, took place later than 125,000 years ago without causing appreciable extinction.

Given the circumstantial association of the faunal crisis with early phases of the Ice Age, we are led immediately to focus on two possible causes: cooling of temperatures and lowering of sea level. The two causes would be expected to operate on very different geographic scales, and this offers us a way to test them against each other. Sea level was lowered globally during glacial episodes, offering the prediction that heavy extinction should likewise have occurred around the world. As exemplified by the fact that California and Japan escaped heavy extinction, the sea level hypothesis fails the test. Is it possible that when the sea dropped to a level near the edge of the continental shelf of eastern North America, there were fewer refuges for mollusks than along the rugged margin of California? This was certainly not a major factor in the differential survival of mollusks along the two coasts. In the western Atlantic, even bivalve species of small body size that were represented by huge populations inhabiting muddy sediments suffered very heavy extinction; reduced area of sea floor could not have eliminated such species because they thrive in vast numbers in muddy lagoons, which certainly existed during low stands of sea level. Furthermore, even western Atlantic species that were geographically widespread experienced much higher rates of extinction than species that were narrowly distributed along the California coast.

In sharp contrast, the geographic pattern of extinction conforms to the predictions of the cooling hypothesis. The Atlantic Ocean north of the equator was bordered by the three great continental ice sheets of the Northern Hemisphere: the Canadian (centered over Hudson Bay), the Greenland, and the Scandinavian. Marginal glaciers would be expected to have had much less impact on the vast Pacific ocean. This prediction is borne out by the results of CLIMAP, an international project designed to map the surface temperatures of the world's oceans during the peak of the most recent glacial episode, about 18,000 years ago. The equatorial Pacific experienced quite minor cooling at this time when compared to modern conditions (which can be taken to approximate those of a typical interglacial interval). On the

The North Atlantic Ocean during the most recent glacial advance, 18,000 years ago. The major oceanic
gyre, part of which is labeled the Gulf Stream, was
cooled by temperatures in the north.

other hand, the western Atlantic did cool substantially, and in the
central Caribbean mean February temperature was lower than today
by some 4°C. In addition, paleobotanical evidence points to severe
climatic cooling along the eastern margin of the United States. The
pollen record reveals that spruce trees, now confined to northern New
England, lived as far south as Georgia. Florida apparently had a temperate climate.

Such severe cooling took place during glacial intervals of the Pleistocene Epoch, but the climate began to deteriorate at the end of early
Pliocene time. Study of deep-sea cores from the northern Atlantic by a
large team led by Nicholas Shackleton of Cambridge University has
revealed that coarse grains were beginning to drop from melting icebergs about 3.2 million years ago, and this is taken to represent the

time when continental ice sheets began to expand. Isotopic shifts indicate another pulse of cooling about 2.5 million years ago, but even this did not yield conditions as cold as those of the Pleistocene Epoch. The thermal changes in the far north are dramatically displayed in the rock record of Iceland. Here temperate molluscan faunas are present in early Pliocene strata, but they give way rather abruptly to coarse sediments deposited by glaciers.

The pattern of extinction within the western Atlantic molluscan fauna to the south points to a dominant role for climatic cooling. We cannot reconstruct the temperature tolerances of all early Pliocene species, but we can examine the tolerances of species that survived the crisis to populate modern seas. The critical place to look is southern Florida, where the climate today is marginally tropical and during early Pliocene time was slightly warmer. In tropical seas anywhere, some species are purely tropical—they are unable to live outside the tropical zone—while others possess broader thermal tolerances which permit them to range into subtropical, or even temperate, zones. It is quite revealing to examine in this light the 57 early Pliocene bivalve species that have survived from the tropical zone of southern Florida. As it turns out, every one of these species today ranges into temperate waters, occurring at least as far north as the Carolinas or around the Gulf Coast to Texas. This situation reveals that a "thermal filter" operated during the mass extinction: All the strictly tropical species of Florida disappeared.

It might seem strange that even early Pliocene faunas that lived along the coast of Virginia suffered heavy extinction. In fact, there was nearly total extinction of species that were restricted to this region. Why did these species not simply migrate southward during intervals of cooling, along with the thermal regime to which they were adapted? The answer is provided by ostracods, small bivalved crustaceans that have left an excellent fossil record studied by Joseph Hazel of the United States Geological Survey. Those ostracod species that have survived from early Pliocene seas of Virginia are restricted to a narrow range of temperature conditions; the Early Pliocene waters in which they lived apparently ranged only from about 14°C in winter to 21°C in summer. In comparison, shallow waters in this region today experience oscillations between about 4 and 24°C. The much greater seasonality today explains why migration was not an option for many bivalve species as seas began to cool down in mid-Pliocene time. Species that were adapted to a narrow range of temperatures could tolerate neither the cold winters nor the hot summers of late Pliocene time, and they could not migrate to the south because summers here were even warmer.

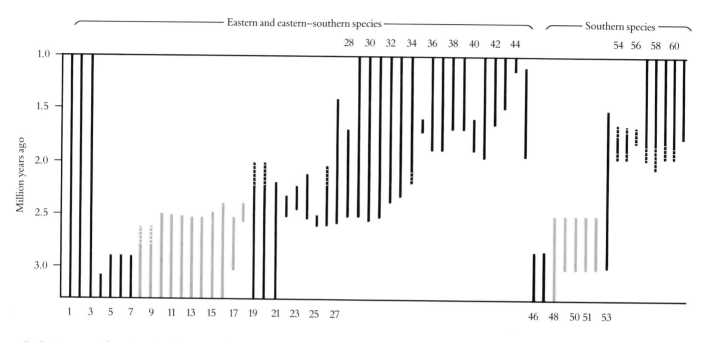

Geologic ranges of species of antelopes in Africa south of the Sahara, showing that numerous species (colored bars) died out about 2.5 million years ago, when the climate changed.

Another interesting pattern relates to the different times that bivalve species died out in the western Atlantic. Most of the victims that had been restricted to a narrow geographic zone and were thus apparently tolerant of only a narrow range of temperature conditions died out early, during late Pliocene time. Probably modest cooling and increased seasonality were responsible. In contrast, most of the victims that had occupied a broader range of latitudes and thus possessed greater thermal tolerance died out later, during the more severe climatic deterioration of the Pleistocene. Working with Sergio Raffi and Rafaella Marasti of the University of Parma in Italy, I have studied the Ice Age extinction of mollusks in the Mediterranean and North Sea. Warm-adapted species of those regions had better escape routes to the south, so the toll was less heavy. Many species that had lived in the North Sea survived in the warmer Mediterranean during glacial intervals, and many species that had lived in the Mediterranean survived along the Atlantic coast of Africa.

The initial impact of the climatic change of the Ice Age on terrestrial faunas is especially evident in Africa, where Elisabeth Vrba of Yale University has found that a large number of antelope species disappeared about 2.5 million years ago. Recall that this was a time

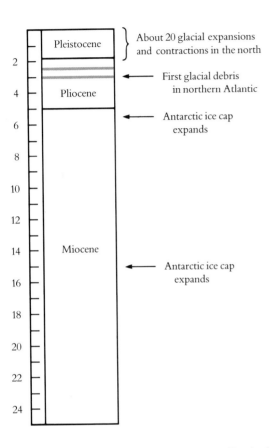

Major events of Neogene time. Severe cooling in the Northern Hemisphere began about 3 million years ago, or a bit earlier.

when there was a pulse of cooling in the North Atlantic. Vrba's conclusion is that climates simultaneously became cooler and drier in Africa, and this is corroborated by the evidence of fossil pollen.

While evidence does not exist of global mass extinction during the Pliocene–Pleistocene interval of climatic deterioration, it is significant that during this time there was a marked increase in the rate of extinction of planktonic foraminiferans, resulting in a substantial drop in the total diversity of this group.

THE DISAPPEARANCE OF ICE SHEETS AND LARGE MAMMALS

Our picture of mammalian extinctions during the Pleistocene Epoch and its immediate aftermath is less detailed than one might expect. The reason for this is that, although Pleistocene mammalian fossils are often of high quality because of their relative youth, the record of mammals is fragmentary: The frequent environmental changes have caused faunas to migrate as glaciers, forests, and grasslands have expanded and contracted or shifted from place to place. As a result, we have nothing like the detailed picture of times of appearance and extinction that is being constructed for Miocene mammals from the fossil record at the foot of the Himalayas, where nearly continuous deposition has worked to the advantage of paleontology. The fragmented nature of the Pleistocene fossil record hinders comparisons with earlier segments of the mammalian record. It is not clear, for example, exactly how severe extinction was during Pleistocene time in comparison to its intensity during earlier geologic intervals. Particularly difficult is the tracking of Pleistocene species through time. In many cases it is not known whether a particular species experienced true extinction or simply evolved enough to be recognized as a new species—a younger one separated from the first by a gap in the fossil record.

Work at the level of the genus, nonetheless, has proved rewarding. S. David Webb of the University of Florida has concluded that the generic record of North American mammals displays six major pulses of extinction since the beginning of late Miocene time, about 10 million years ago. The first occurred about 9 million years ago, and the most recent reached its peak of severity only about 11,000 years ago. This last crisis, which will be discussed in some detail, has been the subject of great controversy; it is remarkable for having affected large mammals almost exclusively, eliminating about 39 North American genera. The most severe of the six pulses identified by Webb is dated

Imperial mammoth and American mastodon, two behemoths that suffered extinction near the end of Pleistocene time. The small ears and woolly fur of the latter, known from rare frozen carcasses, were adaptations to the cold temperatures of the Ice Age.

at approximately 5 million years, which places it more-or-less at the Miocene–Pliocene boundary; this event swept away about 62 genera, almost two-thirds of them being of large body size. The history of the horse family in North America exemplifies the general pattern of the late Neogene mammalian extinctions. Ten million years ago at least 10 genera of horses were present, and this number declined to zero by the end of Pleistocene time via a series of six extinction events. Only the Spaniards' reintroduction of the horse accounts for its presence in the New World today.

Webb has favored late Neogene climatic deterioration as the cause of most of the mammalian extinctions, but acknowledges the possibility that humans had a hand in those that took place about 11,000 years ago. The question whether climatic change or human disturbance (primarily predation) was the primary agent of this final pulse of heavy extinction has been widely debated. A unique feature of this crisis, which occurred as the earth emerged from its most recent interval of glacial expansion, is that it selectively removed large mammals from the ecosystem, leaving a depauperate fauna in our modern world. Before this impoverishment, there were beavers the size of

Giant wombat (top) of the Australian Pleistocene. This animal's skull was about 40 centimeters (about 16 inches) in length. Clovis spear point between the ribs of a victim (bottom), a bison killed by Clovis hunters in the American West.

bears, bisons whose horns spread to nearly 2 meters (about 6 feet), ground sloths 6 meters (20 feet) tall, elephants and lions that dwarfed those of the present day, and a host of other forms that were by our standards gigantic. The extinction of large mammals occurred throughout the globe—even in Australia, where most of the victims, including giant kangaroos, were marsupials. The lowest incidence of extinction on a large landmass is recorded for Africa, where only about eight genera disappeared.

One of the most salient features of this most recent round of extinctions was its timing. In North and South America the majority of extinctions seem to have been tightly clustered at about 11,000 years ago, whereas in Australia they began earlier, perhaps as long ago as 30,000 years. In Europe, most of the extinctions occurred close to 11,000 years ago, but here they were spread over a longer time interval than most of those in North America. In Africa, where extinctions were fewer, they are also less well dated. The relatively high precision of the dating for many extinctions of the past 50,000 years or so comes from the short half-life of carbon 14; carbon dating is the source of virtually all dates for the extinction events in question. Where uncertainty of timing does exist, it is generally attributable to the absence of appropriate materials for dating or to a sparse fossil record. Where fossils are few there is no assurance that the youngest dated individual or population was indeed among the last to exist.

The idea that human activities were the dominant agent of the large mammal extinctions has focused on human hunting and is known as the overkill hypothesis. This idea is inherently reasonable because species of large body size typically have relatively small populations and also find it difficult to hide. As formulated by its foremost proponent, Paul Martin of the University of Arizona, the overkill hypothesis proposes that as human hunters with advanced Stone Age weapons spread throughout the world, they demolished big game and continued to migrate in pursuit of abundant prey.

According to a special case of the overkill scenario known as the blitzkrieg hypothesis, the extirpation was extremely rapid, with hunting parties sweeping away populations almost instantaneously, on a geological scale of time, owing in part to the fact that the victims, like the famous dodo birds of the island of Mauritius, were unwary of humans. Particularly amenable to the blitzkrieg model are the large mammals of the Americas, so many of which disappeared very close to 11,000 years ago.

Any overkill scenario must position effective human hunters in Australia much earlier than this. Although there seems to be abundant

Shasta ground sloth. This large herbivore, descended from a species that migrated from South America, inhabited western North America during the Pleistocene and died out suddenly, about 11,000 years ago.

evidence of occupation as far back as 30,000 years or so, this overkill idea has been attacked with the claim that archaeological evidence fails to demonstrate that the ancient Australian aborigines were any more effective as big game hunters than their living descendants, who do not pursue large prey effectively in large, well-armed groups. On the other hand, tending to support the overkill idea is the rapid human extermination of mammals on small islands much more recently than 11,000 years ago—because humans occupied many small islands only recently. Nonetheless, much of the extinction on islands has resulted from deforestation and other forms of habitat destruction rather than from hunting. The weaponry deemed responsible for the lethal attack on large continental mammals 11,000 years ago is that of the Clovis people of the western United States, whose hunting and butchering sites reveal that they slew giant bison and other large mammals with lances and perhaps stone-tipped missiles launched from throwing sticks.

Over the years, the overkill hypothesis has been pitted chiefly against the assertion that climatic changes swept away the large mammals. The timing in the Americas is appropriate for the climatic hypothesis, in the sense that the last glacial interval ended in many areas between about 12,000 and 10,000 years ago. Opponents, however, point out that the last glacial interval was only one of about 20 that occurred during the Pleistocene Epoch. Why, then, should the most recent glacial episode have had so severe an effect on large mammals? The retort is that the most recent episode was the most severe, or, more particularly, that it ended with the onset of climatic seasonality that was exceptionally severe; in North America, the heavy extinction took place at about the time of glacial withdrawal, which may have introduced climatic instability.

One criticism of the climatic hypothesis is based on the claim that it should predict the demise of small species along with large ones. This prediction is not certain, however, and often cited in favor of the climatic hypothesis is the fact that at the time of extinction, a number of the species that survived underwent dwarfing. This may indicate that vegetational changes worked against large animals. Arthur Phillips of the University of Arizona has cited the specific example of the extinction of the Shasta ground sloth in his opposition to the idea that climate universally played the dominant role in the crisis. This cave-dwelling animal left dung in caverns up to almost exactly 11,000 years ago, and the composition of the fossilized dung reveals a preferred diet of desert plants. Packrat middens from the western Grand Canyon reveal that both desert and woodland plants flourished here at the time when the Shasta ground sloth disappeared, indicating that a varied menu was available and that climatically induced vegetational changes were not responsible for the sloth's sudden demise.

Possibly both hunting and climatic change contributed to the crisis for large mammals, but many participants in the controversy tend to favor one hypothesis or the other. The debate continues.

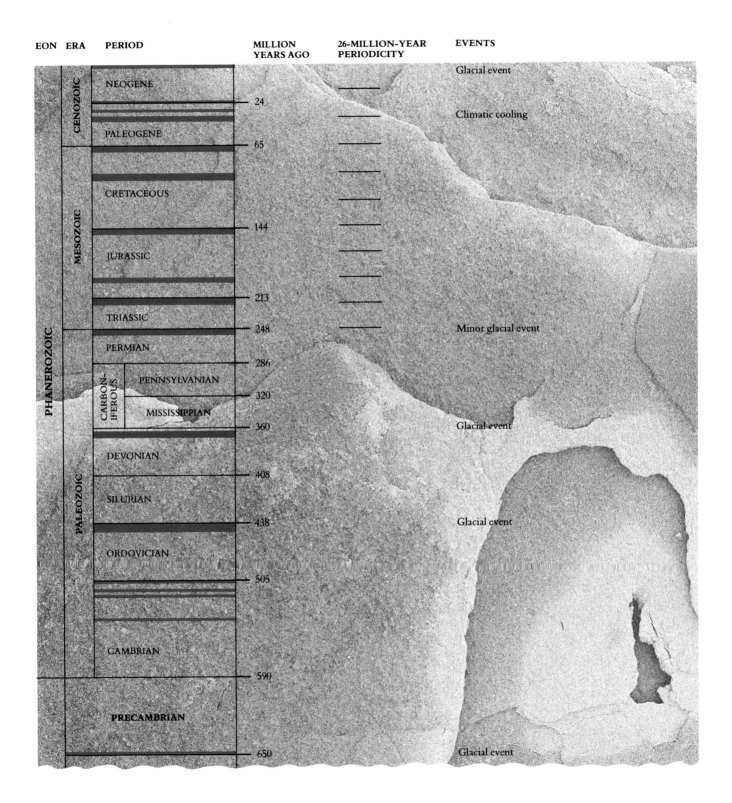

EON	ERA	PERIOD		MILLION YEARS AGO	26-MILLION-YEAR PERIODICITY	EVENTS
	CENOZOIC	NEOGENE		24		Glacial event
		PALEOGENE		65		Climatic cooling
	MESOZOIC	CRETACEOUS		144		
		JURASSIC		213		
		TRIASSIC		248		Minor glacial event
	PALEOZOIC	PERMIAN		286		
		CARBON-IFEROUS	PENNSYLVANIAN	320		
			MISSISSIPPIAN	360		Glacial event
		DEVONIAN		408		
		SILURIAN		438		Glacial event
		ORDOVICIAN		505		
		CAMBRIAN		590		
		PRECAMBRIAN		650		Glacial event

PHANEROZOIC

10 AN OVERVIEW

The dominant theme of this book has been that climatic change, although by no means the only factor in mass extinction, has been the most important one. For the marine realm, the possible agent most commonly placed in competition with climatic change is the reduction of sea-floor area by lowering of sea level. Testifying against a major role for the latter are such conditions as the presence of huge faunas on small areas of sea floor in the modern world and the failure of major episodes of sea-level lowering to cause heavy marine extinction at several times in the past. Neither the major drop near the end of Early Ordovician time nor the one in mid-Oligocene time, which may have been the most severe of all time, was accompanied by significant losses of bottom-dwelling marine life.

THE CASE FOR CLIMATE: A RECAPITULATION

One of the most significant traits of biotic crises has been their tendency to strike simultaneously in the sea and on the land. This correspondence is predicted by most models of mass extinction that assign a dominant role to climatic change because climatic change tends to affect both marine and terrestrial ecosystems. During the past few years we have uncovered firm evidence of glacial episodes or other signs of climatic change at the times of many of the major extinction events, including those of Late Precambrian, Late Ordovician, Late Devonian, Late Cretaceous, and Late Eocene age, and there is nothing to rule out climatic deterioration for any of the other crisis intervals.

Another salient trait of most mass extinctions is the protracted and often pulsatile nature of their timing. Many of these crises were composite events that encompassed several million years. Although it is

possible to invoke the sudden impact on earth of a large extraterrestrial object to explain losses at the very end of the Cretaceous Period,
the total mass extinction occupied several million years, during
which, according to both isotopic (ratio of oxygen 18 to oxygen 16)
and paleobotanical evidence, there was a general trend of climatic
cooling. Similarly, although there is some evidence that a bolide
shower may have erased a few planktonic species in Late Eocene time,
isotopic and paleobotanical evidence reveal that at this time terrestrial
climates experienced a general cooling trend, and a variety of evidence
demonstrates that the deep sea cooled to a near-freezing level, where it
has remained to the present day; the negative effect of the general
cooling trend on many biotas is well established.

Important to our assessment of extraterrestrial causation of mass
extinctions is a recent assertion of Carl Orth and his coworkers at the
Los Alamos National Laboratory, where numerous reliable iridium
analyses have been carried out. These authors have concluded that
there is no case for a significant iridium anomaly at any mass extinction level in the stratigraphic record below the terminal Cretaceous
boundary. Perhaps the strong iridium anomaly at the top of the Cretaceous System is indeed anomalous! This would relegate bolide impacts to at most a minor role in the history of Phanerozoic life.

THE QUESTION OF PERIODICITY

In 1977 Alfred Fischer and Michael Arthur, then both at Princeton
University, proposed that the pattern of mass extinctions during Mesozoic and Cenozoic time suggests that such events may occur regu-
larly, at intervals of about 32 million years. This yielded a dire prediction, because at that time the Late Eocene event was seen as having
occurred about halfway between the terminal Cretaceous event and
the present; the implication was that we should now be entering another crisis interval. The general notion of periodicity has a more
fundamental implication. This is that mass extinctions have an extraterrestrial explanation because it is only astronomical causes that seem
capable of following such a precise schedule: Not only do planets and
smaller bodies rotate around stars with regular timing, but our solar
system adheres to a periodicity in passing through the spiral arms of
the Milky Way. At present, we have no reason to believe that any
earthly cause should behave in a similarly periodic manner.

More recently, David Raup and John Sepkoski of the University of
Chicago have suggested that the clock be reset. Their assertion is that
a periodicity of 26 million years has obtained from Late Permian time

Distribution of crises in the history of marine life during the past 270 million years. These plots, for families (above) and genera (below), reveal times when the percentage of extinction was so high in comparison to earlier and later times that Raup and Sepkoski have judged them to represent mass extinctions (vertical bars indicate the ranges of uncertainty for percentages). Two of these intervals are taken to constitute a single crisis.

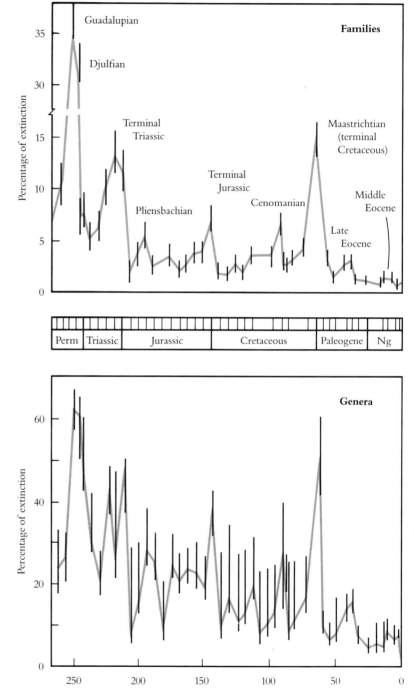

to the present, with the most recent crisis having occurred about 11 million years ago. The initial analysis of Raup and Sepkoski, which they have since expanded, was based on a compilation of the stratigraphic occurrences of families of marine organisms. Originally these authors focused on all peaks in a graph representing the incidence of family-level extinction since mid-Permian time. In the absence of more precise information about timing, they treated each family whose extinction is recorded in a formally recognized geologic age as if it became extinct during the geologic "moment" at the end of the age. They constructed their total graph from the incidences of extinction for 39 such moments. The rising and falling of the rate of extinction formed a series of peaks in the graph. Some of these peaks, including the one representing the end of the Cretaceous Period, coincided with recognized mass extinctions. Others did not. Raup and Sepkoski nonetheless treated the peaks as representing crisis intervals, and they found that these peaks approached 26-million-year periodicity more closely than periodicity of any other wavelength. They further found that the peaks on the graph were positioned closer to peaks exactly 26 million years apart than was at all likely to happen in a system in which the rate of extinction rose and fell randomly, in other words followed a random walk.

The idea of periodicity remains controversial. One complaint has been that the dates employed are demonstrably imperfect because new, and presumably in most cases more accurate, dates for age boundaries are continually being published. Raup and Sepkoski's response is, first, that they have employed more than one published time scale without losing the pattern and, second, that imperfections in the time scale, being essentially random, should weaken rather than strengthen any real periodicity.

Antoni Hoffman of Poland has noted that in a random walk—a system in which the chance that the next step will move up or move down is 50/50—the most probable distance between peaks would be four steps in the temporal sequence; then, given the fact that an average age spanned slightly more than 6 million years, there should automatically be a high percentage of peaks at about 26 (equal to 4 times 6+ million years). Thus, Hoffman has asserted, the finding that many adjacent peaks are about 26 million years apart is not surprising. Stephen Gould of Harvard University has countered that this is, nonetheless, a far cry from Raup and Sepkoski's claim of an extinction peak precisely every 26 million years. It is true that Hoffman's mechanism for pseudoperiodicity is not as strong as he seems to have asserted. On the other hand, the empirical plot does not, in fact, display a significant peak every 26 million years. Three of the peaks in Raup and

Differing time scales that have been proposed for the Jurassic Period in recent years, based on different sets of data, methods of dating, and interpretations. Note that the end of the Pliensbachian Age, where a mass extinction has been recognized by some workers, has been assigned an age as young as 178 million years and as old as 195 million years.

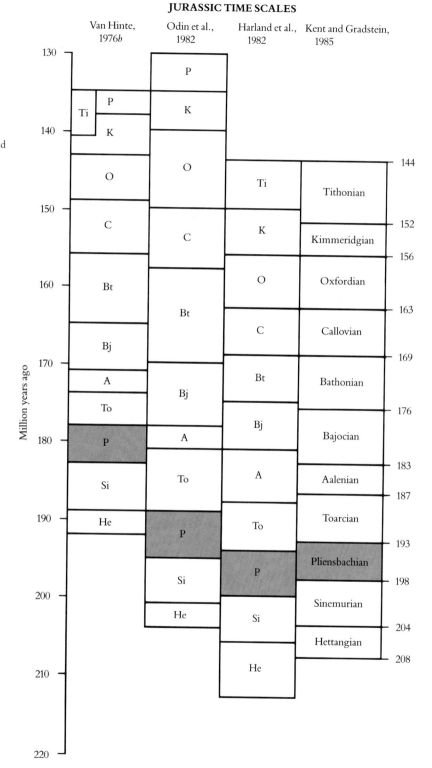

JURASSIC TIME SCALES

Sepkoski's original plot (two that were associated with the same predicted peak) were only marginally above background levels, and these authors have more recently acknowledged that these are not statistically significant peaks.

The discarding of three extinction peaks leads to a perplexing problem. Raup and Sepkoski have continued to test the significant peaks that are present at both the family and the genus level and still assert that they are closer to the peaks of a fitted 26-million-year cycle than is likely to occur by chance. The problem is that, with two predicted peaks missing, there are two intervals in the empirical distribution that are each approximately 50 million years in length. These are the two contiguous intervals that precede the terminal Cretaceous event. Looking backward beyond them, one encounters a different kind of problem, fully acknowledged by Raup and Sepkoski. This is a problem of dating. Not only is there substantial uncertainty about the ages of rocks representing the Late Triassic and Late Permian epochs, but it is not clear where within either interval a peak of extinction should be recognized. Heavy extinction has been attributed to both the Norian and Rhaetian ages of the Late Triassic, but it is considered possible that the two "intervals" overlapped each other substantially. For the Late Permian event, similar, very heavy levels of extinction have been recorded for the penultimate Guadalupian and ultimate Djulfian ages. As noted in Chapter 4, although it has been suggested that the poor exposure of Djulfian rocks may have caused us erroneously to attribute some Djulfian extinctions to the Guadalupian, many apparent Guadelupian extinctions must be real. This argument can be made especially for groups such as fusulinid foraminifers and bryozoans that, when present, are extremely abundant and readily recognized through microscopic examination of rocks; both groups were decimated before the end of Guadalupian time.

What all of this means is that there is not evidence of tight adherance to a 26-million-year periodicity for the interval that extends back some 140 million years from the end of the Cenomanian interval of the Late Cretaceous: there are only four rather than six significant peaks, and at present a strong case for proximity to a predicted peak can be made for only two of these, the late Pliensbachian and the late Tithonian peaks of the Jurassic Period. Furthermore, as noted in Chapter 6 of this book, Anthony Hallam, an expert on Jurassic faunas, has concluded that the Pliensbachian event was not global in scale but restricted to western Europe.

On the other hand, there is little chance that new evidence, including revised dating, will shift the position of the terminal Cretaceous and late Eocene peaks enough to move the duration of the intervening interval very far from 26 million years. There is, however, increased support for a date of about 66.5 million years ago, as opposed to 65, for the end of the Cretaceous (Maastrichtian Age) and of 36.5 million years ago, as opposed to 38, for the end of the Eocene. These modifications yield an estimate of 30 million years, rather than 27, for the interval in between. It should also be recalled that, although the scheme of Raup and Sepkoski assigns all extinctions that occurred during a given age to the end of the age, the Maastrichtian crisis actually began before the end of Maastrichtian time, and the next crisis began before the end of the late Eocene. These facts do not disprove periodicity for the mass extinctions of the last 100 million years, but they do raise important questions. The event alleged to have occurred at the end of middle Miocene time (close to 11 million years ago) also poses problems. There was no real crisis for planktonic foraminiferans at this time—nothing like the substantial decline that occurred during the past 3 million years (the recent glacial interval), and, as we have seen, there is no evidence of heavy mammalian extinctions on the land. For only five marine families is there good evidence of extinction during middle Miocene time, although these were undoubtedly joined by a few others whose demise is not well dated. At the species level, the deep sea may have been the site of the most significant biotic turnover of the middle Miocene interval, and we have evidence that it may also have become markedly cooler at this time.

Raup and Sepkoski's statistical test of periodicity does not demonstrate that the spacing of extinctions closely approximates a 26-million-year cyclicity, but only that the spacing is closer to this than would usually be expected for a random pattern. One possible source of the observed distribution could have been a tendency for certain conditions to reduce the expected number of short intervals between crises, rendering the distribution nonrandom. In particular, the survivors of a crisis interval and their immediate descendants may have been resistant to a second pulse of environmental deterioration following closely upon one that caused the crisis; perhaps it took some time for a large number of new vulnerable families to evolve. In this light, it should be recalled that organic reefs remained weakly developed after a number of mass extinctions. The effect of long recovery intervals would be to space out episodes of heavy extinction. Employing a rigorous mathematical analysis, Jennifer Kitchell of the University of Michigan and Daniel Pena of the University of Wisconsin have suggested a similar source of pseudoperiodicity.

One corollary of the periodicity concept that has received little attention despite its great import is the implication that every significant peak in the Mesozoic–Cenozoic extinction curve is attributable to a single kind of extraterrestrial cause: If every peak forms part of the periodic array, then it must be attributed to the periodic agent. The attribution of all the major crises to such causation would call into question many of the observations and arguments advanced in this book. Do we really need to invoke an extraterrestrial cause for the event that occurred during the latter part of the Eocene Epoch, for example, when we know that at this time both deep-sea waters and terrestrial climates became cold (and remained so to the present)—and when we have a potential earthly explanation for these events in the form of the isolation of Antarctica over the South Pole via the final fragmentation of a large segment of Gondwanaland? Perhaps one might attribute the long-lasting thermal changes to an extraterrestrial triggering mechanism that destabilized Antarctic glaciers in the direction of growth: When an ice cap expands a bit, it tends to expand still further because of increased reflectance of sunlight, and this yields still greater reflectance and continued growth. Even so, it is asking a great deal of something like a brief celestial darkening to yield gross thermal changes that persist for nearly 40 million years. Recall that we also have powerful evidence for tectonically induced climatic causation for at least two earlier, more devastating mass extinctions, those of Late Ordovician and Late Devonian time—two intervals when Gondwanaland moved over the South Pole and accumulated large continental glaciers.

ASTRONOMERS COME DOWN TO EARTH

Hampered by a dearth of evidence, attempts to relate cratering of the earth to mass extinctions have raised the possibility that cratering may have been periodic but not associated with the timing of mass extinctions. Even in the absence of a strong link between cratering and extinctions, astronomers have postulated mechanisms for periodic bombardment of the earth. The astronomical hypotheses constructed to explain a 26-million-year periodicity include perturbation of comets or other bodies—the dislodging of comets from their normal orbits, leading to their collision with the earth. This might happen either during the periodic passage of the solar system through the spiral arms of the Milky Way or during the periodic oscillation of the solar system in its orbital motion through the galaxy. Both of these movements expose comets of the solar system to gravitational disruption by other large bodies. Alternative models invoke the periodic disturbance of the comet cloud at the outer reaches of the solar system either by a hypothetical dark and therefore unseen companion star to the sun or by a similarly hypothetical tenth planet of giant proportions.

Ironically, earthly concentrations of iridium, which first led scientists to seek unearthly causes for mass extinction, are now being cited in opposition to hypotheses that entail periodic extraterrestrial causes. These hypotheses have focused on comet showers as the agents of destruction. Frank Kyte and John Wasson of the University of California at Los Angeles have noted that each of these hypothetical comet showers would have increased the total flux of iridium from extraterrestrial sources for a time ranging from 1 to 3 million years. Searching for evidence of increased iridium concentrations, these geochemists have measured iridium concentrations in a deep-sea core from the Pacific Ocean that represented the interval from slightly before the terminal Cretaceous extinction to about 33 million years ago (slightly after the heavy late Eocene extinctions). The vertical intervals between the samples within the total core represent, on average, not much more than 200,000 years. Such tightly spaced sampling could not fail to uncover high concentrations resulting from an increased flux that lasted from 1 to 3 million years, and yet no high concentrations have been found—not even for the interval of the core representing late Eocene time, when we know that heavy extinction occurred on the land and in the sea. Periodic comet showers heavy enough to disrupt the ecosystem seem to be ruled out for this key interval of time.

Furthermore, in reviewing the astronomical hypotheses for earthly crises, Sepkoski and Raup note that they are all of the ad hoc variety. Two invoke unknown celestial bodies (an invisible star and a tenth planet), none offers independent evidence in favor of a 26-million-year cyclicity, and none explains why two extinction peaks should be lacking. Until such a cyclicity is convincingly demonstrated for mass extinctions, there would seem to be little justification for inventing such astronomical scenarios.

On the other hand, as long as we are making headway in our analyses of patterns of extinction in relation to both terrestrial and extraterrestrial events, our efforts in the realm of geology should move forward. During the past decade, progress in this arena has been nothing short of astounding. Fifteen years ago, the Cambrian, Ordovician, Devonian, and late Eocene crises, among others, had gone largely unnoticed; the inception of a glacial episode in Late Devonian time first came to light as recently as 1985; and only during the past decade have stratigraphers elucidated patterns of sea-level change well

enough to force us to dismiss the idea of a close correspondence between the timing of major events of sea-level lowering and the timing
of marine mass extinctions. More generally, it can be said that within
the past decade most of the facts and ideas described in this book
emerged from the record of rocks and fossils. Given the foundation
now in place, discoveries of the next decade should build an impressive structure of understanding. With this understanding of what preceded us on earth will come a clearer picture of what may be our fate
and that of life around us.

REFERENCES

Alvarez, L. W., 1983. "Experimental Evidence that an Asteroid Impact Led to the Extinction of Many Species 65 Million Years Ago." *Proceeding of the National Academy of Sciences* 80:627–642
> A provocative brief for the idea that an asteroid impact caused the terminal Cretaceous crisis, by an author of the idea.

Alvarez, W., E. G. Kauffman, F. Surlyk, L. W. Alvarez, F. Asaro, and H. V. Michel, 1984. "Impact Theory of Mass Extinctions and the Invertebrate Fossil Record." *Science* 223:1135–1141.
> A collaboration between the Alvarez group and two invertebrate paleontologists, acknowledging that many Late Cretaceous extinctions in the marine realm were of a gradual nature.

Anstey, R. L., 1978. "Taxonomic Survivorship and Morphologic Complexity in Paleozoic Bryozoan Genera." *Paleobiology* 4:407–418.
> Analysis showing that the types of ancient "moss animals" most heavily affected by mass extinctions differed from those most heavily affected by extinction during normal intervals.

Arthur, M. A., J. C. Zachos, and D. S. Jones, 1986. "Primary Productivity and the Cretaceous/Tertiary Boundary Event in the Oceans." *Cretaceous Research* (in press).
> Suggestion that plankton-feeding marine taxa suffered more than deposit-feeders in the Late Cretaceous crisis because the plankton experienced heavy losses.

Aubry, M.-P., 1983. "Late Eocene and Early Oligocene Calcareous Nannoplankton Biostratigraphy and Biogeography." *American Association of Petroleum Geologists Bulletin* 67:415.
> An abstract summarizing the stepwise extinction of tropical species of calcareous nannoplankton during late Eocene and early Oligocene time and the equatorward migration of species from high latitudes.

Bakker, R. T., 1975. "Dinosaur Renaissance." *Scientific American* 232 (April): 58–78
> Argument for the case that dinosaurs were highly active, "warm-blooded" animals.

Bakker, R. T., 1977. "Tetrapod Mass Extinctions—A Model of the Regulation of Speciation Rates and Immigration by Cycles of Topographic Diversity." In A. Hallam, ed., *Patterns of Evolution,* pp. 439–468. Amsterdam: Elsevier.
> Valuable summary of mass extinction patterns for mammal-like reptiles and dinosaurs.

Bakker, R. T., 1980. "Dinosaur Heresy—Dinosaur Renaissance. Why We Need Endothermic Archosaurs for a Comprehensive Theory of Bioenergetic Evolution." In R. D. K. Thomas and E. C. Olson, eds., *A Cold Look at Warm-blooded Dinosaurs,* pp. 351–503. Boulder, Colorado: Westview.
> A multifaceted argument that dinosaurs were "warm-blooded."

Barry, J. C., N. M. Johnson, S. M. Raza, and L. L. Jacobs, 1985. "Neogene Mammalian Faunal Change in Southern Asia: Correlations with Climatic, Tectonic, and Eustatic Events." *Geology* 13:637–640.
> A review of the patterns of extinction of mammals south of the Himalayas during Miocene time.

Benson, R. H., 1975. "The Origin of the Psychrosphere as Recorded in Changes of Deep-Sea Ostracode Assemblages." *Lethaia* 8:69–83.
> The initial article demonstrating that the near-freezing temperatures of the modern deep sea developed during the Eocene–Oligocene transition.

Berggen, W. A., and J. A. Van Couvering, eds., 1984. *Catastrophes and Earth History.* Princeton: Princeton University Press.
> A collection of interesting essays, some of which unfortunately were partly out of date before publication.

Berry, W. B., and A. J. Boucot, 1973. "Glacial-Eustatic Control of Late Ordovician–Early Silurian Platform Sedimentation and Faunal Changes." *Geological Society of America Bulletin* 84:275–284.
> A review of the kinds of marine animals and sediments found throughout the world after the Late Ordovician glaciation and mass extinction.

Bohor, B. F., E. E. Foord, P. J. Modreski, and D. M. Triplehorn, 1984. "Mineralogic Evidence for an Impact Event at the Cretaceous– Tertiary Boundary." *Science* 224:867–869.
> Announcement of the discovery of shocked mineral grains in Cretaceous boundary clay in Montana.

Bohor, B. F., P. J. Modreski, and E. E. Foord, 1985. "A Search for Shock-Metamorphosed Quartz at the K–T Boundary." *Sixteenth Lunar and Planetary Science Conference* (Lunar and Planetary Institute, Houston), Part 1, p. 79.
> Report of the discovery of latest Cretaceous shocked quartz grains outside of North America.

Caputo, M. V., 1985. "Late Devonian Glaciation in South America," *Palaeogeography, Palaeoclimatology, Palaeoecology* 51:291–317
> Documentation of glaciation at a time of major mass extinction.

Caputo, M. V., and J. C. Crowell, 1985. "Migration of Glacial Centers across Gondwana during Paleozoic Era." *Geological Society of America Bulletin* 96:1020–1036.

First report of the growth of glaciers during Late Devonian (Famennian) time in South America, which was the part of Gondwanaland that moved over the South Pole at this time of biotic crisis.

Carter, N. L., C. B. Officer, C. A. Chesner, and W. I. Rose, 1986. "Dynamic Deformation of Volcanic Ejecta from the Toba Caldera: Possible Relevance to Cretaceous/Tertiary Boundary Phenomena." *Geology* 14:380–383.

A report on the discovery that huge, explosive volcanic eruptions can apply enormous pressures to rocks and may be able to produce the kinds of shock features observed in mineral grains found in terminal Cretaceous boundary sediments.

Chi, W. R., and G. Keller, 1985. "Cretaceous/Tertiary Boundary Event, E1 Kef, Tunisia: A Foraminiferal Response." *Geological Society of America Abstracts with Programs* 17:544.

A brief account of the best terrestrial section of later Cretaceous deep-sea sediments, reporting very weak extinction of bottom-dwelling foraminiferans during the terminal crisis.

Cifelli, R., 1969. Radiation of the Cenozoic Planktonic Foraminifera. *Systematic Zoology* 18:154–168.

A classic article pointing out that the planktonic foraminiferans that survived major crises were types adapted to cool water.

Clemens, W. A., J. D. Archibald, and L. J. Hickey, 1981. "Out with a Whimper Not a Bang." *Paleobiology* 7:293–298.

A subjective review, by major figures in the debate, of controversies surrounding biotic changes at the Cretaceous–Paleocene boundary.

Collinson, M. E., K. Fowler, and M. C. Boulter, 1981. "Floristic Changes Indicate a Cooling Climate in the Eocene of Southern England." *Nature* 291:315–317.

Demonstration of how tropical and subtropical floral elements in southern England gave way to more temperate elements under conditions of climatic cooling that began in latest early Eocene time.

Copper, P., 1977. "Paleolatitudes in the Devonian of Brazil and the Frasnian–Famennian Mass Extinction," *Palaeogeography, Palaeoclimatology, Palaeoecology* 21:165–207.

Apparently the first publication to propose that climatic cooling caused the Late Devonian crisis, a major line of evidence being the preferential survival of taxa living in polar regions.

Copper, P., 1984. "Cold Water Oceans and the Frasnian–Famennian Extinction Crisis." *Geological Society of America Abstracts with Programs* 16:10.

A brief summary of evidence that atrypoid brachiopods, which disappeared in the Late Devonian crisis, declined over a period of time.

Corliss, B. H., M.-P. Aubry, W. A. Berggren, J. M. Fenner, L. D. Keigwin, and G. Keller, 1984. "The Eocene/Oligocene Boundary Event in the Deep Sea." *Science* 226:806–810.

A collaborative synthesis demonstrating that heavy extinctions of plankton in the vicinity of the Eocene–Oligocene boundary were not sudden, but spread over several million years.

Dhondt, A. V., 1983. "Campanian and Maastrichtian Inoceramids: A Review." *Zitteliana* 10:689–701.

Documents the gradual decline of inoceramid bivalves during Late Cretaceous time.

D'Hondt, S., and G. Keller, 1985. "Late Cretaceous Stepwise Extinction of Planktonic Foraminifera." *Geological Society of America Abstracts with Programs* 17:557–558.

A brief report on the best terrestrial section of later Cretaceous deep-sea sediments, with evidence that planktonic foraminiferans suffered pulses of extinction, not simply heavy losses at the very end of Cretaceous time.

Dickens, J. M., 1978. "Climate of the Permian in Australia: The Invertebrate Faunas." *Palaeogeography, Palaeoclimatology, Palaeoecology* 23:33–46.

A description of how climates warmed up in parts of Australia in Late Permian time when Pangaea moved northward, off the South Pole.

Dockery, D. T., 1984. "Crisis Events for Paleogene Molluscan Faunas in the Southeastern United States." *Mississippi Geology* 5(2):1–7

An article that attributes Eocene–Oligocene pulses of molluscan extinction in the Gulf of Mexico to episodes of climatic cooling and increased water turbidity.

Douglas, R., and F. Woodruff, 1981. "Deep-Sea Benthic Foraminifera." In C. Emiliani, ed., *The Sea* (7), pp. 1233–1327. New York: Wiley.

Report that includes a summary of isotopic data for deep-sea and planktonic foraminiferans showing a general decline in oceanic temperatures during Late Cretaceous time.

Doyle, J. A., and L. J. Hickey, 1976. "Pollen and Leaves from the Mid-Cretaceous Potomac Group and Their Bearing on Early Angiosperm Evolution." In C. G. Beck, ed., *Origin and Early Evolution of Angiosperms,* pp. 139–206. New York: Columbia University Press.

Documentation of the initial adaptive radiation of flowering plants.

Dutro, J. T., 1984. "The Frasnian–Famennian Event as Recorded by Devonian Articulate Brachiopods in New Mexico." *Geological Society of America Abstracts with Programs* 16:14

A brief summary of evidence that the decline of brachiopods during the Late Devonian crisis was gradual in the New Mexico region.

Ekdale, A. A., and R. G. Bromley, 1984. "Sedimentology and Ichnology of the Cretaceous–Tertiary Boundary in Denmark: Implications for the Causes of the Terminal Cretaceous Extinction." *Journal of Sedimentary Petrology* 54:681–703.

Evaluation of the terminal Cretaceous iridium anomaly in Denmark in light of the activities of burrowing marine animals.

Elder, W. P., 1985. "Biotic Patterns across the Cenomanian–Turonian Extinction Boundary near Pueblo, Colorado." In L. M. Pratt, E. G. Kauffman, and F. B. Zelt, eds., *Fine-grained Deposits and Biofacies of the Cretaceous Western Interior Seaway: Evidence of Cyclic Sedimentary Processes,* pp. 157–169. Tulsa: Society of Economic Paleontologists and Mineralogists.
    A detailed study of mid-Cretaceous extinctions in a region where events may have differed from those elsewhere in the world.

Epshteyn, O. G., 1981. "Late Permian Ice-marine Deposits of the Atkan Formation in the Kolyma River Headwaters Region, U.S.S.R." In M. J. Hambrey and W. B. Harland, eds. *Earth's Pre-Pleistocene Glacial Record,* pp. 270–273. Cambridge: Cambridge University Press.
    Description of the Late Permian glacial marine sediments of Siberia, but with no discussion of the Late Permian geographic situation of the Kolyma block on which they are situated.

Fay, I., and P. Copper, 1982. "Early Silurian Bioherms in the Manitoulin Formation of Manitoulin Island." In M. Copeland and B. Maminet, eds., *Third North American Paleontological Convention Proceeding,* vol. 1, p. 159–163. Toronto: Toronto Business and Economic Service.
    Discussion of rare and poorly developed reefs that lived in Early Silurian time, shortly after the Late Ordovician crisis.

Fischer, A. G., and M. A. Arthur, 1977. "Secular Variations in the Pelagic Realm." *Society of Economic Paleontologists and Mineralogists Special Publications* 25:19–50.
    A classic article suggesting that biotic crises have resulted from changes in the thermal structure of the oceans and also suggesting that these events may have been regularly periodic.

Flügel, E., and G. D. Stanley, 1984. "Reorganization, Development, and Evolution of Post-Permian Reefs and Reef Organisms." *Palaeontographica Americana* 54:177–186.
    Report that includes the observation that Permian reef-building organisms that are absent from Triassic rocks reappear in mid-Triassic deposits.

French, B. M., 1984. "Impact Event at the Cretaceous–Tertiary Boundary: A Possible Site." *Science* 226:353.
    Presentation of the possibility that the Manson, Iowa, crater was the site of latest Cretaceous extraterrestrial impact.

Garrett, P., 1970. "Phanerozoic Stromatolites: Noncompetitive Ecological Restriction by Grazing and Burrowing Animals." *Science* 167:171–173.
    Demonstration of how grazing and burrowing animals restrain the growth of stromatolites in modern seas and have probably done so since early in Phanerozoic time.

Gerstel, J., R. C. Thunell, J. C. Zachos, and M. A. Arthur, 1986. "The Cretaceous/Tertiary Boundary Event in The North Pacific: Planktonic Foraminiferal Results from DSDP Site 577, Shatsky Rise." *Paleoceanography* 1:97–117.
    Presentation of detailed evidence that cool-adapted species of planktonic foraminiferans migrated to low latitudes during latest Cretaceous time, replacing warm-adapted species that suffered extinction.

Gobbett, D. J., 1973. "Permian Fusulinacea." In A. Hallam, ed., *Atlas of Paloeobiogeography,* pp. 152–158. Amsterdam: Elsevier.
    A summary of the evidence that the Fusulinacea became confined to the Tethys in Late Permian time.

Gould, S. J., 1985. "All the News That's Fit to Print and Some Opinions that Aren't." *Discover,* November, pp. 86–91.
    A rejoinder to A. Hoffman's critique of 26-million-year cyclicity for mass extinctions.

Guthrie, R. D., 1984. "Mosaics, Allelochemics and Nutrients." In P. S. Martin and R. G. Klein, eds., *Quaternary Extinctions: A Prehistorical Revolution,* pp. 259–298. Tucson: University of Arizona Press.
A case for the recent extinction of many large mammal species by climatically induced changes in vegetation.

Hallam, A., 1981. "The End-Triassic Bivalve Extinction Event." *Palaeogeography, Palaeoclimatology, Palaeoecology* 35:1–44
    Analysis of the heavy marine extinctions at the end of the Triassic Period that invokes lowering of sea level, a physical change no longer believed to have occurred.

Hallam, A., 1986. "The Pliensbachian and Tithonian Extinction Events." *Nature* 319:765–768.
    Presentation of evidence that two extinction events represented by peaks in the Raup and Sepkoski curve were not global in geographic scale.

Hansen, T. A., 1984. "Bivalve Extinction Patterns in the late Eocene and Oligocene of the Gulf Coast: Relationship to Temperature Drops and Changes in Shelf Area." *Geological Society of America Abstracts with Programs* 16:529.
    An abstract correlating heavy late Eocene and Oligocene extinctions of marine bivalves of the Gulf of Mexico with extinctions of plankton but not with times of sea-level lowering.

Hansen, T. A., R. B. Ferrand, H. A. Montgomery, H. G. Billman, and G. Blechschmidt, 1986. "Sedimentology and Extinction Patterns across the Cretaceous–Tertiary Boundary Interval in East Texas." *Cretaceous Research* (in press).
    An evaluation of the terminal Cretaceous extinction of sea-floor life in the region where the fossil record is most revealing.

Hazel, J. E., 1971. "Paleoclimatology of the Yorktown Formation (Upper Miocene and Lower Pliocene) of Virginia and North Carolina." *Centre de Recherches Pan-SNPA bulletin* 5 (supplement), p. 361–375.
    Demonstration of how the species of the ostracods (small bivalved crustaceans) in the Yorktown Formation of Virginia point to the presence of a highly equable climate shortly before the beginning of the recent ice age.

Hickey, L. J., 1980. "Paleocene Stratigraphy and Flora of the Clark's Fork Basin." *University of Michigan Papers on Paleontology* 24:33–49.

Summary of leaf-margin data that point to a major trend of climatic cooling in Wyoming and Montana during the Cretaceous–Paleocene transition.

Hickey, L. J., 1981. "Land Plant Evidence Compatible with Gradual, Not Catastrophic, Change at the End of the Cretaceous." *Nature* 292:529–531.

Review of the fossil record of flowering plants for Late Cretaceous time, finding that extinction was not severe, with the heaviest losses perhaps occurring at high latitudes.

Hickey, L. J., R. M. West, M. R. Dawson, D. K. Choi, 1983. "Arctic Terrestrial Biota: Paleomagnetic Evidence of Age Disparity with Mid-Northern Latitudes During the Late Cretaceous and Early Tertiary." *Science* 221:1153–1156.

Presentation of the thesis that biotas from the Arctic Circle migrated southward with shifting climates during Late Cretaceous and early Paleogene time.

Hickman, C. S., 1980. "Paleogene Marine Gastropods of the Keasey Formation of Oregon." *Bulletins of American Paleontology* 78:1–112.

Description of the disappearance of warm-adapted snail species in waters off the northwestern United States near the Eocene–Oligocene transition.

Hoffman, A., 1985. "Patterns of Family Extinction Depend on Definition and Geological Timescale." *Nature* 315:659–662.

A critique of Raup and Sepkoski's claim that heavy extinctions have occurred with a periodicity of 26 million years.

Horner, J. R., and R. Makela, 1979. "Nest of Juveniles Provides Evidence of Family Structure Among Dinosaurs." *Nature* 282:296–298.

Report on the discovery of a group of juvenile dinosaurs in Montana that were preserved in a nest where they were apparently fed by one or both parents.

House, M. R., 1985. "Correlation of Mid-Palaeozoic Ammonoid Evolutionary Events with Global Sedimentary Perturbations." *Nature* 313:17–22.

Compilation of data showing how the ammonoids experienced pulses of extinction during the Late Devonian crisis.

Hsu, K. J., 1972. "When the Mediterranean Dried Up." *Scientific American* 227 (December):27–36.

A readable account of the desiccation of the Mediterranean at the end of the Miocene Epoch.

Izett, G. A., and C. L. Pillmore, 1985. "Shock-Metamorphic Minerals as the Cretaceous–Tertiary Boundary, Ratan Basin, Colorado and Mexico Provide Evidence for Asteroid Impact in Continental Crust." *Eos* 46:1149–1150.

Announcement of the discovery of shocked mineral grains of large size and of feldspar composition in the western United States, which suggest a nearby impact site on continental crust.

Jablonski, D., 1986. "Background and Mass Extinctions: The Alternation of Macroevolutionary Regimes." *Science* 231:129–133.

Demonstration that the pattern of mass extinction, with regard to impact on various groups, has often differed from the pattern of normal (background) extinction.

Jiang, M. J., and S. Gartner, 1986. "Calcareous Nannofossil Succession Across the Cretaceous/Tertiary Boundary in East-Central Texas." *Micropaleontology* (in press.)

A detailed picture of the sudden reduction of nannoplankton abundance at the end of Cretaceous time and the final demise of some species early in Paleocene time.

Kauffman, E. G., 1979. "The Ecology and Biogeography of the Cretaceous–Tertiary Extinction Event." In K. Christensen and T. Birkelund, eds., *Cretaceous–Tertiary Boundary Events*, II, pp. 29–37. Copenhagen: University of Copenhagen.

A review of the marine record of the terminal Cretaceous crisis that notes, among other things, the decline of the rudists before the very end.

Keller, G., 1983. "Biochronology and Paleoclimatic Implications of Middle Eocene to Oligocene Planktic Foraminiferal Faunas." *Marine Micropaleontology* 7:463–486.

An evaluation of pulses of cooling and extinction of planktonic foraminiferans.

Keller, G., 1983. "Paleoclimatic Analysis of Middle Eocene Through Oligocene Planktic Foraminiferal Faunas." *Palaeogeography, Palaeoclimatology, Palaeoecology* 43:73–94.

Interpretation of both taxonomic and isotopic changes in planktonic foraminiferans as indicating pulses of cooling and a net cooling trend in the oceanic realm in mid-Cenozoic time.

Keller, G., 1986. "Stepwise Mass Extinctions and Impact Events: Late Eocene to Early Oligocene." *Marine Micropaleontology* (in press).

Argument that a minority of Eocene–Oligocene extinctions of planktonic foraminiferans are attributable to events that produced microtektite layers and a majority of the extinctions to cooling events.

Kennett, J. P., 1977. "Cenozoic Evolution of Antarctic Glaciation, the Circum-Antarctic Ocean, and Their Impact on Global Paleoceanography." *Journal of Geophysical Research* 82:3843–3860.

A classic article explaining how cold temperatures formed in and emanated from circum-Antarctic waters when other continents broke away from Antarctica in late Eocene and Oligocene time, isolating it over the South Pole.

Kennett, J. P., 1985. "Neogene Palaeoceanography and Plankton Evolution." *South African Journal of Science* 81:251–253.

A useful short review of thermal changes in the ocean near Antartica during Miocene time.

Kennett, J. P., and C. C. von der Borch, 1986. "Southwest Pacific Cenozoic Paleoceanography." *Initial Reports of the Deep Sea Drilling Project* 90:1493–1517.
Presentation of a model to explain cooling in the Southern Hemisphere during the Eocene–Oligocene transition as Australia separated from Antarctica.

Kitchell, J. A., D. L. Clark, and A. M. Gombos, in press. "Biological Selectivity of Extinction: A Link Between Background and Mass Extinction." *Palaios.*
An article that suggests that many planktonic diatom taxa survived the Late Cretaceous extinction because they were able to form resting spores.

Kitchell, J. A., and D. Pena, 1984. "Periodicity of Extinctions in the Geologic Past: Deterministic Versus Stochastic Explanations." *Science* 226:689–692.
An evaluation of the distribution of extinction peaks in geological time, concluding that the pattern is pseudoperiodic.

Knoll, A. H., 1984. "Patterns of Extinction in the Fossil Record of Vascular Plants." In M. H. Nitecki, ed., *Extinctions,* pp. 21–68. Chicago: University of Chicago Press.
Demonstration that higher plants have been highly resistant to mass extinction, with data on how these organisms fared during the mass extinction of animals in late Devonian, Permian, and Cretaceous times. Also reviews evidence that the Late Paleozoic transition from the Paleophytic to the Mesophytic flora occurred at different times in different regions of Pangaea.

Kollman, H. A., 1979. "Distribution Patterns and Evolution of Gastropods Around the Cretaceous/Tertiary Boundary." In K. Christensen and T. Birkelund, eds., *Cretaceous–Tertiary Boundary Events* II, pp. 83–87. Copenhagen: University of Copenhagen.
An article that points out that marine snails that had lived in cool northern waters during Late Cretaceous time migrated at least as far south as northern

Africa in the transition to the Paleocene, suggesting the equatorward spread of cool waters.

Kummel, B., 1973. "Lower Triassic (Scythian) Molluscs." In A. Hallam, ed., *Atlas of Palaeobiogeography,* pp. 225–233. Amsterdam: Elsevier.
Review of the impoverished fauna of earliest Triassic time and description of the cosmopolitan occurrence of some of the most conspicuous species.

Kyte, F. T., and J. T. Wasson, 1986. "Accretion Rate of Extraterrestrial Matter: Iridium Deposited 33 to 67 Million Years Ago." *Science* 232:1225–1229.
A report of data on iridium accumulation in the Pacific region since Cretaceous time, showing that there could not have been devastating comet showers at the time of the Eocene-Oligocene crisis.

Logan, A., and L. V. Hills, 1973. *The Permian and Triassic Systems and Their Mutual Boundary.* Canadian Society of Petroleum Geologists Memoir 2.
A valuable compendium of articles that review patterns of Late Permian extinction for particular taxa and geographic regions.

Martin, P. S., 1984. "Prehistoric Overkill: The Global Model." In P. S. Martin and R. G. Klein, eds., *Quaternary Extinctions: A Prehistorical Revolution,* pp. 354–403. Tucson: University of Arizona Press.
A case for the recent extinction of many large mammals by human hunters, presented by the most articulate spokesman for this scenario.

Martin, P. S., and R. G. Klein, eds., 1984. *Quaternary Extinctions—A Prehistorical Revolution.* Tucson: University of Arizona Press.
A broad-based, multiauthored review of the controversy over the cause of the recent heavy extinctions of large mammals.

McElhinny, M. W., B. J. J. Embleton, X. H. Ma, and Z. K. Zhang, 1981. "Fragmentation of Asia in the Permian." Nature 293:212–216.

A reconstruction of the geography of the Tethyan region during Late Permian time, based on paleomagnetism; reviews evidence that the Kolyma block, which accumulated glacial deposits, was positioned in the northern Tethys.

McGhee, G. R., 1982. "The Frasnian–Famennian Extinction Event: A Preliminary Analysis of the Appalachian Marine Ecosystems." *Geological Society of America Special Paper* 190:491–500.
A presentation of data showing that in New York State the Late Devonian mass extinction was spread over some 7 million years and that glass sponges diversified while other groups declined.

McGhee, G. R., J. S. Gilmore, C. J. Orth, and E. Olsen, 1984. "No Geochemical Evidence for an Asteroidal Impact at Late Devonian Mass Extinction Horizon." *Nature* 308:28–31.
Description of unsuccessful efforts to find an iridium anomaly that might be associated with the Late Devonian biotic crisis.

McLaren, D. J., 1970. "Time, Life and Boundaries." *Journal of Paleontology* 44:801–815.
An assertion that the Late Devonian crisis was geologically instantaneous and possibly caused by the impact on the earth of a large extraterrestrial body.

McLean, D. M., 1985. "Mantle Degassing Induced Dead Ocean in the Cretaceous–Tertiary Transition." *Geophysical Monograph* 32:493–503.
Hypothesis that carbon dioxide released with the Deccan Trap lavas in India caused the terminal Cretaceous mass extinction by warming climates via the greenhouse effect.

Michel, H. V., F. Asaro, W. Alvarez, and L. W. Alvarez, 1985. "Elemental Profile of Iridium and Other Elements near the Cretaceous–Tertiary Boundary in Hole 5775B." *Initial Reports of the Deep Sea Drilling Project.* 86:533–538.
Report of a second, smaller iridium anomaly about 50 centimeters (about 20

inches) below the one at the terminal Cretaceous boundary.

Miller, J. F., 1984. "Cambrian and Earliest Ordovician Conodont Evolution, Biofacies, and Provincialism." *Geological Society of America Special Paper* 196:43–67.
Demonstration of how conodonts, not simply trilobites, suffered in the terminal Cambrian crisis, with evidence that sea level fell at the same time.

Officer, C. B., and C. L. Drake, 1983. "The Cretaceous–Tertiary Transition." *Science* 219:1383–1390.
An evaluation by two skeptics of the idea that a bolide impact caused the terminal Cretaceous extinction.

Officer, C. B., and C. L. Drake, 1985. "Terminal Cretaceous Environmental Events." *Science* 227:1161–1167.
A second contribution by the two most vocal skeptics of the terminal Cretaceous impact scenario, focusing on the stratigraphic thickness of the iridium anomaly and the coincident occurrence of other heavy metals that are uncommon in meteorites.

Orth, C. J., J. S. Gilmore, J. D. Knight, C. L. Pillmore, R. H. Tschudy, and J. E. Fassett, 1981. "An Iridium Abundance Anomaly at the Palynological Cretaceous–Tertiary Boundary in Northern New Mexico." *Science* 214:1341–1343.
Description of the terminal Cretaceous iridium anomaly in New Mexico and the associated concentration of fern spores.

Orth, C. J., J. D. Knight, L. R. Quintana, J. S. Gilmore, and A. R. Palmer, 1984. "A Search for Iridium Abundance Anomalies at Two Late Cambrian Biomere Boundaries in Western Utah." *Science* 223:163–165.
Report of failures to find high abundances of iridium at stratigraphic positions where it might be expected if Cambrian mass extinctions resulted from an asteroid impact.

Orth, C. J., J. S. Gilmore, P. Q. Oliver, and L. R. Quintana, 1985. "Iridium Abundance Patterns Across Extinction Bounda-

ries." *Geological Society of America Abstracts with Programs* 17:683.
Summary of results from the Los Alamos group that has conducted the most extensive search for iridium at stratigraphic levels of extinction; the conclusion is that no meaningful anomalies have been detected in rocks older than those at the terminal Cretaceous boundary.

Palmer, A. R., 1984. "The Biomere Problem: Evolution of an Idea." *Journal of Paleontology* 58:599–611.
A thorough review of the record of trilobite mass extinctions in the Cambrian by the paleontologist who discovered them.

Pedder, A. E. H., 1982. "The Rugose Coral Record Across the Frasnian/Famennian Boundary." *Geological Society of America Special Paper* 190:485–489.
A compilation of the species of rugose corals that existed before and after the Late Devonian crisis, showing that reef builders suffered heavy extinction whereas deeper water species did not.

Perth-Nielsen, K., J. McKenzie, and H. Qiziang, 1982. "Biostratigraphy and Isotope Stratigraphy and the 'Catastrophic' Extinction of Calcareous Nannoplankton at the Cretaceous/Tertiary Boundary." *Geological Society of America Special Paper* 190:353–371.
An argument that sparse populations of some nannoplankton species in early Paleocene sediments represent survival rather than reworking because their isotopic compositions differ from those of Cretaceous populations.

Percival, S. F., and A. G. Fischer, 1977. "Changes in Calcareous Nannoplankton in the Cretaceous–Tertiary Biotic Crisis at Zumaya, Spain." *Evolutionary Theory* 2:1–35.
A detailed picture of the sudden reduction of calcareous nannoplankton abundance at the end of the Cretaceous and the final demise of some species early in Paleocene time.

Petuch, E. J., 1984. "An Eocene Asteroid Impact in Southern Florida and the Origin of the Everglades." *Geological Society of America Abstracts with Programs* 17:688.
A brief statement of a proposal that an asteroid impact in southern Florida contributed to late Eocene mass extinction.

Phillips, A. M., 1984. "Shasta Ground Sloth Extinction." In P. S. Martin and R. G. Klein, eds., *Quaternary Extinctions: A Prehistorical Revolution,* pp. 148–158. Tucson: University of Arizona Press.
Presentation of the case that the shasta ground sloth could not have died out from a change of climate and vegetation.

Pillmore, G. L., R. H. Tschudy, C. J. Orth, J. S. Gilmore, and J. D. Knight, 1984. "Geologic Framework of Nonmarine Cretaceous–Tertiary Boundary Sites, Raton Basin, New Mexico and Colorado." *Science* 223:1180–1183.
Description of the depositional environments in which the iridium anomaly and concentration of fern pollen developed at the end of Cretaceous time in the southwestern United States.

Playford, P. E., D. J. McLaren, C. J. Orth, J. S. Gilmore, and W. D. Goodfellow, 1984. "Iridium Anomaly in the Upper Devonian of The Canning Basin, Western Australia." *Science* 226:437–439.
A report of an iridium anomaly stratigraphically close to the Late Devonian interval of mass extinction—but an anomaly associated with fossil algae that concentrated heavy metals.

Prell, W. L., and J. D. Hays, 1976. "Late Pleistocene Faunal and Temperature Patterns of the Columbia Basin, Caribbean Sea." *Geological Society of America Memoir* 145:201–220.
Presentation of CLIMAP data showing that the Caribbean Sea cooled down during Pleistocene time.

Prothero, D. R., 1985. "Mid-Oligocene Extinction Event in North American Land Mammals." *Science* 229:550–551.
Documentation for the first time of a major extinction of mammals about 32

million years ago, when there was a major drop in sea level and a general climatic change.

Prothero, D. R., 1986. "North American Mammalian Diversity and Eocene–Oligocene Extinctions." *Paleobiology* 11:389–405.

Argument that attributes major extinctions of North American land mammals in late Eocene and mid-Oligocene time to climatic changes.

Quinn, J. F., 1983. "Mass Extinctions in the Fossil Record." *Science* 219:1239–1241.

Presentation of a quantitative argument that mass extinctions intergrade with background extinction; includes a response by Raup, Sepkoski, and Stigler.

Raffi, S., S. M. Stanley, and R. Marasti, 1986. "Biogeographic Patterns and Plio-Pleistocene Extinction of Bivalvia in the Mediterranean and Southern North Sea." *Paleobiology* 11:368–388.

An explanation of how climatic cooling eliminated many species of mollusks in European seas during late Neogene time.

Raup, D. M., and J. J. Sepkoski, 1982. "Mass Extinctions in the Marine Fossil Record." *Science* 215:1501–1503.

An article that concludes, on the basis of variations in the rate of extinction of animal families through time, that there have been five primary mass extinctions; these have occurred late in the Ordovician, Devonian, Permian, Triassic, and Cretaceous periods.

Raup, D. M., and J. J. Sepkoski, 1984. "Periodicity of Extinctions in the Geologic Past." *Proceedings of the National Academy of Sciences* 81:801–805.

Provocative analysis of extinction data at the family level, taken to indicate a significant degree of periodicity with a mean interval of 26 million years.

Raup, D. M., and J. J. Sepkoski, 1986. "Periodic Extinction of Families and Genera." *Science* 231:833–836.

An extended analysis of data taken to indicate periodicity for mass extinctions,

with the inclusion of data at the genus level.

Retallack, G. J., 1983. "Late Eocene and Oligocene Paleosols from Badlands National Park, South Dakota." *Geological Society of America Special Paper* 193:1–82.

Illustration of how ancient soils preserved in the South Dakota badlands reveal climatic changes during Eocene–Oligocene time.

Ross, C. A., and J. R. P. Ross, 1982. "Biogeographic Influences on Late Palaeozoic Faunal Distributions." In G. P. Larwood and C. Nielsen, eds., *Recent and Fossil Bryozoa*, pp. 199–212. Fredensborg, Denmark: Olsen & Olsen.

An article that includes a discussion of the restriction of fusulinaceans and bryozoans to the Tethys during Late Permian time.

Sanfilippo, A., W. R. Riedel, B. P. Glass, and F. T. Kyle, 1985. "Late Eocene Microtektites and Radiolarian Extinctions on Barbados." *Nature* 314:613–615.

Argument that an asteroid impact accounted for the extinctions of five species of planktonic radiolarians, based on the presence of an iridium anomaly and a microtektite layer at the critical stratigraphic level.

Schopf, T. J. M., 1974. "Permo-Triassic Extinctions: Relation to Sea-Floor Spreading." *Journal of Geology* 82:129–143.

An attempt to relate the Late Permian crisis in the marine realm to lowering of sea level.

Schopf, J. W., 1976. "How Old Are the Eukaryotes?" *Science* 193:47–49.

Presentation of data showing an increase in the diameter of single-celled fossil algae about 1.4 billion years ago, apparently reflecting the diversification of the earliest eukaryotes.

Sepkoski, J. J., 1982. "Mass Extinctions in the Phanerozoic Oceans: A Review." *Geological Society of America Special Paper* 190:283–289.

A sequel to the 1982 paper by Raup and

Sepkoski, but with more details on the nature of individual mass extinctions.

Sepkoski, J. J., and D. M. Raup, 1986. "Periodicity in Marine Mass Extinctions." In D. K. Elliott, ed., *Dynamics of Extinctions,* pp. 3–36. New York: Wiley.

An expanded version of these authors' case for periodicity of extinctions, with a useful review of the extraterrestrial hypotheses that have been proposed by others to explain it.

Shackleton, N. J., and others, 1984. "Oxygen Isotope Calibration of the Onset of Ice-Rafting and History of Glaciation in the North Atlantic Region." *Nature* 307:620–623.

Description of isotopic changes and ice-rafted debris in deep-sea cores from the North Atlantic Ocean, revealing the pattern of Pliocene cooling.

Sheehan, P. M., 1973. "The relation of Late Ordovician glaciation to the Ordovician–Silurian changeover in North American brachiopod faunas." *Lethaia* 6:147–154.

The first paper to link the Late Ordovician crisis to the onset of continental glaciation.

Sheehan, P. M., 1979. "Swedish Late Ordovician Marine Benthic Assemblages and Their Bearing on Brachiopod Zoogeography." In J. Gray and A. J. Boucot, eds., *Historical Biogeography, Plate Tectonics, and the Changing Environments,* pp. 61–73. Corvallis: Oregon State University Press.

A description of the spread of faunas adapted to cool conditions toward the equator in Late Ordovician time.

Signor, P. W., and J. H. Lipps, 1982. "Sampling Bias, Gradual Extinction Patterns and Catastrophes in the Fossil Record." *Geological Society of America Special Paper* 190:291–296.

Argument that the imperfection of the fossil record may make some sudden extinctions appear to have been spread through intervals of geologic time.

Skevington, D., 1974. "Controls Influencing the Composition and Distribution of Ordovician Graptolite Faunal Provinces."

Palaeontological Association Special Papers in Palaeontology 13:59–73.

Presentation of evidence that planktonic graptolite zones were compressed toward the equator in Late Ordovician time.

Sloan, R. E., 1969. "Cretaceous and Paleocene Terrestrial Communities of Western North America." *Proceedings North American Paleontological Convention (E)*. Lawrence, Kansas: Allen Press.

A useful, now slightly dated, summary of biotic changes in terrestrial communities during the Cretaceous–Paleocene transition.

Sloan, R. E., 1985. "Periodic Extinctions and Radiations of Permian Terrestrial Faunas and the Rapid Mammalization of Therapsids." *Geological Society of America Abstracts with Programs* 17:719.

A brief presentation of evidence that mammal-like reptiles suffered pulses of extinction in Late Permian time.

Sloan, R. E., J. K. Rigby, L. Van Valen, and D. Gabriel, 1986. "Gradual Extinction of Dinosaurs and the Simultaneous Radiation of Ungulate Mammals in the Hell Creek Formation of McCone County, Montana." *Science* 232:629–633.

A provocative article that concludes, first, that dinosaurs declined gradually in Late Cretaceous time and, second, that at least eight species survived into the Paleocene Epoch.

Smit, J., 1982. "Extinction and Evolution of Planktonic Foraminifera After a Major Impact at the Cretaceous/Tertiary Boundary." *Geological Society of America Special Paper* 190:329–352.

An early review of data revealing the sudden extinction of planktonic foraminiferans; the isotopic data, based on whole rock samples, are problematical and the survival of several minute species into the Paleocene is not reported.

Smit, J., and A. J. T. Romein, 1985. "A Sequence of Events Across the Cretaceous–Tertiary Boundary." *Earth and Planetary Science Letters* 74:155–170.

A review of terminal Cretaceous events as depicted in deep-sea sections, with a discussion of microtektite-like spherules; fails to consider the survival of very small planktonic foraminiferans.

Stanley, S. M., 1984. "Marine Mass Extinction: A Dominant Role for Temperature." In M. H. Nitecki, ed., *Extinctions*, pp. 69–117. Chicago: University of Chicago Press.

A compendium of evidence that climatic change has been the primary cause of mass extinctions.

Stanley, S. M., 1984. "Mass Extinctions in the Ocean." *Scientific American* 250 (June):64–72.

A general discussion of the role of climate in mass extinction.

Stanley, S. M., 1986. "Anatomy of a Regional Mass Extinction: Plio–Pleistocene Decimation of the Western Atlantic Bivalve Fauna." *Palaios* 1:17–36.

Evaluation of the pattern of marine extinction in eastern North America during the recent Ice Age, offering evidence that climatic cooling was the cause.

Stanley, S. M., 1986. *Earth and Life Through Time*. New York: W. H. Freeman and Company.

Text that includes a survey of the history of life that introduces the groups of animals and plants discussed in this book as well as the setting in which they lived.

Stanley, S. M., and L. D. Campbell, 1981. "Neogene Mass Extinction of Western Atlantic Molluscs." *Nature* 293:457–459.

An assessment of a large volume of data revealing that there was a regional mass extinction in the western Atlantic Ocean during Pliocene and Pleistocene time.

Stitt, J. H., 1977. "Late Cambrian and Earliest Ordovician Trilobites, Wichita Mountains Area, Oklahoma." *Oklahoma Geological Survey Bulletin* 124:1–79.

Documentation of two Cambrian crises for trilobites and argument for the hypothesis that climatic cooling was responsible.

Surlyk, F., and M. B. Johansen, 1984. "End-Cretaceous Brachiopod Extinctions in the Chalk of Denmark." *Science* 223:1174–1177.

A detailed account of the sudden extinction of brachiopods that lived on chalky sea floors in Europe during Late Cretaceous time.

Taylor, M. E., 1977. "Late Cambrian of Western North America: Trilobite Biofacies, Environmental Significance, and Biostratigraphic Implications." In E. G. Kauffman and J. E. Hazel, eds., *Concepts and Methods of Biostratigraphy*, pp. 397–425. Stroudsburg, Pennsylvania: Dowden, Hutchinson & Ross.

Presentation of the case that Cambrian trilobites experienced crises when cool waters moved from the margin of North America up into shallow seas.

Vail, P. R., R. M. Mitchum, and S. Thompson, 1977. "Global Cycles of Relative Changes of Sea Level." *American Association of Petroleum Geologists Memoir* 26:83–97.

A classic paper introducing the first general results of a technique for estimating relative changes in global sea level.

Vail, P. R., J. Hardenbol, and R. G. Todd, 1984. "Jurassic Unconformities, Chronostratigraphy and Sea-level Changes from Seismic Stratigraphy and Biostratigraphy." *American Association of Petroleum Geologists Memoir* 36:345–362.

A detailed study of sea-level changes during the Jurassic Period, concluding that there was not a general decline at the end of the period, when mass extinction occurred.

Van Valen, L. M., 1984. "Catastrophes, Expectations, and the Evidence." *Paleobiology* 10:121–137.

A thoughtful, lengthy review of a major publication that examined the question of whether bolide impacts have caused mass extinctions.

Van Valen, L., and R. E. Sloan, 1977. "Ecology and the Extinction of the Dinosaurs." *Evolutionary Theory* 2:37–64.

Presentation of the case that mammals replaced dinosaurs during latest Cretaceous time in western North America as climates and floras were changing.

Vidal, G., and A. H. Knoll, 1982. "Radiations and Extinctions of Plankton in the Late Proterozoic and Early Cambrian." *Nature* 297:57–60.
Documentation of the drastic decline of planktonic algae close to the end of the Cryptozoic Eon, when the earth experienced a major glacial episode.

Vrba, E. S., 1985. "African Bovidae: Evolutionary Events Since the Miocene." *South African Journal of Science* 81:263–266.
Summary of late Neogene extinctions of antelopes in Africa, showing heavy losses about 2.5 million years ago.

Ward, P. D., and P. W. Signor, 1983. "Evolutionary Tempo in Jurassic and Cretaceous Ammonites." *Paleobiology* 9:183–198.
Demonstration that certain groups of ammonoids were characteristically resistant to the mass extinctions that struck down others.

Ward, P. D., and J. Wiedmann, 1983. "The Maastrichtian Ammonite Succession at Zumaya, Spain." In T. Birkeland, ed., *Symposium on Cretaceous Stage Boundaries. Univ. of Copenhagen, Abstracts.*
Description of a gradual decline and final disappearance of ammonoids before the top of the Cretaceous at an important site in Spain.

Watts, W. A., 1980. "The Late Quaternary Vegetation History of the Southeastern United States." *Annual Review of Ecology and Systematics* 11:38–409.
Report of the occurrence of spruce as far south as Georgia and of temperate climates in Florida in late Pleistocene time.

Webb, S. D., 1984. "Ten Million Years of Mammalian Extinctions in North America." In P. S. Martin and R. G. Klein, eds., *Quarternary Extinctions: A Prehistorical Revolution,* pp. 189–210. Tucson: University of Arizona Press.
Argument that the extinction of species of large mammals in North America 11,000 years ago was the last of six pulses of extinction during the past 10 million years.

Wicander, E. R., 1975. "Fluctuations in a Late Devonian–Early Mississippian Phytoplankton Flora of Ohio, U.S.A." *Palaeogeography, Palaeoclimatology, Palaeoecology* 17:89–108.
A description of the decline of the acritarchs at the time of the Late Devonian crisis.

Wolbach, W. S., R. S. Lewis, and E. Anders, 1985. "Cretaceous Extinctions: Evidence for Wildfires and Search for Meteoritic Material." *Science* 230:167–170.
Report of the discovery of fluffy aggregates of carbon at the Cretaceous–Paleocene boundary that are taken to signal the spread of wildfires across major continents.

Wolfe, J. A., 1978. "A Paleobotanical Interpretation of Tertiary Climates in the Northern Hemisphere." *American Scientist* 66:694–703.
A summary of the author's very important use of leaf-margin analysis to show that a series of cooling events occurred in western North America and along the Gulf Coast between Mid-Eocene and Mid-Oligocene time.

Wolfe, J. A., in press. "Late Cretaceous–Cenozoic History of Deciduousness and The Terminal Cretaceous Event." *Paleobiology.*
A discussion of how the terminal Cretaceous crisis selectively eliminated evergreen species of land plants.

Wolfe, J. A., and G. R. Upchurch, in press. "Vegetational, Climatic, and Floral Changes at the Cretaceous-Tertiary Boundary."
Documentation of heavier extinction of North American land plants in the south than in the north and the preferential survival of deciduous species.

Wolfe, J. A., and G. R. Upchurch, in press. "Leaf Assemblages across the Cretaceous–Tertiary Boundary in the Raton Basin, New Mexico and Colorado." *Proceedings of the National Academy of Sciences.*
Presentation of evidence that in New Mexico heavy extinction of land plants resulted from a brief pulse of cooling.

Zachos, J. C., and Arthur, M. A., 1986. "Paleoceanography of the Cretaceous/Tertiary Boundary Event: Inferences from Stable Isotopic and Other Data." *Paleoceanography* (in press).
A synthesis of evidence that calcareous plankton underwent a major decline in productivity at the end of the Cretaceous Period that lasted at least 1 million years.

Zinsmeister, W. J., 1982. "Late Creaceous–Early Tertiary Molluscan Biogeography of the Southern Circum–Pacific." *Journal of Paleontology* 56:84–102.
Demonstration that heavy extinction of mollusks occurred at high latitudes in the Southern Hemisphere during the Eocene–Oligocene transition.

ILLUSTRATION CREDITS

Illustrations by
Alan Iselin
Brenda Booth

CHAPTER 1

page 2
Jay Bader, Cincinnati Museum of Natural
History

page 3
Novosti Press Agency

page 4
left, From G. Cuvier and A. Brongniart,
Description Geologique Environs de Paris, 1822;
right, Chip Clark

page 6
Bridgeman Art Library/Art Resource

page 7
Douglas Henderson

page 15
After Raup and Sepkoski, 1982

page 16
Steven M. Holland, Cincinnati Museum of
Natural History

page 17
David Jablonski, University of Chicago

page 19
left, Chip Clark; right, William Berry, University of California, Berkeley

CHAPTER 2

page 22
After H. F. Osborn

page 23
After F. Press and F. Siever, *Earth,* New
York, W. H. Freeman and Company, 1986

page 24
left, Margaret Bradshaw, Canterbury
Museum

page 25
After A. Holmes

page 26
Hjalmar R. Bardarson

page 27
After F. Press and R. Siever, *Earth,* New
York, W. H. Freeman and Company, 1986

page 30
Peter Molnar, MIT

page 31
After R. K. Bambach, C. R. Scotese, and
A. M. Ziegler

page 32
After R. K. Bambach, C. R. Scotese, and
A. M. Ziegler

page 33
Adapted from A. G. Smith and J. C. Briden

page 34
Colin Montreath, Hedgehog House

page 37
After R. H. Macarthur and E. O. Wilson

page 38
Olive Schoenberg

page 39
After Stanley, 1984

page 41
Philip Alan Rosenberg/Pacific Stock

page 43
Swedish Museum of Natural History

page 44
Drawing by Sydney Parkinson, The British
Museum

CHAPTER 3

page 50
top, J. W. Schopf, University of California,
Los Angeles; bottom, S. M. Awramik, University of California, Santa Barbara

page 51
Steven M. Stanley

page 52
From G. Playford and R. Dring, "Late De-
vonian Acritarchs from the Carnarvon Basin,
Western Australia," in *Special Papers In Pale-
ontology No. 27,* London, The Paleontological
Association, 1981; photograph by Geoffrey
Playford

page 54
George E. Williams, Broken Hill Proprietary
Co. Ltd.

page 55
Exhibit by Chase Studio, photograph by
Chip Clark, National Museum of Natural
History

page 56
Chip Clark

page 57
top, Wilhelm Stürmer; left, after
I. T. Zhuravleva

page 58
After C. Lochman-Balk

page 60
Anita Harris, USGS

page 61
Steven M. Stanley

CHAPTER 4

page 66
After J. J. Sepkoski

page 67
top, Chip Clark; middle, Peter Ward, University of Washington; bottom, Charles Arneson

page 68
From R. Levi-Setti, *A Photographic Atlas of Trilobites,* Chicago, University of Chicago Press, 1975, photograph by Riccardo Levi-Setti.

page 69
Chip Clark

page 70
left, Lynton Land, University of Texas, Austin; right, Chip Clark

page 71
Chip Clark

page 72
The British Museum (Natural History)

page 75
The British Museum (Natural History)

page 76
Exhibit by George Marchand and Chase Studio, photograph by George Baldwin, National Museum of Natural History

page 77
After H. K. Erben

page 79
left, Chip Clark; right, exhibit by Chase Studio, photograph by Dan Rockafellow, Nebraska State Museum

page 80
After S. M. Stanley, *Earth and Life Through Time,* New York, W. H. Freeman and Company, 1985

page 83
left, Chip Clark; right, The British Museum (Natural History)

page 84
From P. E. Playford, "Devonian Great Barrier Reef of the Canning Basin, Western Australia," *Petroleum Geologists,* 64:814–840, 1980, photograph by Phillip Playford.

page 88
After J. C. Crowell

CHAPTER 5

page 92
left, The British Museum (Natural History); right, Chip Clark

page 94
right, John Shaw

page 96
right, Carnegie Museum of Natural History

page 97
Chip Clark

page 99
Mark Hallet

page 102
National Park Service

page 103
Chip Clark

page 104
Lysbeth Corsi/Focus on Nature

CHAPTER 6

page 110
top, John Stanley, University; bottom, Daniel Varner

page 111
Field Museum of Natural History, Chicago

page 113
Douglas Henderson/Petrified Forest Museum Association

page 114
Suzanne Swibold/Tyrrell Museum of Palaeontology

page 115
Douglas Henderson/Collection of Los Angeles County Museum of Natural History

page 118
left, Chip Clark
right, Field Museum of Natural History, Chicago and the artist, Charles R. Knight

page 119
top left and right, Daniel Varner; bottom, Mark Hallett

page 120
Chip Clark

page 122
Daniel Varner

page 123
top left, Michael Hoban, California Academy of Sciences; bottom left, right, Mitchener Covington, Florida State University

page 124
Biostatigraphy Research Group, British Geological Survey

page 125
After S. M. Stanley, 1984

page 126
left, Megan Rohn; right, David Dilcher, Indiana University

page 127
From P. E. Crane, E. M. Friis, and K. R. Pederson, "Lower Cretaceous Angiosperm Flowers: Fossil Evidence on Early Radiation of Dicotyledons," *Science,* 232, 1986

page 128
After E. G. Kauffman

page 129
Photo Archives, Denver Museum of Natural History

CHAPTER 7

page 134
Walter Alvarez, University of California, Berkeley

page 136
Ocean Drilling Program, Texas A&M University

page 140
After P. D. Ward and J. Wiedmann, 1953

page 141
Gerta Keller, Princeton University

page 143
Gerta Keller, Princeton University

page 144
Gerta Keller, Princeton University

page 147
Mitchener Covington, Florida State University

page 150
top left and right, bottom left and right, Katharina Perch-Nielsen; middle, Anthony Ekdale, University of Utah

page 151
After F. Surlyk and M. B. Johansen, 1984

page 153
left, Chip Clark; right, The British Museum (Natural History)

page 155
From J. Horner and J. Gorman, *Maia, A Dinosaur Grows Up,* illustrated by Douglas Henderson, Museum of the Rockies, 1985

page 157
After C. J. Orth et al., 1981

page 158
After J. A. Wolfe, 1978

page 162
Painting by Zdeněk Burian collection of Zdeněk Spinar

page 163
Camera Hawaii

page 164
Bruce Bohor, USGS

page 166
USGS

page 167
From W. Wolbach, R. Lewis, and E. Anders, "Cretaceous Extinctions: Evidence for Wildfires and Search for Meteoritic Material," *Science,* 230, 1985

page 168
Jet Propulsion Laboratory

page 170
After R. Douglas and F. Woodruff

CHAPTER 8

page 174
Chip Clark

page 175
Smithsonian Institution, National Museum of Natural History

page 176
David Dockery, Mississippi Department of Natural Resources

page 177
Gerta Keller, Princeton University

page 178
Gerta Keller, Princeton University

page 181
Richard Benson, Smithsonian Institution

page 182
After R. Douglas and F. Woodruff

page 183
After J. A. Wolfe, 1978

page 184
William Garnett

page 186
Field Museum of Natural History, Chicago and the artist, Charles R. Knight

page 188
After J. P. Kennett and C. C. von der Borch, 1986

CHAPTER 9

page 192
John Shaw/Tom Stack & Assoc.

page 193
Chip Clark

page 194
After J. Hays

page 196
Peter Molnar, MIT

page 197
Steven M. Stanley

page 200
After Steven M. Stanley, 1984

page 202
After E. S. Vrba, 1985

page 204
Painting by John Dawson, The George C. Page Museum, Los Angeles County Museum of Natural History

page 205
top, Peter Schouten, Australia Museum Trust; bottom, Photo Archives, Denver Museum of Natural History

page 206
Painting by John Dawson, The George C. Page Museum, Los Angeles County Museum of Natural History

CHAPTER 10

page 211
After Raup and Sepkoski, 1986

page 213
After D. V. Kent and F. M. Gradstein

INDEX

Acid rain, 47, 168

Acritarchs (dormant resting stages of an unknown type of fossil algae), 52–54, 70, 78, 82, 93

Adaptation, 1, 75, 148

Adaptive radiation(s) (the rapid origins of many new species or higher taxa from a single ancestral group): ammonoids, 110; angiosperms, 127; animal life: Neogene, 192–93; corals, 69; dolphins, 191; foraminiferans, 176; herbaceous plants, 192; invertebrates, 71; mammal-like reptiles, 99; mammals, 8, 112–113, 173, 174; marine organisms, 110; nautiloids, 67; Ordovician Period, 66; post-crises, 75; rugose corals, 86; songbirds, 173; teleost fish, 123; trilobites, 57

Aerosol(s) (a gaseous suspension of minute droplets of liquid suspended in the atmosphere), 168, 171

Africa, 10, 22, 27, 28–29, 32, 99; extinctions, 53, 202–203, 205; glacial deposits, 72; glaciers, 88

Age of Dinosaurs (the Mesozoic Era). *See* Mesozoic Era (Age of Dinosaurs)

Age of Mammals, 5, 162, 169

Ages, 8

Agnostids, 56, 63

Alaska, 185, 191

Albedo (the percentage of solar radiation that is reflected from the surface of the earth), 35

Alberta, Canada, 156, 159, 160, 161

Albertosaurus, 155

Aleutian Islands, 27

Algae, 1, 85, 86, 92, 93, 102, 174; filamentous, 50; floating, 154; fossil, 87; mass extinction, 18–19; Ordovician, 70; single-celled 53; single-celled planktonic, 123–124; symbiotic, 125; *see also* Calcareous algae

Alligators, 159

Alps, 116

Alvarez, Luis, 133, 161, 165, 166

Alvarez, Walter, 133

American mastodon, 204

Ammonoids (extinct cephalopods with chambered shells like that of the modern pearly nautilus), 76, 77, 82, 85, 91, 92, 131, 153; declines, 97, 116, 140, 169; declines, followed by final extinction, 154–155; extinctions, 18, 121, 128–129, 153–154, 174; fossil, 153; late Paleozoic, 97; periodic extinctions, 139; preponderance of, 109–110; recovery of, 91, 117

Amphibians, 19, 77, 78, 95–96; species–area curve, 37

Anders, Edward, 165–166

Andes, 27

Angiosperms (flowering plants, including grasses and hardwood trees), 13, 45, 126, 156, 173; changes in: Eocene–Oligocene, 183–185; Cretaceous, 127–131, 169; fossils, 127, 136, 138; herbaceous, 192; leaves with entire margins, 183

Animals: declines, 137; diversification, 50, 51, 54, 85; invaded land, 77; mass extinctions, 19, 98–99; Neogene Period, 192–193; size of, and survival, 100; terrestrial, 17, 95–96, 182

Anoxic waters (characterized by the absence of oxygen), 45–46, 85

Anstey, Robert, 16

Ant Atoll, 41

Antarctic separation, 186–189

Antarctica, 22, 34, 53, 99, 100, 101; deep-sea sediments, 194, 195; glaciers, 88, 194, 195, 196; position of, 33; position of, in relation to South Pole, 129, 216

Antelope, 10, 202–203

Anthropocentrism, 7

Apennine Mountains, 134

Appalachian Mountains, ancestral, 32, 80–81, 82

Aquilapollenites botanical province, 156

Archaeocyathids, 56, 57

Archaeopteryx, 121

Arthropods, 56

Arthur, Michael, 147, 148, 154, 210

Asaro, Frank, 133

Asia, 24, 29, 32, 33, 98; faunal interchange with North America, 185; flora, 159; southern, 30

Asthenosphere (the dense, dough-like layer of the earth below the lithosphere), 26, 27, 136

Astronomical hypotheses, 216–218

Aswan Dam, 195

Atlantic Ocean, 5, 33, 129, 187, 195; effect of glaciers on, 199–200; extinctions in, 11, 37; formation of, 32, 81; southern, 27

Atrypoids (a group of Paleozoic brachiopods that became extinct in the Late Devonian crisis), 82

Aubry, Marie-Pierre, 180–181

Australia, 22, 24, 33, 56, 101, 102, 129; Antarctica attached to, 187–188; extinctions in, 53, 205; glaciation, 54, 88; human hunters, 205–206; reefs, 83–84, 85

Background extinction (extinction of the sort that takes place continually during intervals of time not characterized by catastrophic regional extinction or global mass extinction), 11, 13, 15, 16, 17, 18, 22, 198

Baculites, 153–154

Badlands of South Dakota, 184, 185

Bakker, Robert, 112, 113, 128, 155

Baleen whales (whales that feed by sieving zooplankton from the water), 174

Barry, John, 195–196

Bats, 8, 173, 174

Bays, 46, 147

Beavers, 204–205

Bed(s), 3–4

Belemnoids (extinct squidlike cephalopods in which gas occupying an internal shell was balanced by a cigar-shaped counterweight), 117, 118

Benson, Richard, 181

Bering Strait, 185
Beuf, Serge, 72
Biblical deluge, 5, 6
Biotic crises, 1, 6, 17, 131, 193; ancient, 43–45; causes of 21–22, 36–47; early, 49–63; glaciation and, 102; major, 7–8; periodicity of, 18–19, 210–216; protracted, pulsatile, 176; simultaneity of land and sea, 209; *see also* Mass extinction(s)
Biotic deterioration, 169–170
Birds, 121, 173, 192–193
Bison, 205, 206
Bivalves (a class of mollusks characterized by two shell halves; examples are clams, mussels, scallops, and oysters), 42, 67, 153, 154, 171, 174; declines, 116, 169, 198; extinctions, 16, 123, 138–139, 149, 198–199; migration option, 201; preponderance, 110; recovery, 91, 117; reef-building, 109; thermal tolerance, 201–202; *see also* Rudists
Black muds, 45, 86, 121
Blitzkrieg hypothesis (a special case of the overkill hypothesis, invoking the sudden spread of advanced human hunters over many areas of the world about 11,000 years ago), 205–206
Body heat, 96, 113
Body size, 16–17, 100, 120
Bohor, Bruce, 164
Bolide(s) (an extraterrestrial body, such as a meteor or comet), 166–167, 168, 210
Boucot, Arthur J., 75
Boundary clay(s) (the clay layer separating Cretaceous and Paleocene sediments in some parts of the world), 133, 134, 136, 164, 166, 167; foraminiferan fossils, 144, 145; nannoplankton, 147; Raton Basin, 156
Boundary layer: Cretaceous–Neogene boundary, 136
Bovidae, 193
Braarudosphaera bigelowi, 147, 153
Brachiopods (lamp shells) (a group of invertebrate animals characterized by two shell halves but unrelated to bivalve mollusks), 58, 67–68, 71, 78, 110, 151; declines, 81–82, 97, 116; distribution, 72; Ordovician, 69; recovery, 91; sudden extinctions, 149, 151–152
Brazos River, Texas, 152–154, 169
Breadfruit plants, 43, 44
Bromley, Richard, 151

Bryozoans (a group of animals that colonize the sea floor; today these "moss animals" grow on rocks, docks, ships' hulls, etc.), 68, 70, 71, 75, 92, 102, 110, 149; declines, 97, 100, 103–104; extinction patterns, 16; lacy, 91–92; Ordovician, 16

Calcareous algae, 42, 57, 75, 86, 92, 101, 105, 106
Calcareous nannoplankton (an important group of phytoplankton in Mesozoic and Cenozoic seas, especially in warm seas), 124, 143, 145–147, 148, 154; decline, 169; evolution, 124; extinctions, 167, 180; recovery, 152
Calcareous sponges, 101, 103
Calcium carbonate, 56–57, 75, 124, 144, 151, 177
California, 16, 194
Cambrian crisis, 217
Cambrian Period, 19, 42, 49, 55–56, 61, 62, 65; Early, 56; Late 56, 59, 63
Campanian Age, 137, 138
Campbell, Lyle, 198
Canada, 16, 32, 37, 53; ice sheet, 199; reefs, 76, 83–84, 85
Canning Basin (Western Australia), 84, 85
Cannonball Sea, 171
Caputo, Mario V., 87, 88, 89
Caravaca, 142
Carbon dating (radiometric dating that employs the radioactive isotope carbon 14), 205
Carbon dioxide, 35–36, 168
Carbon 13/carbon 12 isotopic ratio, 146, 149, 154
Carboniferous Period, 82, 87, 91, 92, 93, 95; Late, 92
Caribbean Sea, 11, 41, 129, 171, 200
Carnivores, 95, 112, 123
Carnivorous reptiles, 113
Carter, Neville, 164
Cascade Range, 29
Catastrophe(s), 5, 6, 7, 8; agents of, 21–47
Catastrophism (the outmoded belief that sudden, violent, and widespread events caused by supernatural forces formed most of the rocks visible at the earth's surface), 5
Cenomanian Age, 128–129, 214
Cenozoic Era, 127, 175, 177; life forms, 173–174; mass extinctions, 19, 210; tempo-

ral divisions, 135–136
Cephalopoda, 66, 76, 117
Ceratopsians (horned dinosaurs of Cretaceous age), 129
Chalk (fine-grained limestone, usually consisting mainly of skeletons of Calcareous nannoplankton), 124
Chalk deposition, 109, 124, 145–146, 151, 152; Denmark, 149, 151
Chance factors, 10
Chi, W. R., 143–144, 149
China, 53, 67, 99, 162
Chordata, 11
Cifelli, Richard, 148, 176
Circumantarctic gyre (the circular current that has encircled Antarctica during the latter part of the Cenozoic Era), 186–187, 188, 189, 200
Clams, 16, 67, 125
Clark, David, 167
Classes, 16, 40, 75, 174
Clast (a solid product of erosion that may be deposited in sediment), 103
Clemens, William, 161
Cleveland Shale, 82
CLIMAP (the international project that produced a map of global temperatures for the most recent time of maximum glacial advance, 18,000 years ago), 199
Climate(s), 19, 21, 33–36, 45, 196–197; dry, 93–94, 99, 105, 162, 185–186, 203
Climatic change, 10, 61, 74, 102–105; Eocene Epoch, 188–189; lasting, 189; Neogene time, 191, 192, 193; North America, 183, 192; plankton and, 148–149; volcanism and, 164; *see also* Cooling
Climatic change as agent of mass extinction, 19, 36, 40–45, 47, 54, 63, 65, 72, 74, 75, 85, 87, 91, 100, 106, 117, 137, 141, 148, 149, 168, 169–171, 173, 175, 176, 204–205, 206–207, 209–210, 216; and disappearance of dinosaurs, 162
Clinopyroxene, 179
Clovis people, 205, 206
Coal deposits, 93, 94, 96, 99, 156
Coiled cephalopod mollusks, 76
Collinson, Margaret, 184–185
Comet cloud, 217
Comet showers, 179, 217
Comets, 167, 216; *see also* Extraterrestrial causes (mass extinctions)

Competition, ecological, 10, 13, 67, 85, 125, 128, 157, 162

Competitive displacement, 13, 42, 126

Compositae, 192

Conifers (cone-bearing seed plants, including pines and spruces), 13, 93, 94, 99, 111, 128, 156

Conodonts (extinct eel-shaped swimmers of unknown relationships; their minute teeth are abundantly preserved in rocks of Paleozoic and Triassic age), 58, 60, 70–71, 78, 85, 116, 117

Continental drift (the movement of continents with respect to one another over the surface of the earth), 22–30; history of, 30–33

Continental shelf (a continental margin flooded by the sea), 36–37, 38–39

Continents: colliding along subduction zones, 29; movement of, 21, 22–30, 47; pole encounters, 65, 72, 103, 107; position of, 31–33, 35

Convection (rotational flow of a fluid that results from imbalances in density, which often result from differences in temperature), 29

Cooling, 11, 22, 72, 73, 75, 103–105, 129; as agent of Late Devonian mass extinction, 87; Antarctic separation as model for, 186–189; as cause of mass extinctions, 106, 117, 199–203, 216 (see also Glaciation); Cenozoic Era, 177; and crises on land, 183–186; evidence of, 82–86; and extinction pulses: Eocene–Oligocene interval, 178, 179, 180, 183–184, 185, 188–189; global, 100–101; from high latitudes, 72, 106; Miocene Epoch, 194–195; Northern Hemisphere, 203; pulses of, 149; regional, 16–17; and terrestrial plants, 156–160; western region, North America, 159–160; see also Oceanic cooling

Copper, Paul, 81–82, 83

Coral reefs, 41, 116–117

Corals, 41, 42, 47, 57; declines, 97, 103–104; dominance, 110, 124, 125; modern, 79, 85; Ordovician, 69–70, 71; recovery, 92, 117; reef-building, 71, 109, 110, 122, 174

Coring (technique), 136, 141, 142; see also Deep-sea cores

Coriolis force (the force, resulting from the earth's rotation, that diverts currents clockwise in the Northern Hemisphere and counterclockwise in the Southern Hemisphere), 105

Crabs, 67, 123, 174

Cratering, 216

Cretaceous–Neogene boundary, 136

Cretaceous–Paleocene boundary, 135–136, 141, 142, 143, 149, 151, 153, 154, 163, 164; environmental change in, 155–160; extinction of dinosaurs at, 161; iridium anomaly at, 165

Cretaceous Period, 8, 17, 42, 43, 45, 121, 215; Early, 33; marine life, 122–126, 138; late, 13, 17, 128, 171; mass extinctions, 13, 18, 141, 148; sea level, 39; vegetation, 173–174

Cretaceous–Tertiary boundary, 135, 154

Crinoids (sea lilies) (relatives of starfish with branched arms that collect food particles from sea water), 68–69, 70, 76, 92, 97, 110

Crocodiles, 113; marine, 117–118, 119, 121, 122; terrestrial, 129

Crocodilians, 112

Cross beds, 104

Crowell, John C., 87, 88, 89

Crust (the outermost layer of the lithosphere, consisting of less dense rocks than those that lie below), 25; continental, 32, 101; movement of, 25–28; new, 136

Cuvier, Georges, 2–3, 4, 5, 6, 7; Recherches sur les Ossemens Fossiles, 5

Cyanophytes (Cyanophyta) (blue-green algae) (phytosynthetic, prokaryotic organisms, some types of which produce stromatolites), 50–51, 52, 85

Darwin, Charles, 5, 6

Dating, 197, 205; problem of, 214–215

Deccan traps, 163

Dockery, David, 176

Deep sea: cold waters at bottom of, 178, 181–182, 186–189; physical-chemical change in, 148

Deep-sea cores, 142, 177, 178, 200; hiatuses in, 178–179, 180; Miocene Epoch, 195; Pacific Ocean, 217

Deep Sea Drilling Project, 177; Hole 577, 148, 149; Site 577B, 165

Deep-sea life: mass extinctions, 195, 215; see also Sea-floor life

Deep-sea trenches, 26, 27, 136

Denmark, 142, 149–152, 166; Stevns Klint, 149–151, 152

Deserts, 23, 105

Devine, Joseph, 164, 167–168

Devonian crisis, 65–89, 217; temporal pattern of, 79–81

Devonian Period, 75, 76, 77, 81; Early, 31; Late 83, 91; major events of, 73; reefs, 83–86

Dhondt, Annie, 138

D'Hondt, Steven, 144, 145

Diatoms (one of the most important groups of phytoplankton of late Mesozoic and Cenozoic time), 123, 174, 188, 194, 195; centric, 167; evolution of, 124

Dinoflagellates (one of the most important groups of phytoplankton of the Mesozoic and Cenozoic eras), 123, 124, 148, 167, 174

Dinosaur National Monument, Utah, 118

Dinosaurs, 13, 22, 109–131, 137, 156; body size, 113–114, 120; digestion, 114; diversity, 129, 160, 161; extinction of, 1, 6, 7, 8, 13, 17, 18, 19, 36, 42, 47, 65, 114, 117, 126, 131, 133, 155; footprints of, 114, 115; last, 127–131; minor extinctions, 121; progressive decline, 160–162, 169; rise of, 111–115; small, 121; social behavior, 114, 115, 129; survival into Paleocene, 137

Diplodocus, 118–119

"Disaster forms," 147, 153

Distal factor of mass extinction (in a chain of events that results in mass extinction, one of the events removed from the actual agent of extinction), 7

Diversity of life, 49, 65, 66; sea floor, 37–39

Djulfian Age, 97, 100, 214

Dolomite (a mineral or rock consisting of calcium magnesium carbonate and usually occurring with limestone), 117

Dolphins, 111, 174, 191

Dragonfly, 96

Drake, Charles, 163–164, 167–168

Dropstone(s) (a stone dropped to the bottom of a lake or ocean from a melting body of ice afloat at the surface), 87, 101, 103

Duckbilled dinosaurs. See Hadrosaurs

Dune (a hill of sand piled up by the wind), 23; deposits, 104, 105

Dunkleosteus, 79

Dust, 21, 22, 167

Dutro, J. Thomas, 81

Dwarfing, 207

Earth: as bar magnet, 30; origin of, 49
Earth history: divisions of, 8, 49, 135
Earthquakes, 27
Ecosystem (organisms that live together in nature, together with the environment they occupy), 91; climatic change and, 191, 193; *see also* Marine ecosystem; Terrestrial ecosystem
Ekdale, Alan, 149–151
El Chichon, 168
El Kef, 142, 143–144, 145, 148
Elephants, 114
England: climate, 45, 191; shallow seas, 196
Environmental change, 10, 17, 155–160; and extinction of dinosaurs, 114; and fauna migrations, 203
Eocene Epoch, 135, 178, 185, 214, 215, 216, 217; climatic change, 188–189, 191; cooling 183–186; sea-floor life, 174–175
Eocene–Oligocene boundary, 175, 186–189
Eocene–Oligocene interval, 176–177; extinction pulses, 178–182
Eons, 8
Epochs, 8
Equatorial zone, 43, 45
Eras, 8
Eukaryote(s) (an advanced cell, such as characterizes plants and animals, that includes a nucleus and chromosomes), 52–53
Eurasia, 33, 39
Europe, 32, 81, 98, 164; continental drift, 25; extinction events, 121, 175–176, 205; shallow seas, 40
Evaporation, 46, 51
Evaporite salts, 105
Evolution, 5, 11, 59, 92, 117, 174, 203; global, 13; iterative, 176; marine food web, 123–124
Evolutionary rebounds, 85, 91–93, 129
Evolutionary turnover: dinosaurs, 128–131
Extinction (the total disappearance of a species or groups of species), 5, 6, 11, 19; causes of, 10–11; episodes of heavy, 109; fact of, 1–2; mild: Miocene Epoch, 193–196; nature of, 10–11; sudden: sea-floor, 149–155; *see also* Background extinction; Mass extinction(s); Regional extinction(s)
Extinction pulses, 45, 82, 99, 100, 105, 106, 129, 137, 145, 149, 155, 168, 169, 170, 176, 178, 198, 203–207; survivors of, 215
Extinction rate, 13–15

Extraterrestrial causes (mass extinctions), 18, 22, 36, 41, 46–47, 60, 81, 133–134, 149, 163–167, 210, 216, 217
Extraterrestrial objects: striking earth, 143, 144, 149, 179

Famennian Age, 77, 81, 82, 85, 87
Families, 11, 13, 75, 175; new, 174; extinctions, 13–15, 40, 122, 211
Faults, 23, 28, 29
Fauna: impoverished, 97, 198; mass extinctions, 65; Triassic, 112
Faunal turnover, 129, 179, 185, 196
Feeding, 95; dinosaurs, 113–114, 115; fish, 123
Fern event, 156–157, 158
Fern spores, 157
Ferns, 111, 156–157, 169
Ferguson Ranch (Montana), 161
Fischer, Alfred, 146, 147, 210
Fish, 82, 85, 86, 109, 111; armored, 19; bony, 92; evolutionary history, 78; jawed, 76–77; jawless, 76; sport, 123; teleost, 123, 174
Fish Clay, 149–151, 152
Floras, terrestrial, 99; climatic change and, 191–192; *see also* Plants
Florida, 196, 198, 200, 201
Florida Everglades, 179
Florida Keys, 41
Flowering plants. *See* Angiosperms
Food supply, 22, 100, 162
Food webs, 155, 174
Foraminiferans (an amoeba-like single-celled marine organism that secretes a skeleton), 110, 124, 171, 174, 177, 193; declines, 176–177; *see also* Planktonic foraminiferans
Forests, 77, 93, 192, 203
Fossil(s) (a remnant or trace of ancient life), 5, 49
Fossil record, 1–2, 11, 49, 138, 218; acritarchs, 93; angiosperms, 127; animals, 54–55; birds, 173; brachiopods, 152; conodonts, 58; cyanophytes, 50; dinoflagellates, 124; dinosaurs, 114, 115, 118, 129, 156, 160–162; eukaryotic life, 52; evidence about climate, 45; evidence of Pangaea, 22–23; fish, 76, 77; flowers, 127; foraminiferans, 141–145; graptolites, 71; incomplete, 97, 117; invertebrates, 14; leaves, 159;

mammals, 203, 205; molluscan faunas, 197; nannoplankton, 145–147, 154; Neogene extinctions, 193; Ordovician, 71; plants, 45, 93; pollen, 127, 159, 200, 203; prokaryotic, 50; reptiles, 116; trilobites, 59
Fossilization (the process of becoming a fossil), 5
Frasnian Age, 77, 81, 82, 85, 87
Frasnian–Famennian boundary, 77, 82, 86
Frasnian–Famennian crisis, 82
French, Bevan, 165
Fusulinaceans, 97, 100, 103–104
Fusulinid(s) (a group of large foraminiferans that died out in the Late Permian crisis), 92–93

Gabriel, Diane, 160
Garrett, Peter, 50
Gartner, Stefan, 154
Gastropods (mollusks known informally as snails; most species are crawling animals with coiled shells), 38, 67, 91, 110, 153, 174, 176; cool-adapted, 171; declines, 116; extinctions: Pliocene, 198; predaceous, 123; recovery, 117
Genera, 11, 75, 174; disappearance of, 175, 185, 211; distribution, 100, 106, 109
Geographic pattern (mass extinctions), 100, 148; Pliocene extinctions, 199–203
Geography: and agents of catastrophe, 21–47; world, 102–105
Geological record, 5–6
Geology, 80, 217–218
Gerstal, Jennifer, 148
Giant wombat, 205
Girtyocoelia, 103
Gizzard stones (the stones that an animal such as a bird or dinosaur employs to grind food in its digestive tract), 114, 118
Glacial deposits, 61, 72, 87, 200, 201
Glaciation (the creeping of large masses of ice over the surface of the earth), 79, 87–89, 129; cycles of, 19; Gondwanaland, 73, 74; Late Permian, 105; late Precambrian, 54; and mammalian extinctions, 206–207; and mass extinctions, 37, 53–54, 65, 100, 102–103, 106, 107, 209; Northern Hemisphere, 189, 191, 199; and Ordovician and Devonian crises, 65–89, 217; South Polar, 72–75

Glaciers, 23–24, 135, 203; Antarctica, 188; and climatic change, 35–36; expansion of, 177, 216; melting back, 196

Glass sponges, 82–83

Global hydrological cycle (the movement of water from sea to air to sea again, often via the land), 35, 73, 177

Globigerapsis, 179

Globigerines (a group of planktonic foraminiferans that has been unusually resistant to mass extinction), 148, 176

Globotruncanidae, 148

Glossopteris flora (the late Paleozoic flora that was widely distributed in Gondwanaland), 22–24, 99

Gobi Desert, 94, 105

Gombos, Andrew, 167

Gondwanaland (the large southern continent that during latest Precambrian and Paleozoic time included South America, Africa, peninsular India, Antarctica, and Australia), 24, 29, 97, 99; evidence for, 24–25; framentation of, 32–33, 129, 188, 216; glaciation, 25, 87–89; Late Ordovician time, 73, 74; position of South Pole relative to, 31, 72, 73, 74, 87, 88, 89, 100, 102; position of, 30–31, 83

Gould, Stephen, 212

Grand Canyon (Arizona), 104

Graptolites (colonial Paleozoic animals, most species of which floated in the ocean), 18, 19, 71, 72

Grasses, 127, 173–174, 192

Grasslands, 191–192, 193, 203

Great Bahama Bank, 51

Great Barrier Reef, 84

Great Britain, 10, 81; climatic cooling, 184–185; *see also* England

Great Lakes region (U.S.), 75

Greenhouse effect (the trapping of heat near the earth's surface by carbon dioxide in the atmosphere, which allows warming sunlight to reach the earth), 35–36, 168

Greenland, 16, 31, 43, 54, 77, 185; climate, 45; ice sheet, 199; position of, 31–32, 33

Ground sloths, 2, 205, 207

Guadalupian Age, 97, 214

Guembelitria cretacea, 144–145, 148

Gulf of Mexico, 42, 129, 171, 176

Gulf Stream, 200

Gymnosperms (plants characterized by naked seeds; conifers are examples), 94–95, 99, 111, 128

Gyre, mantle, 28

Hadrosaurs (duckbilled dinosaurs, a diverse Late Cretaceous group), 7, 114, 115, 129, 155

Hall, James, 4, 80–81

Hallam, Anthony, 116, 121, 214

Hansen, Thor, 152, 154, 176

Hardwood trees, 13, 45, 93, 127

Hawaiian archipelago, 38

Hazel, Joseph, 201

He, Qiziang, 146

Hedbergella, 148

Hell Creek Formation (Montana), 160, 161

Herbaceous plants, 192

Herbivores, 95, 99, 112, 162

Hess, Harry, 25, 27

Heterohelicidae, 148

Hexacorals (the group of corals alive today, named for the hexagonal symmetry of their skeletons), 110

Hickey, Leo, 159

Hickman, Carole, 176

Higher life, 54, 77; beginning of, 49–63

Himalayas, 29, 30, 33, 195, 196, 203

Hoffman, Antoni, 163, 212

Homo sapiens, 12

Horner, Jack 114

Horse family, 173, 193, 204

House, Michael, 82

Hudson Bay, 37, 199

Human species, 8, 191; as cause of mammalian extinctions, 8, 204, 205–206, 207

Hutchison, Howard, 159

Hydrogen chloride, 168

Hydrogen cyanide, 167

Hypothetico-deductive method, 41–42

Ice Age (the recent interval of continental glaciation in the Northern Hemisphere, which began about 3 million years ago), 2, 11, 16, 37, 53, 135, 165, 177, 189; extinctions, 37, 38; faunal crisis and, 199; shallow sea life in, 74; volume of glaciers in, 35

Ice caps, 16, 195; disappearance of, 203–207; Northern Hemisphere, 199, 200

Icebergs, 101, 194, 200

Iceland, 201

Ichthyosaur ("fish lizard"), 111, 116, 117, 121, 122

Ichthyostega, 77, 79

Impact scenario (Cretaceous), 47, 165–167

Imperial mammoth, 204

India, 24, 99, 162; peninsular, 22, 29, 30, 33

Indian–Australian plate, 23, 30

Indian Ocean, 33, 187

Inoceramids (a group of Mesozoic bivalve mollusks that died out in the terminal Cretaceous crisis), 138–139, 169

Insects, 95

Interglacial age, 191, 199; Pleistocene, 198–199

Invertebrates (animals without backbones), 55, 71, 81; major groups of, 14; marine, 18, 116, 122, 138, 152–154, 169

Iridium, 18, 46–47, 60, 81, 86, 167; and extraterrestrial-cause hypothesis, 217; seafloor deposits, 153

Iridium anomaly (an exceptionally high concentration of the rare element iridium in a sedimentary stratum), 6–7, 86, 133–134, 136, 210; Fish Clay, 151; foraminiferan deposits, 143; Late Cretaceous, 161, 162; 163–165, 166; New Mexico, 157; Raton Basin, 156, 157

Isotopic data, 177, 178

Izett, Glen, 164

Jablonski, David, 17

Jaw(s), 76, 77, 111

Jefferson, Thomas, 2

Jiang, Ming-Jung, 154

Johansen, Marianne, 151, 152

Jones, Douglas, 154

Jurassic–Cretaceous transition, 122

Jurassic Period, 121, 136, 214; life in, 116, 117–122; time scales for, 211, 213

Kangaroos, 205

Kansas, 137

Kauffman, Erle, 129; 140–141

Keller, Gerta, 143–144, 145, 148, 149, 178, 179, 180

Kennett, James, 186, 188

Kilauea (Hawaii) volcano, 163

Kingdom(s), 11

Kitchell, Jennifer, 167, 215

Knoll, Andrew H., 17, 53–54, 99

Kollmann, Heinz, 171

Kolyma (terrain), 101, 103

Krakatoa (volcano), 164

Kyte, Frank, 217

Labyrinthodont amphibians, 115
Lagoons, 46, 51, 147
Lake Tanganyika, 29
Lamina(s), 3
Late Cretaceous event, 65, 117, 133–138, 144–145, 147, 149, 153, 161, 162, 174, 178, 210, 214; catastrophic hypothesis, 163–171; climatic change and, 209; plant losses in, 156
Late Devonian crisis, 16, 77, 78–82, 91, 93, 95, 100, 101, 139, 216; cause of, 87; climatic change and, 209; glaciation, 88–99, 102; patterns shared with other crises, 106–107
Late Eocene crisis, 188–189, 210, 217; climatic change and, 209
Late Ordovician crisis, 16, 71–72, 86, 100, 101, 216; climatic change and, 209; and glaciation, 102; patterns shared with other crises, 106–107
Late Permian crisis, 109–110, 214; effect on terrestrial life, 98–99; patterns shared with other crises, 106–107
Late Precambrian crisis, 209
Late Triassic crisis, 115–117
Latitude, 30
Latitudinal bias, 171
Leaf margin analysis (the use of the incidence of smooth-margined leaves in a fossil flora to estimate ancient climatic temperature), 159, 160
Leaf shapes, 136
Leaves, 127–128; entire-margin, 158, 159, 183–184; fossil, 159
Lewis, Roy, 165–166
Life: classification of, 12; on land, 93–96; see also Diversity of life; Higher life
Life position, 125
Limestone (a sedimentary rock that consists primarily of calcium carbonate; most limestones are formed mainly of shell debris and other biologically produced materials), 57, 60, 61, 117, 124; tropical, 91
Limestone deposition, 63, 75, 101, 103, 106
Limiting factors (aspects of the environment that control the distribution and abundance of species and that can become agents of extinction), 10, 22, 45–46
Lipps, Jere, 97
Lithification (the process by which soft sediment turns into hard rock), 4

Lithosphere (the outer rigid shell of the earth, situated above the crust and including the crust and upper mantle and divided into plates), 26–27, 28
Lizards, 96, 122
Local extinction. See Regional extinction(s)
Locomotion, 95, 112; dinosaurs, 114, 115, 129; fish, 123
London Clay, 185
Longitude, 30
Lycopods (Lycopodium) (club moss) (spore-bearing plants that were the most important coal producers of late Paleozoic time), 93–94, 111
Lyell, Charles, 5–6
Lystrosaurus (the most abundant genus of mammal-like reptiles immediately after the terminal Permian crisis), 99, 112

Maastrichtian Age, 137, 138–139, 145, 151, 162, 170, 215; extinctions, 154–155
Maastrichtian–Paleocene boundary, 140
McGhee, George, 81, 82, 83, 86
Mackay glacier, 34
McKenzie, Judith, 146
McLaren, Digby, 79
Magma (naturally occurring molten rock), 27, 29
Magnetic field, 21, 30; polarity reversals, 28, 143
Magnetism: deep-sea floor, 27–28
Mamenchisaurus, 119
Mammals (Mammalia), 7–8, 11, 112–113, 120, 185, 215; adaptive radiation, 174; disappearance of large, 203–207; diversification, 161, 162, 175; dominance, 133, 173; effect of climatic deterioration on, 185–186; Late Cretaceous, 114, 162; Miocene Epoch, 195–196; Neogene Period, 193
Mammoth, 2, 3, 204
Manson, Iowa, crater, 165
Mantle (the zone of the earth's interior below the crust and consisting of denser rock), 25, 26, 29, 35, 136
Marasti, Rafaella, 202
Marine ecosystem, 82, 100, 106, 110, 117, 131; depletion of, 155; effect of climatic change on, 209; recovery, 122, 124–125
Marine invertebrates, 18, 116, 122, 138, 169; biotic change, 152–154

Marine life, 57, 71, 109–111, 122–123, 174; Cretaceous, 122–126; distribution of, 75, 106; distribution of crises in, 211; diversity, 91; effect of cooling on, 82–86; effect of mass extinctions on, 133; evolutionary recovery, 91–93, 129; extinction patterns, 154–155; extinction rates, 13–15; extinctions, 8, 36–40, 167, 171, 175–182, 209; family-level extinctions, 211, 214, 215; Jurassic, 117–118; mass extinctions, 17, 18, 19, 65, 71–72, 78–79, 89, 91, 96–98, 100, 114–117, 121, 218; Neogene Period, 191; new forms of, 66, 67–71; protracted extinctions, 137–141, 169–170; reef-building, 40–41, 42
Marl (sediment consisting of a mixture of carbonate sediment and clay), 152
Marsupials, 205
Martin, Paul, 205
Mass extinction(s) (the extinction of many taxa on a global scale during a brief interval of geologic time), 1–19, 59, 62, 73, 212; and adjustment to environmental change, 155; causes of, 7, 21–47, 58–63, 99–101, 106–107, 209; Cretaceous Period, 128–129; early 49–63; Eocene–Oligocene, 193–196; first, 49, 52, 53–54; geography and, 21–47; Late Cambrian, 61; nature of, 11–17; patterns in, 17–19, 41–42, 65, 91, 99–101, 106–107, 137–138, 154–155, 178–179; Pliocene Epoch, 196–203; proximate agents of, 7, 21–22, 36; protracted, pulsable, 97, 98, 99, 128–129, 141–147, 168–171, 175, 178, 209–210; simultaneity of land and sea, 209; Triassic, 115, 117; trilobites, 56–58; see also Extinction pulses
Mediterranean Sea, 144, 195, 202
Megalonyx jeffersoni, 2
Mesophytic Flora (the flora that prevailed during the Mesozoic Era before flowering plants became dominant), 95, 99, 105, 111
Mesosaurus, 22
Mesozoic–Cenozoic extinction curve, 215–216
Mesozoic Era (Age of Dinosaurs), 6–7, 8, 24, 79, 81, 96, 97, 109–131, 174; catastrophic end of (hypothesis), 163–171; marine life, 138; mass extinctions, 19, 39, 42, 47, 115–117, 139, 210; new life forms in, 109, 110; Pangaea in, 32; terminal extinction, 124, 133–174; terrestrial change,

155–160

Metabolism: ectothermic, 113; endothermic, 113, 114

Meteor crater: Arizona, 166

Meteor-striking-earth theory, 6, 7, 22, 46–47; *see also* Extraterrestrial causes (mass extinctions)

Meteorites, 165, 166, 179

Mice, 192–193

Michel, Helen, 133

Microfossils, 178

Microtektite(s) (a very small tektite), 143, 179

Mid-Atlantic ridge, 23, 25, 26, 27

Midocean ridges, 23, 25, 26, 28, 29, 35, 136

Midocean spreading, 27, 33–35

Milky Way, 210, 216

Miller, James F., 61

Miocene Epoch, 135, 191, 193, 215; mild extinction, 193–196

Miocene–Pliocene boundary, 204

Mollusks (a phylum of invertebrate animals that includes bivalves, gastropods, and cephalopods), 17, 38, 55, 57, 67, 174, 197; declines, 138–139, 169, 182, 197–198; extinctions, 176, 201–202; fossil, 153–154; migrating, 196–197; predominance, 109, 110, 117, 122; See also Bivalves; Cephalopoda; Gastropods

Monera (kingdom), 50

Mongolia, 114

Monoclonius, 155

Montana, 115, 156, 160, 161, 162, 164

Montmartre (Paris), 4

Morrison Formation, 118–119, 121

Mosasaurs (large marine lizards of the Cretaceous Period), 122, 137

Mountain building, 29, 116, 139

Multicellular life, 49, 52, 54

Murphy, Margaret, 186

Mussels, 16, 67

Nannofossil species, 150

Nannoplankton. See Calcareous nannoplankton

Natural selection, 6

Nautiloids (swimming, carnivorous mollusks characterized by a chambered shell; the pearly nautilus is the only living nautiloid genus), 66–67, 76, 77, 85

Neogene Period, 135, 191–207

New Mexico, 81, 156, 158, 159, 162, 164, 171; reef complex, 102; shocked mineral grains, 164, 165

New York State, 4, 32, 76, 80–81, 82, 83

New Zealand, 68

Nile River, 195

Nitecki, Matthew, 163

Nitrous oxide, 166

Norian Age, 214

North America, 24, 25, 31–32, 81, 98; climatic change, 183, 192; faunal interchange with Asia, 185; interior seaway, 128, 128, 137–138, 156, 160, 171; latitudinal bias in extinctions, 171; mammalian extinctions, 205, 206; regional mass extinctions, 16–17; shallow seas, 39, 58, 81, 92; trilobite extinctions, 56–57, 61, 63; western region, 156–162, 183–184

North American plate, 29

North Atlantic, 197, 203

North Dakota, 42, 171

North Pole, 103

North Sea, 202

Northern Hemisphere: climatic change, 103–105, 203; glaciation, 19, 189, 191, 199; ice sheets, 194, 199, 201

Nothosaurs, 111

Nuclear winter, 167

Ocean currents, 178, 180, 186–187, 188–189

Oceanic cooling, 63, 116, 169–170, 171, 177–178, 179, 181–182, 186–189, 193–194, 215, 216

Oceanic crust, 25–26, 27, 28, 29

Oceans, 4, 21; alkalinity, 168; restructuring of (middle Miocene), 193–196; temperature, 169–170 (*see also* Oceanic cooling); thermal structure, 181; *see also* Deep sea

Octopuses, 66, 67

Officer, Charles, 163–164, 167–168

Old Red Sandstone continent (continent formed in mid-Paleozoic time, comprising North America, Greenland, Scotland, and Scandinavia), 32, 80, 81

Old Red Sandstone deposit, 32, 81

Olenellids (the oldest kind of trilobite, restricted to the Early Cambrian), 56

Olenid (a kind of trilobite that lived in cool waters and survived the marine crises of Late Cambrian time), 63

Oligocene Epoch, 135, 178, 185, 193; cooling in, 183–186; sea level, 39, 40, 209

On the Origin of Continents and Oceans (Wegener), 22

Opportunists, 59, 147, 157

Orders, 11, 16, 75, 174, 175

Ordovician crisis, 79, 91, 217; glaciation and, 65–89

Ordovician Period, 31, 61, 66, 77; Early, 209; major events of, 73; recovery in, 66–71; Late, 67

Orth, Carl, 210

Osteichthyes (the bony fish group that includes most fish of the modern world), 111

Ostracods (small crustaceans that are housed in a hinged shell), 181, 201

Overkill hypothesis (the idea that the impact of Stone Age hunting caused the extinction of many large mammals), 205–206, 207

Oxygen, 21; level of dissolved, as agent of mass extinction, 36, 45–46, 63, 85, 121

Oxygen isotope ratios, 169–70, 177, 178, 179, 181, 182, 193–194, 210

Oysters, 16, 67

Ozone layer, 167, 168

Pacific Ocean, 28, 129, 187, 199; temperatures, 170, 182

Pacific plate, 23, 29

Pakistan, 195

Paleocene Epoch, 135, 147, 171, 173–189; dinosaurs in, 161, 162

Paleogene Period, 135, 173, 174, 175; major events of, 186

Paleomagnetism (the magnetism of a rock, developed from the earth's magnetic field when the rock is formed), 30

Paleophytic Flora (the flora, dominated by spore-bearing plants, that prevailed during the Paleozoic Era), 105

Paleozoic Era, 7, 42, 81, 95, 99; glacial deposits, 87, 88–89; major events of, 98; late interval: taxonomic groups in, 91–93; marine life, 67–68, 71; mass extinctions, 8, 19, 39, 42, 65, 67, 72, 96, 116; new life forms, 76, 77; reef growth, 42, 79

Paleozoic–Mesozoic transition, 110

Palmer, Allison, 58–59, 63

Pangaea (the supercontinent that included nearly all of the earth's continental crust

Pangaea (*continued*)
near the end of the Paleozoic Era), 32, 97–98, 99, 100, 102, 105; evidence for existence of, 22–23, 24; fauna, 112; formation of, 32; fragmentation of, 33, 116; Late Permian time, 101; location of, 103
Paris Basin, 3, 5
Pearly nautilus, 66, 67, 76
Pedder, A. E. H., 86
Pelagic life (life that floats or swims in the upper zone of the ocean), 37
Pena, Daniel, 215
Pennsylvania, 93
Perch-Nielsen, Katharina, 146
Percival, Stephen, 146
Periodicity, 18–19, 210–216
Periods, 8
Permian crisis, 65, 91–107, 112, 133, 138
Permian Period, 87, 91, 92, 93–94, 100, 105, 214; animal life, 95–96; Early, 92; Late, 32, 91, 101; mass extinctions, 96–98; reef complex, 102, 103; sea level, 39
Petroleum reservoirs, 76, 84
Petuch, Edward, 179
Phanerozoic Eon, 49, 50, 53, 55, 71, 101
Phillips, Arthur, 207
Photosynthesis, 36, 50, 123, 125, 146; shutdown of, 167
Phyla, 11, 75
Phytoplankton, 51, 93, 109, 123, 174; cold-adapted, 188; extinctions, 149, 154, 167; fossil, 136; photosynthesis, 146
Placoderms (armored fish of Paleozoic age that barely survived the late Devonian mass extinction), 77, 78, 79, 81, 82, 92
Placodont reptile, 110
Plankton, 19, 52, 70, 138, 154, 168; and climate, 148–149; cold-water, 186; extinctions, 170, 176–177, 182, 195; and ocean cooling, 194; warm-adapted, 171
Planktonic foraminiferans, 141, 144, 153, 168, 203, 215; extinction pulses: Eocene–Oligocene interval, 178–182; globigerine, 148; new forms, 145; temporal extinction pattern, 141–145
Planktonic life, 51–52
Plants, 17, 36, 77, 93–95, 217; extinctions, 99, 171; first, 77; periodic transformations, 99; taxonomic identification, 136; Triassic, 111–112; *see also* Angiosperms; Terrestrial life, plant

Plate(s) (a segment of the earth's lithosphere that moves independently over the earth's interior), 22, 23, 28–29
Plate tectonics (the study of the movements and interactions of lithospheric plates), 22, 29–30, 33, 103; model for inception of psychosphere, 186–189
Pleistocene Epoch, 11
Plesiosaurs (large swimming reptiles of Mesozoic seas), 118, 119, 122, 137
Pliensbachian Age, 121, 213, 214
Pleistocene Epoch, 135, 191, 198, 203; glacial intervals, 200–201, 206
Pliocene Epoch, 11, 135, 191, 196–203
Po River, 195
Polarity, 28, 30
Poles, 7, 45–46, 101; continents encroaching on, 103, 107, 129; and deep-sea cooling, 186, 194; glacial expansion at, 177, 178
Pollen, 127–128, 156, 157; fossil, 159, 161
Pollen record, 127, 200, 159, 203
Posture, upright, 95, 96
Precambrian time, 49–53, 62
Predation, 10; as cause of mammalian extinction, 204, 205–206, 207
Predator/prey ratio (the ratio between the weight of predators in an ecosystem and the weight of their prey), 113
Predators, 13, 70, 77, 92, 99, 112; dinosaur, 119–20, 129; marine, 174; mobile, 66–67; swimming, 76, 77, 82, 117–118
"Primary Time," 7
Primates, 8, 173
Prokaryote(s) (a simple cell, such as that of a bacterium, that lacks a nucleus and chromosomes), 49–50, 52
Prothero, Donald, 185
Protozoans, 51
Proximate factor of mass extinction (the immediate agent causing mass extinction), 7, 21–22, 36
Pseudoperiodicity, 212, 215
Psychrosphere (the mass of cold water that occupies the deep sea today), 181, 186, 188
Pterosaurs, 120–121
Pyrite, 144

Quetzalcoatlus, 121, 129–131
Quinn, James F., 15

Radiation, 21, 35, 36, 41, 107
Radioactive dating, 143

Radiolarians (marine zooplankton that are relatives of foraminiferans but secrete a skeleton of silica), 179
Radiometric dating (the use of naturally occurring radioactive materials to date rocks by measuring the amounts of these materials relative to the amounts of materials produced by their decay), 54, 59, 184, 197
Raffi, Sergio, 202
Rain forests, 158
Random walk (stepwise change in some variable that moves upward or downward with equal probability at each step), 212, 215
Raton Basin (New Mexico), 156, 157
Rats, 192–193
Raup, David M., 13, 15, 210–214, 215, 217
Recent (Holocene) Epoch, 135, 191
Recherches sur les Ossemens Fossiles (Cuvier), 5
Recovery(ies), 65, 75–77, 85, 91–93, 101, 129, 215
Red Sea, 28
Reef builders, 40–41, 42, 56, 71, 75–76, 139–141; dominant, 124–125; Ordovician, 69–70; Mesozoic Era, 79; Permian, 101; *see also* Bivalves; Corals; Rudists; Tabulates
Reef community, 79, 97, 105, 106, 110; collapse of Devonian, 83–86; Cretaceous, 124–126; Triassic, 116–117
Reefs, 57, 75, 101, 106, 215; coral, 41, 116–117; Devonian, 86; late Paleozoic, 92; Late Permian, 103; rudist, 131
Refrigeration, 78–79; *see also* Cooling
Regional extinction(s) (the extinction of many taxa in a particular geologic region), 11, 16–17, 198–199
Reproductive behavior: dinosaurs, 114; marine reptiles, 117; plants, 93, 99
Reptiles (Reptilia), 11, 13, 95–96, 112, 113; declines, 137; flying, 1, 120–121, 129–131; mammal-like, 8, 23, 95, 96, 98–99, 115; marine, 110–111, 116, 117–118, 121, 174; species–area curve, 37; warm-adapted, 159, 160
Retallack, Gregory, 185
Rhaetian Age, 214
Rhone River, 195
Rifting, 28–29, 33
Rigby, Keith, 160
Riss-Würm glacial interval, 199
Rock magnetism (technique), 53, 57, 72, 83, 87, 88

Rock record, 6, 74, 149, 218; evidence of continental drift, 23–24

Rocky Mountains, ancestral, 129, 156

Rodents, 173

Romein, A. J. T., 143

Rudists (reef-building bivalve mollusks that died out in the terminal Cretaceous crisis), 124–126, 131, 169, 171, 174; periodic extinctions, 139–141

Rugose corals (Rugosa), 69, 71, 75, 76, 86, 97; distribution, 100

Saharan Desert, 72

Salinity (the salt content of natural water), 22, 51; as agent of mass extinction, 36, 46

Salt deposits, 93, 195

San Andreas Fault, 29

Sandstone(s) (sedimentary rock formed by the cementation of sand), 4, 80–81

Sanfilippo, Annika, 179

Sauropods (the group of dinosaurs that included the largest species of all time), 118–119, 121

Scandinavia, 16, 31, 53, 61, 63; ice sheet, 199

Scaphites, 153

Schizophytes (Schizophyta) (prokaryotes of the type informally termed bacteria), 50

Schopf, J. William, 52

Scotland, 53

Sea anemones, 69

Sea floor, 7, 209; spreading, 27, 33–35

Sea-floor life, 36, 37, 39, 56, 123, 209; in anoxic waters, 45, 46; change in: Eocene Epoch, 174–175; effect of sea-level lowering on, 74–75; gradual improverishment of, 138–141; sudden extinctions of, 149–155

Sea level, 7, 21, 124, 196; change in, 33–36, 100, 106, 116, 217–218; and cooling, 180; lowered, 39, 73–74, 93–94, 101, 105, 121–122, 162, 184, 185, 195

Sea-level lowering as agent of mass extinctions, 36–40, 60, 61, 73–74, 106, 170–171, 176, 209, 218

Sea positions: change in, 21

Sea urchins, 57, 110, 174

"Secondary Time," 7

Sediment(s) (material deposited at the earth's surface by water, ice, or air), 3, 4, 5, 7, 23–24, 36, 136; Antarctica, 194, 195; glacial, 45, 53; see also Turbidity

Sedimentary rock (a rock formed by the consolidation of loose sediment by compaction or by precipitation of cement from a watery solution), 4

Sedimentary record: climatic change, 47; hiatuses in deep-sea, 177–179

Sedimentation (the accumulation of sediment), 3–4

Sepkoski, J. John, 13, 15, 210–214, 215, 217

Shackleton, Nicholas, 200

Shale(s) (rock formed by compaction of clay and tending to break easily along horizontal planes), 80–81, 87

Shallow seas, 36, 37, 39, 42, 60, 124, 152, 196; anoxic, 46; cooling of, 83; extinctions in: Miocene Epoch, 195; North Atlantic, 58, 92, 105; regression of, 61, 74, 75

Shark Bay (Western Australia), 51

Sharks, 77, 78, 92, 92

Shasta ground sloth, 206, 207

Sheehan, Peter, 72, 75

Shocked minerals (grains displaying microscopic fractures produced by very high pressures), 164, 165

Siberia, 3, 103, 185

Signor, Philip, 97, 139

Silurian Period, 71, 73, 75, 89

Single-celled organisms, 49–50, 52

Skeleton(s), 4, 49, 55–56, 57, 77, 93, 125, 177, 178; internal, 117; silica, 82; sponges, 70; trilobites, 56; type of, and extinctions, 148

Skevington, David, 72

Sloan, Robert, 98–100, 105, 160, 161, 162

Smit, Jan, 143

Snails, 17, 67, 153, 174

Snakes, 192–193

Soils, 185

Solar system, 210, 216, 217

Songbirds, 173, 192–193

South Africa, 22, 100

South America, 22, 24, 61, 100, 121, 129, 162; Antarctica attached to, 187–188; glacial deposits, 87, 88; mammalian extinctions, 205, 206; position of, 27, 32

South Pole, 31, 181, 186; encroachment of Antarctica on, 129; Ordovician glaciation, 72–75; position of, 83, 88; position of Gondwanaland relative to, 31, 72, 73, 74, 87, 88, 89, 100, 102

Southern Hemisphere, 24, 100, 103, 194

Soviet Union, 53, 100

Spain, 139, 169

Speciation (the origin of a new species from another species), 18

Species, 75; classification of, 11–13; cool-adapted, 178, 180; disappearance, replacement, 1–2, 5, 7, 10–11, 13, 40, 122, 175, 185; distribution, 40–41, 100, 106, 109–110; extinctions, 179; new, 6, 11, 59, 97, 174; origin of, 5–6; warm-adapted, 180, 202

Species–area hypothesis (the idea that reduced area of sea floor at times of lowered sea level results in mass extinction), 37–40

Spiny foraminiferans, 178

Sponges, 42, 55, 70, 71, 92, 102, 105, 110; calcareous, 101, 103

Spore (the reproductive structure of ferns and other seedless plants), 93, 157

Squid, 66, 67

Starfish, 4, 68

Stegosaurs, 119–120, 121

Stitt, James, 63

Straits of Gibraltar, 195

Stratigraphic (pertaining to stratigraphy) record, 136, 142, 198–199

Stratigraphy (the study or the relationships of strata in time and space), 3–5

Stratum, strata (a discrete layer of sedimentary rock), 3–4

Stromatolite(s) (a layered sedimentary structure formed by threadlike cynophytes), 50–51, 58, 85

Stromatoporoids (an extinct group of sponges that secreted layered skeletons and were important contributors to reefs until the Late Devonian crisis), 70, 71, 75, 79, 85

Subduction (descent of a slab of the earth's lithosphere into the asthenosphere along a trench in the deep sea), 27, 28, 29

Subduction zone(s), 23, 27, 28, 29

Submarine trenches, 38

Subsidence (depression of a region of the earth's crust), 7

Sulfuric acid, 168

Sun, 22, 35; companion star of, 217

Supernova explosion, 21

Supratidal zone, 50–51

Surlyk, Finn, 151, 152

Suture(s) (the juncture between two plates that have been united along a subduction zone), 29, 32, 81
Swamp flora, 93–94
Swamps, 4, 93, 96, 99

Tabulates (an extinct group of colonial corals that were important contributors to reefs until the Late Devonian crisis), 69–70, 71, 75, 76, 79, 85
Tallgrass prairie, 192; see also Grasslands
Taxon, taxa (a group of organisms united in a particular category in the classification of life), 11–13, 75, 174; and mass extinctions, 13, 16, 18, 40, 122, 129; post-crisis recovery, 91–93
Taylor, Michael, 63
Teeth, 110; differentiated, 95, 96; horses, 193; nothosaurs, 111; placodonts, 110
Tektite(s) (a tiny grain of glassy texture produced by the impact on earth of an extraterrestrial object), 143
Teleosts (the advanced group of bony fish, which includes most living fish species), 123, 174
Temperature, 47, 101, 106; and leaf margins, 159; mean annual, 183; tropical Pacific Ocean, 170, 182; volcanism and, 168
Temperature change. See Climatic change
Temporal pattern in mass extinctions, 97–98, 99, 141–147, 148–149, 176; foraminiferans, 141–145; Late Cretaceous, 136–137; mammalian, 205, 206; Pliocene regional, 198–199; protracted and pulsatile nature of, 209–210
Terrestrial crises: cooling and, 183–186
Terrestrial ecosystem: Cretaceous, 127–128; effect of climatic change on, 209; long-term transformation interrupted by pulse of sudden change, 160, 161, 169
Terrestrial habitats: dinosaurs, 114; Triassic, 111–112
Terrestrial life, 93–96, 100, 113, 118, 129; animal, 17, 95–96, 182; changes in: Mesozoic Era, 155–160; climatic change and, 191–192, 202–203; Late Permian event and, 98–99; plant, 78, 109, 155–160, 162
Tethyan region, 100, 105

Tethys (the tropical seaway that spread westward from the Pacific Ocean during the Mesozoic Era), 97–98, 103–105, 116–117, 128
Texas, 102, 103, 152–154
Thecodonts, 112, 113, 114
Therapsids (advanced mammal-like reptiles that suffered heavy losses in the terminal Permian crisis), 95, 96, 112
Thermal change, 63, 201, 216
Thermal filter, 201
Thermal tolerance, 148, 201–202
Thingvellir graben, 26
Thoracosphaera, 153
Thunell, Robert, 148
Timofeev, B. F., 52
Titanotheres (rhinoceros-like mammals that died out in the mid-Oligocene mass extinction), 185
Tithonian Age, 214
Toba (volcano), 164
Transcontinental Arch (a narrow uplift that transected North America from north to south during Paleozoic time, sometimes standing as an island above shallow seas), 81
Trees, 93–94, 159, 200
Triassic–Jurassic boundary, 117
Triassic Period, 97, 109–111; Early, 100–101; Late, 214
Triassic System, 110
Tridacna, 125
Trilobites (Paleozoic marine arthropods that were especially abundant during the Cambrian Period), 54–58, 59, 63, 65, 67, 71, 76, 78, 97; decline, 92; Early Cambrian, 56; extinctions, 18, 19, 61; fossil, 68; geologic range: Late Cambrian, 59
Tropical life forms: effect of cooling on, 83, 104; extinctions, 17, 18, 86, 89; preferential extinction of, 42–45, 91, 106, 149, 171, 176, 178; thermal tolerance of, 201–202
Tropics: biotas compressed in, 106; climatic change, 40–41
Turbidity (the condition of natural water that is charged with suspended sediment), 22, 47
Turnover rates, 18

Turtles, 112, 122–123, 137, 159
Tyrannosaurs (Cretaceous dinosaurs, the largest terrestrial carnivores of all time), 129

Ultraviolet radiation, 168
United States, 114, 118–119, 196, 200
Upchurch, Garland, 157–159
Ural Mountains, 32
Vail, Peter, 40, 121, 180
Van Valen, Leigh, 160, 161, 162
Vegetation, 173–174, 192–193, 207
Vertebrates (animals with backbones), 19, 77, 95, 99–11, 112, 120–121; mammal-like, 91; marine, 122–123, 137–138
Vidal, Gonzalo, 53–54
Volcanic emissions, 21, 41–42
Volcanism as cause of mass extinctions, 163–165, 167–168, 171
Volcanoes, 27, 29, 163
Vrba, Elisabeth, 202–203

Waders, long-legged, 173
Ward, Peter, 139
Warming, 102–103, 170
Wasson, John, 217
Water temperature, 174, 177, 178, 181–182, 188; see also Oceanic cooling
Webb, S. David, 203–204
Weeds, 127, 192, 193
Wegener, Alfred, 25; On the Origins of Continents and Oceans, 22
West Indies, 37
Western Australia: Late Devonian reef, 84
Whales, 8, 173, 174, 175, 191
White Cliffs of Dover, 124
Wicander, E. Reed, 82
Wiedmann, Jost, 139
Wildfire hypothesis, 166
Wisconsin glacial interval, 199
Wolbach, Wendy, 165–166
Wolfe, Jack, 157–159, 183
Wyoming, 45, 156, 158, 159–160, 162

Zachos, James, 148, 154
Zinsmeister, William, 176
Zooplankton, 51, 136
Zumaya, Spain, 139, 140, 142, 146